The Demise of the American Convention System, 1880–1911

JOHN F. REYNOLDS

University of Texas at San Antonio

CAMBRIDGE UNIVERSITY PRESS
Cambridge, New York, Melbourne, Madrid, Cape Town, Singapore, São Paulo

Cambridge University Press
32 Avenue of the Americas, New York, NY 10013-2473, USA

www.cambridge.org
Information on this title: www.cambridge.org/9780521859639

First published 2006

Printed in the United States of America

A catalog record for this publication is available from the British Library.

Library of Congress Cataloging in Publication Data

Reynolds, John Francis.
The demise of the American convention system, 1880–1911 / John F. Reynolds.
    p.   cm.
Includes bibliographical references and index.
ISBN-13: 978-0-521-85963-9 (hardback)
ISBN-10: 0-521-85963-8 (hardback)
    1. Political conventions – United States – History.   2. Nominations for office – United
States – History.   3. Political parties – United States – History.   I. Title.
JK2255.R49 2006
324.273'015609034–dc22   2005036293

ISBN-13 978-0-521-85963-9 hardback
ISBN-10 0-521-85963-8 hardback

To My Teachers:
Bill and Peter
and David O.
and
Richard M. and Richard L.
and especially for Rudy,
who insisted on a second book

Contents

Acknowledgments

A book fifteen years in the making accumulates a mountain of debt of the pecuniary and nonpecuniary kind. I am grateful for the opportunity to acknowledge the professional assistance and many kindnesses tendered me over the years from many quarters. The early stages of the project required extensive research into newspapers on microfilm that were tracked down and accessed through the diligent efforts of Sue McCray in the University of Texas at San Antonio's interlibrary loan office. Every history department deserves a bibliographer on the library staff like Dr. Richard H. McDonnell, who combines his mastery of content with a command of search engines and Boolean logic. Paulo J. Villarreal skillfully digitized and cleaned up the many images in the text that originated from scratchy microfilm. Also at San Antonio, the indomitable Sheryl S. McDonald, the very able Anastasia J. Peña, and the same technologically savvy Paulo Villarreal have run the History Department with such efficiency and quiet professionalism that I could steal time to put the finishing touches on the manuscript, for which I am most thankful.

The numerous research trips that highlighted my summers were supported in part by the university's Division of Behavioral and Cultural Sciences, through its director, Raymond R. Baird. My sincerest thanks to the staff at the Bancroft Library at the University of California at Berkeley; the Department of Special Collections at the Stanford University Library; the Bentley Historical Library at the University of Michigan; the Archives at the University of Colorado at Boulder Libraries; the Sinclair New Jersey Collection at Rutgers University; and the public libraries of Denver, Newark, and San Francisco. I must single out the late Charles F. Cummings of the Newark Public Library for his ready assistance in tracking down material. A development leave from the University of Texas at San Antonio allowed me time to think and write my way through my research notes and emerge with a manuscript.

A number of scholars read and commented on earlier versions of the work given as papers or circulated as drafts. Among my San Antonio colleagues Patrick J. Kelly, in the History Department, volunteered to read some of the earliest chapters in the rough. As on most matters of importance, I have come to rely on James C. Schneider, who lent his meticulous editorial skills to the manuscript and, most especially, prodded me think about the work's broader implications. Diane B. Walz, in the College of Business, generously tutored me on the finer points of binary logistic regression as it applied to the roll call analysis. I am also much obliged to my friends in the politics network of the Social Science History Association, who were subjected to yearly updates on my progress. Philip VanderMeer read and commented on early drafts and offered encouragement. Howard L. Reiter offered much constructive criticism to the critical early drafts from the vantage point of political science. Peter H. Argersinger read the work with his usual care, helped me better hone my argument, and set me straight on some particulars. Late in the process I had the pleasure of meeting with Alan Ware, who had recently produced his own work on the direct primary but was generous to a fault in assisting me in seeing this work to fruition. I count myself fortunate in having Lewis Bateman in the editorial chair for this work, as he was for my previous book; my manuscripts will follow him wherever he goes. Susan Greenberg diligently scrubbed the text clean of ungrammatical stains and improved on the clarity. Mary E. Lennon has endured my many absences, joined in repeated discussions of the work's content and merit, and read and reread and corrected the text without ever once asking, "Aren't you done yet?" And that, I suppose, is why I married her.

Abbreviations

DEN	*Detroit Evening News*
DFP	*Detroit Free Press*
DP	*Denver Post*
DR	*Denver Republican*
DSG	*Daily State Gazette* (Trenton)
DT	*Denver Times*
LAT	*Los Angeles Times*
NA	*Newark Advertiser*
NEN	*Newark Evening News*
NSC	*Newark Sunday Call*
NYT	*New York Times*
RMN	*Rocky Mountain News*
SFC	*San Francisco Chronicle*
SFE	*San Francisco Examiner*
TTA	*Trenton True American*

The Demise of the American Convention System, 1880–1911

I

Introduction

The hundred or so delegates arriving at California's state capitol in July 1865 for the Union Party's county convention came prepared for trouble. For weeks past, up and down the state, Republicans (who had temporarily taken up the "Union" label) had watched their local primaries and county conventions thrown into turmoil. Sacramento's primaries had been more disorderly than most, marred by charges of "ruffianism," bribery, and assorted frauds. Many blamed the bruising contest on a headstrong governor determined to land himself in the U.S. Senate. The so-called Short Hair faction championed his cause, meeting stiff resistance from a clique dubbed the "Long Hairs." Now, the two factions glared at one another from opposite sides of the Assembly Chamber.[1] The chair of the county committee called the delegates to order and brought up the first order of business, the selection of a temporary secretary. Each side of the room had a candidate for the post. Following a voice vote, the presiding officer announced that the position had gone to the choice of the Long Hairs. The proceedings immediately erupted into cacophonous bedlam. Short Hair delegates screamed for "fair play" and a formal ballot to decide the issue. They bombarded the chair with questions and motions. A few minutes later, when the chair's choice for secretary advanced toward the podium, a phalanx of Short Hairs blocked his path. Verbal ripostes gave way to shoving, pushing turned to punching, fisticuffs escalated to hickory canes. A reporter from the *Sacramento Union* looked on as the battle was joined.

---

[1] On the background to the contest see Winfield J. Davis, *History of Political Conventions in California, 1849–1892* (Sacramento, Calif., 1893), pp. 213–19. The term "short hair" implied that members of the group, described as San Francisco "roughs," had recently

A Typical Republican County Convention, A. D. 1890.

FIGURE 1.1. Denver's Republican primaries in 1890 resulted in a bitter fight between two factions dubbed the "Gang" and the "Smashers." The county convention included about 117 delegates elected on the Gang slate and 74 for the Smashers; 62 seats were claimed by both sides. Nothing approximating the violence depicted here occurred at the county convention, but the temporary chair's rulings on behalf of the Smashers did prompt the Gang to walk out and organize a separate Republican county convention. (*RMN*, Sept. 11, 1890, p. 1.)

"Spittoons flew from side to side like bomb shells.... Inkstands took the place of solid shot. Pistols were drawn and used as substitutes for clubs."[2] Those who had come unarmed grabbed the cane-bottomed armchairs and broke them over the heads of their antagonists. After five minutes of combat the Long Hairs retreated, some by way of the window, while others

served in prison where the cropped haircut was the order of the day. The presumably more respectable Long Hairs championed other senatorial aspirants.

[2] *Sacramento Union* quoted in The *San Francisco Evening Bulletin*, July 27, 1865, p. 2.

carried their bruised or unconscious comrades from the building. Each faction, whatever was left of it, organized a separate county convention and appointed competing sets of delegates to go to the state convention, appealing to the latter to sort things out.

The violence that marred the Sacramento County Convention was shocking even by California standards, but it was the aftermath of the political pandemonium that commands attention. Within a year, the same legislative chamber that had been the scene of battle (its chairs now bolted to the floor) witnessed the passage of the nation's first law to regulate the nominating process. Republican legislators – over the opposition of Democrats – pressed for state oversight of their party's often tumultuous proceedings. The "Porter Law" did not require much change in how political parties did business,[3] but it did mark a significant point of departure in the nation's political development. Political parties, the bane of the nation's first generation of politicians, had won recognition in the eyes of the state. In time, other states followed California's lead. Laws appeared around the nation in the 1880s outlawing fraud in primaries and conventions. Subsequent legislation converted party primaries into official elections and in doing so converted the Republican and Democratic organizations from private associations into semipublic agencies. Eventually the states replaced the party convention with what the political scientist Austin Ranney has dubbed "the most radical of all party reforms adopted in the whole course of American history."[4] The direct primary pushed party leaders aside and allowed the voters to designate their parties' candidates for elective office. The new system of direct nominations allegedly gave rise to the candidate-centered version of electioneering that would characterize American politics over the century that followed. The relationship between party nominating procedures and elective office-seeking strategies during the Gilded Age and the Progressive Era constitutes the core of the study that follows. Numerous scholars have argued that American politics at the turn of the twentieth century experienced a profound transformation in its processes and purposes. This work seeks to understand how much of that change was foreshadowed by Sacramento's belligerent Republican delegates.

The nominating convention served as an important bulwark to Democratic, Whig, and Republican Party supremacy during the "party period"

[3] *Statutes of California* (1865–66), No. 359, pp. 438–40. The law is discussed in more detail in Chapter 5.
[4] Austin Ranney, *Curing the Mischiefs of Faction: Party Reform in America* (Berkeley, Calif., 1975), p. 18.

spanning the last two-thirds of the nineteenth century.[5] The caucus and the convention predated the U.S. Constitution,[6] but became important to the nominating process only during the Jacksonian Era. Politicians integrated local party meetings with county, state, and national nominating bodies into a "convention system." The organizational structure first took shape in the closely contested Middle Atlantic region. It advanced state by state during the 1820s and 1830s as electoral competition took hold around the nation. The convention system's appeal rested on the democratic principle of taking the nominating power away from cliques of political insiders and investing it in "the people." Voters empowered delegates to designate their parties' nominees for elective office in county or legislative conventions, or to select other delegates to attend congressional, state, or national nominating bodies. Political parties came to dominate American politics during the nineteenth century in part because the convention system bestowed legitimacy on their deliberations and imposed some order and discipline in a highly decentralized electoral environment. The convention system maximized a party's vote by ensuring but one party choice for every elective position. In addition, the partisan bodies called into being at various stages of the process provided opportunities for organization and publicity. The earliest nominating conventions were not so much decision-making bodies as they were public relations exercises designed to embellish a candidacy with the stamp of public approbation. "The convention owed its ascendancy to its superior ability to meet the theoretical and practical requirements of democratic politics: candidates nominated by conventions, wrapped in the mantle of popular sovereignty and backed by an organization no independent could equal, were likely to be elected."[7] The convention system brought structure to political parties and linked the parties more securely to the electorate.

---

[5] Joel H. Silbey, *The American Political Nation, 1838–1893* (Stanford, Calif., 1991), pp. 59–64.

[6] G. B. Warden, "The Caucus and Democracy in Colonial Boston," *New England Quarterly* 43 (Mar. 1970): 19–45. The convention concept can be traced back to England's "Convention Parliament" of 1660, which invited Charles II to take the throne after the death of Oliver Cromwell. See Edmund S. Morgan, *Inventing the People: Popular Sovereignty in England and America* (New York, 1988), pp. 94–95 and 107–21.

[7] James S. Chase, *Emergence of the Presidential Nominating Convention, 1789–1832* (Urbana, Ill., 1973), p. 292. On the spread of the convention from state to state during the 1820s, see Richard P. McCormick, *The Second American Party System: Party Formation in the Jacksonian Era* (Chapel Hill, N.C., 1966); Frederick W. Dallinger, *Nominations for Elective Office in the United States* (New York, 1903), pp. 4–45; Charles P. Spahr, "Method of Nomination to Public Office: An Historical Sketch," in *Proceedings of the Chicago Conference for Good City Government and the Tenth Annual Meeting of the*

The waning of the party period not coincidentally brought an end to the nominating convention in most states. Between 1900 and 1915, the shortcomings of the nomination process occupied the attention of many prominent scholars, crusading journalists, and several eminently practical politicians. The list of prominent academics who interested themselves in the subject included the historians Carl Becker and Charles A. Beard, the economist John R. Commons, and the founder of modern-day political science, Charles Edward Merriam.[8] They placed their faith in a system of direct primaries, investing the electorate with the final authority in designating a party's choice of nominees. Arguments over the merits of direct nominations filled up many pages of the popular and scholarly press. Direct primaries were widely prescribed as an antidote to boss rule during the Progressive Era. Supporters of the reform insisted that they had to battle entrenched party interests to put the new nominating procedures in place. "It is well known history," testified the author of Colorado's direct primary law in 1923, "that these changes in our election laws were secured against the bitterest opposition of old-time politicians who were unwilling to surrender their long enjoyed privileges, including their power to manipulate conventions, nominate officials, and control legislation for the benefit of themselves and of the special interests they served."[9] All but a handful of states had abolished the convention system by World War I.

As it was the reformers who seemingly emerged victorious in the contest over nominating procedures, it was their version of events that initially found its way into the history books. Alan Ware has aptly titled these early works documenting the origins of the direct primary as "heroic." They portray progressive reformers bringing democracy to a corrupt and boss-ridden political system that mostly served powerful, corporate

National Municipal League [1904], ed. Clinton Rogers Woodruff (Philadelphia, 1904), pp. 321–27.

[8] Charles A. Beard, "The Direct Primary Movement in New York," *Proceedings of the American Political Science Association* 7 (1910): 187–98; Carl Becker, "The Unit Rule in National Nominating Conventions," *American Historical Review* 5 (Oct. 1899): 64–82; Charles Edward Merriam, "Some Disputed Points in Primary Election Legislation," *Proceedings of the American Political Science Association* 4 (1907): 179–88. Commons's interest and involvement in the movement is documented by his presence at the National Conference on Practical Reform of Primary Elections; see its *Proceedings of the National Conference on Practical Reform of Primary Elections, January 20 and 21, 1898* (Chicago, 1898), p. 23.

[9] Edward P. Costigan, "Remarks of ... at Austin Texas, Feb. 9, 1923," Box 38, "General Personal" file, Edward P. Costigan Papers, The Archives at the University of Colorado at Boulder Libraries.

interests.[10] The exposés of muckraking journalists combined with the political leadership of Wisconsin's governor Robert M. La Follette to galvanize public opinion and force legislatures to take action. These narratives fit neatly into an interpretive framework that viewed the progressive movement as a revolt by middle-class citizens who felt threatened by mammoth corporations and political machines answerable to no one. The direct primary stood out as one of many reforms of the era "awakening the people to a widespread interest in participation in political affairs."[11] The direct election of U.S. senators, the secret and official ballot, voter registration laws, women's suffrage, and limitations on corporate campaign contributions all helped wrest power from the hands of venal, political manipulators.

Scholarly interest and support for the direct primary cooled in the years following its implementation. Inevitably perhaps, the new electoral device did not live up to expectations. Voter turnout in primaries often proved anemic. The costs of running for office skyrocketed, and it was hard to make the case that the voters had selected a better class of elected officials.[12] By midcentury, the direct primary's reputation suffered further as it became associated with perceived deficiencies in the American political system. In the wake of the New Deal, scholars had come to harbor a renewed respect for the Democratic and Republican organizations. "Political parties created democracy," affirmed the political scientist E. E.

[10] Alan Ware, *The American Direct Primary: Party Institutionalization and Transformation in the North* (Cambridge, U.K., 2002), p. 15. Works in this genre would include Ransom E. Noble, *New Jersey Progressivism Before Wilson* (Princeton, N.J., 1946), pp. 130–35; and George L. Mowry, *The California Progressives* (Berkeley, Calif., 1951). Buttressing this historiographical outlook on the Progressive Era was the odious reputation of Gilded Age politics made famous by such works as Matthew Josephson, *The Politicos, 1865–1896* (New York, 1938); Richard Hofstadter, *The American Political Tradition and the Men Who Made It* (New York, 1948), pp. 211–39; and Morton Keller, *Affairs of State: Public Life in Late Nineteenth Century America* (Cambridge, Mass., 1977), pp. 238–83.
[11] Allen Fraser Lovejoy, *Robert M. La Follette and the Establishment of the Direct Primary in Wisconsin, 1890–1904* (New Haven, Conn., 1941), p. 8.
[12] Karl F. Geiser, "Defects in the Direct Primary," *Annals of the American Academy of Political and Social Science* 106 (Mar. 1923): 31–39. This issue of the *Annals* includes a number of studies on the workings of the reform in Wisconsin, Iowa, New York, Maine, Indiana, South Dakota, and California. Other monograph-length works include Ralph Simpson Boots, *The Direct Primary in New Jersey* (New York, 1917); Boyd A. Martin, *The Direct Primary in Idaho* (New York, 1947); James K. Pollock, *The Direct Primary in Michigan, 1909–1935* (Ann Arbor, Mich., 1943); Victor J. West, "Round Table on Nominating Methods: The Development of a Technique for Testing the Usefulness of a Nominating Method," *American Political Science Review* 20 (Feb. 1926): 139–43; Ware, *Direct Primary*, pp. 227–54.

Schattschneider, "modern democracy is unthinkable save in terms of the parties."[13] They connected the voters to their elected officials and held the latter accountable for their actions, thereby making government more responsive to public opinion. Yet, scholars drew sharp contrasts between the Democratic and Republican parties in the United States and their European counterparts. Whereas elections in other Western democracies were fought over issues dividing the parties, those in the United States revolved instead around the personal qualities of the candidates. The relatively weak and "irresponsible" political parties in the United States did not offer the electorate meaningful choices or seek to implement a partisan agenda once in power. The American Political Science Association's "Committee on Political Parties" issued a much-heralded report in 1950 detailing many of these deficiencies in the party system. It traced the problem back to the nation's unique political institutions and practices, most notably the direct primary. "[T]he inability of party organizations in the United States to control the party in government... begins with the failure to control the nominations."[14] "The direct primary has been the most potent in a complex of forces pushing toward the disintegration of the party," complained one scholar.[15] Since the APSA's report in 1950, the candidate-centered character of electoral politics in the United States has become ever more apparent.[16] Television, electioneering consultants, and campaign finance laws have all greatly exacerbated a condition many trace back to the direct primary. A call for a revival of the political

---

[13] Ranney, *Mischiefs of Faction*, p. 5

[14] Frank J. Sorauf, *Party Politics in America*, 2nd ed. (Boston, 1972), pp. 228–29; Committee on Political Parties of the American Political Science Association, "Toward a More Responsible Two Party System," *American Political Science Review* 44 (Sept. 1950): 15–84. Not all political scientists believed that American political parties were in need of repair. Many concurred that parties in the United States lacked a level of programmatic content equivalent to like bodies in Europe, but they believed that such flexibility was appropriate or inevitable given the nation's political institutions and culture. See Leon D. Epstein, *Political Parties in the American Mold* (Madison, Wis., 1986), pp. 30–37.

[15] David B. Truman, "Party Reform, Party Atrophy, and Constitutional Change: Some Reflections," *Political Science Quarterly* 99 (Winter 1984–85): 649.

[16] Scholarly concern about candidate domination over the electoral process and the consequent decline of political parties became paramount only in the 1970s. The spread of presidential primaries surely played a role in bringing the phenomenon to scholarly attention. See Martin P. Wattenberg, *The Rise of Candidate-Centered Politics: Presidential Elections of the 1980s* (London, 1991), pp. 156–65; Hedrick Smith, *The Power Game: How Washington Works* (New York, 1987); Alan Ware, *The Breakdown of Democratic Party Organization, 1940–1980* (Oxford, 1985), pp. 143–74; John F. Bibby, "Party Organizations, 1946–1996," in *Partisan Approaches to Postwar American Politics*, ed. Byron E. Shafer (New York, 1998), pp. 151–60.

convention (sometimes tinged with nostalgia) appeared in the scholarly literature and popular press.[17]

Whether they endorsed or deplored the direct primary, much of the past literature has understood reform as something imposed on political parties from without.[18] In more recent years, however, historians and political scientists have paid closer attention to the ways the major parties used reform to protect their own interests. V. O. Key, Jr., and others have argued that direct nominations served as a mechanism to ensure one-party rule. Parties that enjoyed majority status in a state made the direct primary the main arena of political contests, rendering all other parties and the general election almost irrelevant. Key's insight certainly seemed applicable to the Democratic monopoly on power across the Solid South as well as to Republican rule in many northern states prior to the 1930s.[19] Key's work anticipated the "new institutionalism" that characterizes much current political history, especially as practiced by political scientists. This approach to American politics argues that political parties and the politicians who run them are fully capable of using reform to their advantage.[20] The adoption of the official or secret ballot around

[17] The APSA's model nominating system retained the direct primary, though closing it off to all but persons who affiliated with the party. It proposed to precede the primary with a convention (or "party council") where party leaders could issue a collective judgment on prospective nominees and consider a platform. See Committee on Political Parties, "More Responsible Two Party System," pp. 72–73. See also Herbert McClosky, "Are Political Conventions Undemocratic?" *New York Times Magazine*, Aug. 4, 1968, p. 10; Ranney, *Mischiefs of Faction*; Nelson W. Polsby, *Consequences of Party Reform* (Oxford, 1983); Arthur Schlesinger, Jr., "Faded Glory," *New York Times Magazine*, July 12, 1992, p. 14; Tom Wicker, "Let Some Smoke In," *New York Times Magazine*, June 14, 1992, p. 34.

[18] Arthur S. Link and Richard L. McCormick, *Progressivism* (Arlington Hts., Ill, 1983), p. 32; Ranney, *Mischiefs of Faction*; Bibby, "Party Organizations," p. 152; Michael E. McGerr, *The Decline of Popular Politics: The American North, 1865–1928* (New York, 1986); Martin Shefter, *Political Parties and the State: The American Historical Experience* (Princeton, N.J., 1993), pp. 76–81; Eric Falk Petersen, "The Adoption of the Direct Primary in California," *Southern California Quarterly* 54 (Winter 1972): 363–78.

[19] V. O. Key, Jr., *Politics, Parties and Pressure Groups*, 5th ed. (New York, 1964), pp. 375–76; and see his essay "The Direct Primary and Party Structure: A Study of State Legislative Nominations," *American Political Science Review* 58 (Mar. 1954): 1–26. See also E. E. Schattschneider, *The Semi-Sovereign People* (New York, 1960). Other scholars have called into question the cause-and-effect relationship between direct nominations and electoral competition, an issue discussed more thoroughly in Chapter 4.

[20] Paul Pierson and Theda Skocpol, "Historical Institutionalism in Contemporary Political Science," in *Political Science: The State of the Discipline*, ed. Ira Katznelson and Helen V. Milner (New York, 2002), pp. 693–721. See also, in the same volume, Karen Orren and Stephen Skowronek, "The Study of American Political Development," pp. 722–54.

1890 is cited as one such episode. State regulation of the ballot became a means to inhibit maverick candidates, third parties, and independent action on the part of the electorate.[21] Most recently, the political scientist Alan Ware has challenged the conventional account that credits reformers with forcing the direct primary on urban, party machines.[22] Party regulars took up the measure to better administer an increasingly unwieldy nomination process, especially in the more densely populated cities.

The present work elaborates on Ware's argument with the insight of the new institutionalist framework. Attention focuses on the role of elective office seekers in the restructuring of the nomination process. It argues that past studies have put the cart before the horse by treating the origins of the candidate-centered campaign as an unintended consequence of direct nominations. A fundamental premise shaping the analysis that follows maintains that before one could implement or even imagine a direct primary, one first needed to have candidates. When the convention system was in its prime in the 1880s it compelled ambitious office seekers to maintain a low profile. The nominating process took hardly any official notice of candidates and deplored the very existence of "chronic office seekers." Delegates assumed responsibility for recruiting the best candidates for each office following the oft-repeated dictate that "the office should seek the man." Party leaders used these partisan conclaves to quietly negotiate a slate of nominees for an array of offices that would satisfy all the party's factional elements. Almost no one considered it feasible to expect voters to choose candidates for major offices without knowing who the "available men" were.

Of course, it was never quite so simple nor the candidates quite so passive as the partisan press would have it. Prospective nominees and their friends worked quietly behind the scenes, but found their scope of action bounded by party customs intended to promote harmony. Beginning at the local level, candidates mounted progressively more aggressive and

[21] Peter H. Argersinger, "'A Place on the Ballot': Fusion Politics and Anti-Fusion Laws," in *Structure, Process and Party: Essays in American Political History*, ed. Peter H. Argersinger (Armonk, N.Y., 1992), pp. 150–71; John F. Reynolds and Richard L. McCormick, "Outlawing 'Treachery': Split Tickets and Ballot Laws in New York and New Jersey, 1880–1914," *Journal of American History* 72 (Mar. 1986): 835–58.
[22] Ware, *Direct Primary*. Historians of the current day offer a more complex narrative outlining the origins and impact of the direct primary. See Richard L. McCormick, *From Realignment to Reform: Political Change in New York State, 1893–1910* (Ithaca, N.Y., 1981), pp. 243–47; Philip R. VanderMeer, *The Hoosier Politician: Officeholding and Political Culture in Indiana, 1896–1920* (Urbana, Ill., 1985), pp. 35–36.

disruptive campaigns to capture nominations for minor offices. Candidates for gubernatorial or congressional seats were more coy about making their ambitions known, but by 1900 even they had learned that it paid to be assertive in promoting one's availability for party honors. The appearance of "hustling candidates" contesting primaries and conventions coincides with new modes of electioneering introduced around this time; candidates and even parties toned down their strictly partisan appeals to capitalize on issues or personalities during the general election.[23]

The appearance of a more visible and active body of elective office seekers posed a special problem for the convention system. Candidates recruited scores of paid and unpaid agents, traveled extensively to meet with local notables, took a more active part in conventions, and, most importantly, worked to elect delegates committed to their candidacy. Primaries became more popular and conventions more unruly as aspirants struggled for control. It became more difficult for parties to function in their accustomed manner – as was demonstrated in Sacramento as early as 1865 and less spectacularly elsewhere in the decades that followed. Although cities often served as the settings for ugly political brawls inflicting open wounds on the parties, this was not precisely a problem of adapting the nomination process to function in a more urbanized setting. The hustling candidates who dominated and manipulated primaries and conventions posed a bigger challenge for party managers. The rapid and relatively uncontroversial adoption of the direct primary represented an effort by officeholders and party officials to adapt the electoral system to an increasingly candidate-centered political culture. Legal and institutional changes did not give rise to the nation's more candidate-centered electoral system; rather, candidate domination of the nominating process required a new set of rules encompassed by the direct primary and other reforms to follow.

Any study of American politics, particularly one focusing on its electoral machinery, must take account of the federal governing structure and the decentralized and multilayered character of its political parties. Like most progressive measures, the direct primary was an issue for state

[23] McGerr, *Decline of Popular Politics*; Philip J. Ethington, "The Metropolis and Multicultural Ethics: Direct Democracy Versus Deliberative Democracy in the Progressive Era," in *Progressivism and the New Democracy*, ed. Sidney M. Milkis and Jerome M. Mileur (Amherst, Mass., 1999), pp. 195–96; Richard Jensen, *The Winning of the Midwest: Social and Political Conflict, 1888–1896* (Chicago, 1971), pp. 165–77; Thomas R. Pegram, *Partisans and Progressives: Private Interest and Public Policy in Illinois, 1870–1922* (Urbana, Ill., 1992), p. 155.

governments, not the national one. The appropriate research strategy is an in-depth case study approach with the state as the unit of analysis. Putting the reform into context also requires understanding how the nomination process fared in the waning years of the convention system. The state nominating convention offers the best vantage point to examine changes in how candidates secured their party's nomination. In theory, the state convention represented the final authority in Democratic and Republican party matters. Documenting the proceedings of the state convention as well as of the local caucuses and county conventions that preceded it reveals how it was that candidates, party officials, and voters became frustrated with the process. Ultimately, it was state legislators who enacted the direct primary, and roll call analysis can identify those most responsible for this and other statutes regulating the nominating process. The story opens when the state convention and the party period were in full flower during the 1880s. It concludes with the abolition of state nominating conventions around 1910.

The choice of states for analysis, or more particularly the reasons for their selection, is obviously a matter of some consequence. It will not be contended here that the four northern states singled out can be characterized as "representative" of the nation as a whole. No set of four or perhaps even a dozen states can possibly serve such a purpose. The choice of New Jersey, Michigan, Colorado, and California rests on their diversity rather than in their collective profile. They offer an assortment of characteristics with some relevance to the evolution of the nominating process. The presence or absence of electoral competition, the level of urbanization, the importance of third parties, and the role of women and minority voters all shaped dissimilar political landscapes. The historian is also entirely at the mercy of her or his primary sources. The presence in each state of major research repositories with a wide selection of newspapers and relevant manuscript collections was another important factor in their selection.[24] The decision to exclude states affiliated with the Confederacy recognizes that the nominating systems put in place in the Southern states about this time set them apart. The "white primary" served not least of all to disfranchise minorities. Southerners alone employed the "runoff primary" (between the two top vote getters in the initial primary) in place of a

---

[24] Among the sites that proved most useful were the Archives at the University of Colorado at Boulder Libraries, the Bentley Historical Library at the University of Michigan, the Bancroft Library at the University of California at Berkeley, the Colorado Historical Society in Denver, and the California State Library in Sacramento.

general election.[25] White supremacy was not at the heart of the debate over the direct primary outside the South, where racial minorities were far smaller in size.

The socioeconomic and political characteristics in Table 1.1 allow for a brief sketch of each of the selected states.[26] New Jersey, by far the most urban and industrial state in the mix, was representative of the emerging "Metropole." Booming industries in the center of the state drew a sizable immigrant population. First came the "old immigrants" (Irish and German) followed, after 1890, by the new variety (from Italy, Russia, and Austria-Hungary). Two large cities, Newark and Jersey City (each with over 100,000 residents in 1880), together with a half dozen other municipalities with ten thousand or more inhabitants, account for New Jersey's highly urban profile. Suburbanization was the newer and more dramatic trend at the turn of the century. Bedroom communities sprouted outside the state's largest cities – allowing the percentage of citizens living in "rural" areas to remain constant over time.[27] New Jersey's African American population was the largest of the sampled states, but it was nonetheless small and did not grow faster than the white population. The Garden State's agricultural sector was relatively small and shrinking. The truck farmers and dairy producers in the southern and western portions of the state did not share the hardships of farmers elsewhere in the nation. Consequently, Populism did not take root in the state, and the electorate evinced little interest in any other third parties. During the Third Party System (1856–92), New Jersey was closely contested in state and national elections. Democrats managed to keep a lock on the governor's mansion and usually on one or more branches of the legislature. Like other urban centers, the state deserted the Democratic Party with the Depression of 1893 and became a Republican bastion in presidential

---

[25] Peter H. Argersinger, "Electoral Processes in American Politics," in *Structure, Process and Party*, p. 60. Ware also confines his analysis to northern states, arguing that "the South was a different country" with respect to its electoral arrangements; see *American Direct Primary*, pp. 168, 18–20. On the origins and workings of the white primary, see J. Morgan Kousser, *The Shaping of Southern Politics: Suffrage Restriction and the Establishment of the One Party South, 1880–1910* (New Haven, Conn., 1974), pp. 72–80; O. Douglas Weeks, "The White Primary, 1944–1948," *American Political Science Review* 42 (June 1948): 500–510.

[26] Demographic data taken from the United States Bureau of the Census's published *Population* volumes for *Tenth* and *Thirteenth* censuses. Electoral data taken from Paul T. David, *Party Strength in the United States* (Charlottesville, Va., 1972).

[27] "Rural," as the Census Bureau defines it, refers to incorporated places with populations under 2,500.

TABLE I.I. *Socioeconomic and Political Characteristics of Selected States,*
1880 and 1910

	New Jersey (%)	Michigan (%)	Colorado (%)	California (%)
1880				
Population				
Rural	24.8	72.6	36.2	48.8
Agriculture	14.9	42.2	13.4	21.1
Trade/transportation	16.7	9.6	15.3	15.2
Manufacturing/mining	40.5	23.0	46.8	31.4
White	96.5	98.6	98.4	88.7
African/American	3.4	0.9	1.3	0.7
Other	0.0	0.4	0.4	10.6
Foreign born	19.6	23.7	12.0	21.3
Election Data				
Presidential vote (1880–1892)				
Republican	47.6	49.5	50.5	46.3
Democratic	49.9	43.2	32.0	48.6
Other	2.5	7.3	17.5	5.1
Off-year gubernatorial vote (1882–1890)				
Republican	45.6	46.3	48.0	44.5
Democratic	49.6	47.1	47.9	48.3
Other	4.8	6.6	4.1	7.2
1910				
Population				
Rural	24.8	52.8	49.3	38.2
Agriculture	7.5	30.2	25.3	20.3
Mining	0.6	3.3	8.4	2.8
Manufacturing	45.8	32.6	22.3	26.5
Transportation	8.7	6.3	9.5	9.4
Trade	12.1	9.4	11.6	13.7
Other	25.4	18.3	23.0	27.2
White	96.4	99.1	98.0	95.0
African American	3.5	0.6	1.4	0.9
Other	0.1	0.3	0.5	4.0
Foreign born	26.0	21.3	16.2	24.7
Election Data				
Presidential vote (1896–1908)				
Republican	57.1	60.8	39.2	55.2
Democratic	38.6	35.1	56.9	37.4
Other	4.3	4.1	3.9	7.4
Off-year gubernatorial vote (1894–1910)				
Republican	48.8	56.2	44.9	45.0
Democratic	47.6	38.2	47.6	41.9
Other	3.6	5.6	7.5	13.1

elections.[28] Although the G.O.P. held a virtual lock on the state government from 1893 through 1909,[29] Democrats posed a credible threat when they did not share the ballot with one of their unappealing presidential nominees. The governor was the only official elected statewide, so state conventions in New Jersey had less business to conduct than those of other states. Governors could not succeed themselves at the end of their three-year terms. A guaranteed open seat in a usually competitive electoral environment made for lively times when the state convention rolled around.

Michigan presents many of the characteristics of the prototypical Midwestern state. It had by far the largest agricultural sector of the four states across the time period. Farming was confined mainly to the most heavily populated, southern tier of counties. Farther north the lumber industry dominated. Mining towns dotted the Upper Peninsula (above the Straits of Mackinac). Michigan's relatively large foreign-born population in 1880 was mainly an accident of geography: 38% were born in Canada. Although the relative size of the immigrant population was falling slightly, a higher proportion of them were Europeans by 1910 (disproportionately from Central Europe) and living in urban areas. Industrialization took hold in the state during this time, primarily in Detroit and in its smaller rival, Grand Rapids. The Great Lakes State was identified with the Republican heartland. "Anybody can carry Michigan,"[30] Senator Roscoe Conkling of New York once sneered. The observation was true enough if he meant to apply it to "any Republican," or – to be more precise – "any Republican presidential candidate."[31] The national ticket regularly trounced the opposition during the late nineteenth century, and the margin only widened after 1896. Strictly state elections, however, were another matter during the Third Party System. A powerful Greenback Party combined with the Democrats to elect their fusion gubernatorial choice in 1882. Even after the third party disappeared later in the decade, Democrats managed to elect a governor on their own in 1890. Thereafter, Michigan's Democrats bordered on extinction – losing state elections in lengthening landslides and electing scarcely any state

[28] Samuel T. McSeveney, *The Politics of Depression: Political Behavior in the Northeast, 1893–1896* (New York, 1972).
[29] Republicans retained the governorship during this period and controlled every legislature except when the lower house (the assembly) went to the Democrats in the 1906 election.
[30] *DFP*, Aug. 19, 1886, p. 1.
[31] Arthur Chester Millspaugh, *Party Organization and Machinery in Michigan Since 1890* (Baltimore, 1917), pp. 10–11.

legislators. Few states better illustrated the one-party Republican Party rule associated with the "system of 1896."[32]

Colorado exhibited a split personality indicative of its geographic location on the Great Plains and the Rocky Mountains. Mining dominated the economy of the Centennial State when it entered the Union in 1876, but agriculture soon took hold of the eastern half of the state. Denver was by far the state's largest city (35,000 in 1880) and growing at an astounding pace. Even with two hundred thirteen thousand residents by 1910, however, the city was far smaller than San Francisco, Detroit, or Newark. The foreign-born population was relatively small, but these numbers do not reflect the presence of a large and long-standing "Mexican" population in the southernmost counties. As in Michigan, Colorado's governors were elected every two years. Here too the G.O.P. sweep in presidential years during the 1880s did not materialize in off years. Colorado elected Democratic governors in 1882 and 1886. The demand for an inflated currency using silver animated both major parties but met its warmest reception among the Populists.[33] The latter elected a governor and many legislators in 1892. Populist rule brought with it the adoption of women's suffrage in 1894. The period of 1892 to 1898 was one of profound partisan confusion as first Colorado's Democrats and then its Republicans cut their ties with their national affiliates over the silver issue. During this time dual (state and national) Democratic and Republican organizations met in conventions, and nominated competing tickets. An era of electoral instability followed. William Jennings Bryan ran off with 84.1% of the vote in 1896, Theodore Roosevelt carried the state handily in 1904, and Bryan barely squeaked through four years later. Off year gubernatorial elections remained competitive even after 1900. Drastic changes in party fortunes in Colorado corroborate scholarly opinion that voters in the West were less closely tied to the major parties than were Americans elsewhere.[34]

---

[32] E. E. Schattschneider coined the term "system of 1896" to describe an era of noncompetitive elections, waning public interest in politics, and tightening control by political elites. It overlaps with the Fourth Party System (1896–1928). See Schattschneider, *Semi-Sovereign People*, pp. 78–85. See also Walter Dean Burnham, "The System of 1896: An Analysis," in *The Evolution of American Electoral Systems*, ed. Paul Kleppner et al. (Westport, Conn., 1981), pp. 147–202.

[33] James Edward Wright, *The Politics of Populism: Dissent in Colorado* (New Haven, Conn., 1974).

[34] A number of studies argue that partisan roots did not sink so deeply into the electorate west of the Mississippi. See Paul Kleppner, "Voters and Parties in the Western States, 1876–1900," *Western Historical Quarterly* 14 (Jan. 1983): 49–68; Martin Shefter,

No state's politics was more thoroughly shaken up by the progressive movement than California's. With a population of two hundred thirty-four thousand in 1880, San Francisco was by far the largest city in the sample – and among the largest in the nation. In California, agriculture and industry grew at the expense of mining after the Civil War. The Chinese (and later the Japanese) represented a considerable portion of the state's population, but California's Constitution denied them citizenship until 1926; Asian Americans were thoroughly shut out of the political process. The major state officers served four-year terms after their election in even numbered, off years. The longer terms enhanced the value of the offices and ensured that conventions in the Golden State were the most elaborate of all. State offices remained electorally competitive throughout the time frame, although Republicans dominated the legislature after 1896.[35] Third parties thrived, beginning with the rabidly anti-Chinese Workingmen's Party of the 1870s and continuing through the Socialist parties at the outset of the twentieth century. In later years, California acquired a reputation for the antipartisan excesses of its progressive reforms. Little wonder the state pioneered in the development of the modern-day, mass media–oriented system of campaign management.[36]

Understanding the evolution of the nominating process offers clues as to how and why political development in the United States followed a different trajectory than that of other Western democracies. The convention system and the direct primary that replaced it represented two distinctive features of American politics. Both institutional arrangements helped preserve the nation's two-party political system at a time when mass-based political parties and multiparty systems emerged in Europe and later around the globe. The United States would enter the twentieth century with both relatively weak parties and domineering political personalities, in part because of institutional changes of the Progressive Era. The appearance of the direct primary followed in the footsteps of

"Regional Receptivity to Reform: The Legacy of the Progressive Era," *Political Science Quarterly* 98 (Autumn 1983): 459–83; Elizabeth S. Clemens, *The People's Lobby: Organizational Innovation and the Rise of Interest Group Politics in the United States* (Chicago, 1997), pp. 73–81.

[35] Michael Paul Rogin and John L. Shover, *Political Change in California: Critical Elections and Social Movements* (Westport, Conn., 1970).

[36] Robert B. Westbrook, "Politics as Consumption: Managing the Modern American Election," in *The Culture of Consumption: Critical Essays in American History, 1880–1980*, ed. Richard Wrightman Fox and T. J. Jackson Lears (New York, 1983), pp. 145–73; Thomas Goebel, *A Government by the People: Direct Democracy in America, 1890–1940* (Chapel Hill, N.C., 2002), pp. 158–84.

past electoral reforms, and blazed a path for those to come. The convention system was constructed "from the top down" by rival political elites during the early part of the nineteenth century. After 1900 a new generation of politicians reinvented the nomination process to accord with their more aggressive style of electioneering. The decisive role played by the office-seeking class in shaping the nation's political processes remains one of the notable and recurring motifs of American political history.

2

The Search for Harmony

The Convention System in the Party Period

I

"Do you know much about politics?" inquired the editor of the *San Francisco Examiner* of reporter Annie Laurie in the late summer of 1890. "Of course I do," she shot back. "I always have a candidate, and I would vote for him if I could and – and that's all there is in it, isn't it?" The editor peered at her pensively. After a long silence he suggested that the Democratic State Convention at nearby San Jose would be "an object lesson for you." Laurie eagerly got packing. For three full days she sat demurely in the reporters' gallery with a male colleague she deferred to as "Mr. Worldly Wise." Laurie learned about "bolts" and "breaks" and "trades" and the many happenings on the convention floor that were not at all what they seemed. And she learned to be grateful. "I never think of the turmoil and excitement of those eventful hours without thanking my lucky stars that I do not have the vote."[1]

Laurie's visit to the convention left her with some vivid memories. Above all, she recalled the noise and congestion that rattled her composure. Men and women packed the galleries and the aisles. Delegates and spectators emitted a low roar as they awaited the opening gavel. "Every single man was in earnest – dead earnest. So much so that he never listened to a word his friends said, but just talked on, as if unconscious that there was another voice raised in the place." (This body of delegates, she

---

[1] "Annie Laurie" was the pen name of Winifred Sweet Black, a pioneering woman journalist who expressed little sympathy for the suffrage cause during the 1890s. See Philip J. Ethington, *The Public City: The Political Construction of Urban Life in San Francisco, 1850–1900* (Cambridge, U.K., 1994), p. 316.

THE BORDER LINE BETWEEN THE BLISS AND FERRY PUSH.

SCENE IN THE GRAND RAPIDS CONVENTION WHILE THE RESULT WAS STILL IN DOUBT.

FIGURE 2.1. The bedlam unloosed at Michigan's Republican State Convention of 1900 is rendered in this drawing from a reporter on the scene. The overheated delegates are shouting out the names of their respective gubernatorial favorites (Aaron T. Bliss and Dexter M. Ferry) while vigorously waving their fans. Bliss emerged with the nomination only after nineteen roll calls. (*DEN*, June 29, 1900, p. 3.)

was assured, was an unusually orderly and well-behaved crowd.) Nothing prepared her for the tumultuous racket that broke out once the convention got down to business. The participants, a term that embraced the audience as much as the delegates, shrieked, howled, and pounded the floor with their canes at numerous junctures in the program. "Every man in that hall was possessed of a burning desire to talk. Those that didn't care to talk just yelled. There was a man sitting near me who had a most marvelous voice. It was like the bellow of an enraged locomotive. Just behind him sat an elderly man, who emitted short, sharp barks whenever he grew excited, which was early and often." The clamor was deafening when the "break" came on the fourth roll call for governor. The delegates went "insane." Hats and canes flew about, and the assembly joined in a pandemic of handshaking. No one was immune from the delirium on the floor. The women in the balconies "knocked on the rail with their fans. One extremely sedate woman rose and frantically opened and shut a white parasol with far more vigor than grace." Worldly Wise claimed that Laurie herself "shrieked audibly." "I know I did nothing of the sort," she assured her readers.

Throughout the exercise, Worldly Wise instructed his charge not to become engrossed by the official proceedings. The long and eloquent speeches, which Laurie followed closely, convinced no one. Empty gestures abounded, as when speakers nominated men for posts everyone knew they would decline. Much of the real work of the convention took place elsewhere. The outcome of the gubernatorial contest was settled during negotiations carried on after the convention adjourned on the first day. The secret discussions involved "trades," deliberations never hinted at from the podium, whereby supporters of candidates for different offices joined forces. It was a humbling experience for the female reporter, but an enlightening one. "Whether I know any more about politics as they are than I did before I went I cannot say," she concluded. "I certainly do know considerably more about politics as they seem."[2]

Part deliberative body, part spectacle, and part pandemonium, the state convention occupied an exalted place in Gilded Age politics. Understanding how and why the parties structured the nominating process as they did offers insight into the era's political culture: the set of values and expectations common citizens and their "betters" harbored about governance, the proper role of political parties, and the political elite.[3] The convention

---

[2] *SFE*, Aug. 24, 1890, p. 13.
[3] Ronald P. Formisano, "The Concept of Political Culture," *Journal of Interdisciplinary History* 31 (Winter 2001): 393–426.

system flourished amid traditions grounded in the ideology of republicanism. The longstanding notions of deference, the mistrust of ambition, and the craving for harmony that characterized the mindset of the
nation's founding generation were passed down to their partisan-minded
nineteenth-century offspring. But the convention system dealt in substance
as well as in symbols. It served as an imperfect outlet for public opinion,
furthered or terminated the careers of elective office seekers, crafted public policy on a range of issues, and promoted party unity. This chapter
explores the workings of the nominating system during the 1880s – when
the convention system was in its prime. The process commenced with the
call for the state convention and concluded when partisans at the grassroots ratified the actions of the delegates. Like the San Francisco reporter,
this chapter examines the public face of the Democratic and Republican
parties. It offers an idealized model of how the system was supposed to
work. Subsequent chapters will explore the gap Laurie detected between
"politics as they are" and "politics as they seem."

II

The responsibility for setting the nomination process in motion fell to
the parties' state committees. The members, commonly one from each
county in the state, came together in late spring or early summer. Certain
mundane matters, such as the date and place for the state convention, were
ordinarily uncontroversial. The selection of a site for the convention might
provoke a friendly rivalry among local boosters. The state convention of a
major party was an economic boon for any city. California's Republicans
put up three thousand dollars for their Los Angeles meeting in 1886 to
pay for accommodations and renting and decorating the hall. The five
hundred to one thousand delegates brought in their wake a small army of
journalists and interested onlookers of both sexes for a two- or three-day
political extravaganza. State committees looked for a bidder who offered
the right set of inducements. In 1890 the city of Sacramento sealed its
bid with the G.O.P. by promising to pick up the tab for most expenses.
The state committee was also impressed by the city's half million dollar
brewery and one hundred thousand dollar ice machine.[4]

The decision about the convention date raised strategic considerations.
State committees shunned early conventions ordaining a lengthy campaign that left their nominees "tired in body, mind and pocket."[5] Most

---

[4] *LAT*, Aug. 20, 1886, p. 4; *SFE*, Apr. 24, 1890, p. 5.
[5] *SFE*, May 4, 1894, p. 2; *DFP*, June 28, 1894, p. 1; July 18, 1880, p. 4.

state conventions surveyed in this study occurred in September. August was also a common choice, and anything earlier or later was rare.[6] The majority party in each state was more likely to schedule its state convention first.[7] The minority party waited, hoping to capitalize on whatever opportunities the dominant party presented it by bungling the nomination process. If, for example, an important constituency was overlooked in filling out the majority party's ticket, the minority party arranged its own selections to exploit any lingering ill will. An unpopular or controversial nomination choice by the majority party might spur otherwise reluctant candidates to accept or even to seek a nomination from the minority party. The leaders of the majority party knew that their opponents were watching and hoping to see them come apart at the seams.

The apportionment of delegates was one weighty matter taken up by the state committee that could provoke dissent. Space considerations of the available opera houses or other potential venues, and the problems of managing a teeming and unruly mass of delegates, dictated that state conventions stay within a range of about five hundred delegates in the 1880s.[8] The apportionment formula differed from state to state but did not differ much between the major parties within a state. Michigan's Democrats and Republicans used the same formula: two delegates for every county plus one for every five hundred total votes cast for governor in the last general election.[9] California's rules followed Michigan's, except that they used the vote of the respective parties rather than the total vote. In Colorado the lack of consistent guidelines on apportionment caused discord in both parties. It instigated an "animated debate" at the Republican

---

[6] Of the 92 conventions surveyed, 7 were held in June, 6 in July, 26 in August, 50 in September, and 3 in October.

[7] In Republican-dominated Colorado, the G.O.P. convention preceded the Democratic one in 6 of 7 gubernatorial elections between 1880 and 1892; after the state went over to the Democrats in 1896, the Democratic state convention appeared on the calendar first in 6 of 8 elections between 1896 and 1910. This pattern also explains why the party that was first in the field was more likely to carry away the honors on election day. Amid forty-six elections surveyed for this study, the party that nominated its gubernatorial candidate first won the office 65% of the time.

[8] The mean size of state conventions in the 1880s in all four states amounted to 520. New Jersey Democrats upped the apportionment from one in every 100 Democratic voters to one in every 200 in 1880 because it was hard for them to accommodate, much less control, the 990 delegates who took their seats that year. *NA*, Sept. 2, 1880, p. 1. State convention size grew over the period as larger facilities became available, doubling to about one thousand delegates by 1910.

[9] *DFP*, Aug. 13, 1880, p. 8. Previously, the Democrats tied apportionment to representation in the state legislature. For Republican apportionment, see *Detroit Tribune*, May 5, 1876, p. 1.

State Committee meeting of 1880. Eventually the task of allotting each county's delegate count was assigned to a special committee whose report was accepted only "after considerable debate." The full state committee amended the document to grant some counties additional seats for unstated reasons. A few weeks later, Democrats went through a like exercise, producing an apportionment from a committee that also followed no explicit criteria.[10]

The apportionment of delegates usually privileged sparsely populated counties, though the disparity was not great. Table 2.1 uncovers evidence of malapportionment of urban versus rural counties. It first calculates the electoral weight of the county containing each state's largest city as a percentage of the statewide party vote for president over three elections. It then matches these results with the like percentage of delegates hailing from that locality in the following state convention.[11] The county of San Francisco, for example, accounted for 26.7% of the statewide popular vote cast for the Democratic candidate for president in 1880; the city's representation at the ensuing state convention amounted to 23.6% of all delegates in attendance. Although urban areas generally did not receive an allotment of seats equivalent to their voting strength in the preceding general election, the shortfall rarely exceeded three percentage points. Table 2.1 also details how the "smallest counties" fared by a similar standard. The latter were defined as those in the bottom half of counties ranked by the party's total vote for president. In 1880, a total of 76 counties in Michigan turned in election returns. The votes from the 38 counties that recorded the lowest number of votes for the Democratic presidential candidate accounted for 11.0% of the Democrat's statewide total. These small counties represented 12.2% of the total number of delegates attending the state convention of 1882. Small counties typically sent more than their "fair share" of delegates to the state convention based on the party's vote for president. The rule of ensuring every county a minimum of one or two delegates benefited small counties in Michigan[12] and California.

---

[10] *RMN*, Apr. 23, 1880, p. 8; July 23, 1880, p. 8; Aug. 28, 1884, p. 3.

[11] In Colorado the disruption and confusion that overtook the Democratic Party in 1892 (when two state parties took the field, one endorsing the Populist candidates) dictated that comparison be based on the 1888 vote.

[12] Michigan's rural Republicans were the exception to the rule after 1896. The G.O.P. based apportionment on the total vote cast for governor (rather than on the vote for the Republican candidate). In 1904, Theodore Roosevelt won the support of 79% of the voters in the state's smallest counties, but this did not earn these counties extra representation at the state convention of 1906.

TABLE 2.1. *Apportionment at State Conventions for Urban and Rural Counties Paired with the Party Vote for President in the Previous Election*

	Year	Democrats			Republicans		
		Election (%)	Convention (%)	Difference (%)	Election (%)	Convention (%)	Difference (%)
County with Largest City							
California	1880	26.7	23.6	-3.1	23.7	20.9	-2.9
	1892	26.2	23.2	-3.0	20.7	19.3	-1.4
	1904	20.2	22.3	2.1	19.4	18.8	-0.6
Colorado	1880	17.0	15.8	-1.2	15.3	13.8	-1.5
	1888	22.6	21.6	-1.1	23.2	10.2	-13.0
	1904	28.9	21.8	-7.2	24.3	21.5	-2.8
Michigan	1880	11.4	9.1	-2.4	8.7	9.0	0.2
	1892	13.6	11.8	-1.9	11.8	11.9	0.0
	1904	14.6	13.8	-0.8	13.4	13.8	0.4
New Jersey	1880	16.0	15.7	-0.3	17.2	16.4	-0.8
	1892	18.8	16.8	-2.0	18.6	18.2	-0.4
	1904	23.1	22.3	-0.8	20.6	20.3	-0.3
Smallest Counties							
California	1880	26.7	21.9	-4.8	23.7	21.8	-2.0
	1892	16.7	19.6	2.9	15.8	18.5	2.7
	1904	18.2	18.3	0.2	12.9	12.7	-0.2
Colorado	1880	17.8	17.7	-0.1	18.2	20.6	2.3
	1888	18.1	15.5	-2.5	18.5	22.6	4.1
	1904	11.4	13.5	2.1	12.5	17.3	4.8
Michigan	1880	11.0	12.2	1.2	14.1	14.8	0.7
	1892	15.7	17.2	1.6	15.3	16.4	1.1
	1904	12.4	13.8	1.4	19.8	13.8	-6.0
New Jersey	1880	24.0	25.5	1.5	23.6	25.8	2.2
	1892	20.1	23.4	3.3	20.3	22.4	2.2
	1904	18.2	25.2	7.0	18.6	25.0	6.3

In New Jersey the political clout of the smaller counties increased as a result of a 1904 law that allotted one delegate for each election district however small.[13] While a modest level of malapportionment characterized state party conventions of the era, and may have been getting worse in New Jersey and Colorado, the convention's shortcomings in this respect pale in comparison to those of contemporary state legislatures.[14] By basing representation mainly on party votes in recent elections, the major parties preserved the state convention's representative character.

Following the state committee's call, the county committees got busy arranging for a delegation. The decentralized character of American political parties dictated that state committees leave the method of selecting delegates to the discretion of their local affiliates. The county committee often confined its duties to naming the time and place of the county convention and fixing the number of delegates to represent each township or ward. Local practices bearing on the date and precise procedures for appointing county delegates, the use of proxies, the application of the unit rule, and the qualifications of voters varied widely. In 1882 the Colorado Democratic State Committee took the unusual step of "recommending" that the counties hold their conventions on Saturday, the 16th of September. Few counties heeded the committee's counsel, however, and it did not venture to make similar suggestions in later years.[15] Owing to the Porter Law of 1866, California's Democratic and Republican organizations exercised greater supervision over the delegate selection process than did parties elsewhere. The law authorized the state committees to impose guidelines bearing on voter qualifications to participate in primaries and caucuses. Democrats in 1886 empowered county committees to set their own eligibility guidelines when they issued their calls. California's Workingmen's Party State Convention of 1879 gave voice to a long tradition of suspicion of central authority when it affirmed: "That the W. P. C. of each county in this State shall prescribe its own rules and regulations for the

[13] *New Jersey Laws* (1904), Chap. 241, p. 416. In 1907, for example, the township of South Cape May cast but one vote for the Democratic candidate for governor, but Cape May County was still entitled to another delegate to the 1910 state convention. *NEN*, Sept. 16, 1910, p. 1.

[14] State constitutions commonly assigned legislative seats in a manner that inflated the influence of rural areas. In New Jersey, for example, each county was assigned one seat in the state senate. For patterns elsewhere, see Peter H. Argersinger, "The Value of the Vote: Political Representation in the Gilded Age," in *Structure, Process and Party: Essays in American Political History*, ed. Peter H. Argersinger (Armonk, N.Y., 1992), pp. 69–102.

[15] *RMN*, Sept. 4, 1882, p. 3; Sept. 6, 1884, p. 8; Sept. 3, 1886, p. 4.

government of the party organization in its own territory, notwithstanding anything in the Constitution of the State organization of the W. P. C. to the contrary."[16] Local autonomy was enshrined as a guiding principle of party governance during the Gilded Age

Most state delegates during the 1880s were chosen in county conventions composed of delegates who themselves had been selected in caucuses or primaries. The county convention that appointed state delegates might be one of several such bodies called into being during an election year. In some cases, the same county convention might select all the delegates to state, legislative, and other nominating bodies, and then choose its candidates for county offices. In other places or times, separate caucuses and county conventions were called to appoint delegates to specific conventions or to settle on the local ticket. New Jersey's parties mandated that voters meet in their precincts or election districts to elect the state delegates, and thereby dispensed with a county convention. In Woodbury, New Jersey, in 1880 the Democratic voters met at the courthouse at 8:00 P.M. on August 26th to select a delegate to the state convention. They met again on September 21st to pick a delegate to attend a congressional-nominating convention meeting the next day in a nearby county. The practice of direct nominations prevailed in many New Jersey counties when it came to more local races. For example, the choice of candidates for Gloucester County offices and the state legislature was left in the hands of the county's voters, who convened in mass conventions just two or three weeks before the general election.[17]

In the Garden State, as elsewhere, cities and towns tended to select their delegates by ballot in a "primary,"[18] while a "caucus" – or simple meeting – obtained in smaller towns and rural areas.[19] When balloting was called for, a preliminary meeting nominated a slate and enjoined others to arrange the voting procedures. The Democrats in the city of Burlington, New Jersey, took the unusual step of publishing a set of rules in 1877 regarding the conduct of their primaries. They specified an initial meeting of voters in each district to nominate individuals for delegates to state,

---

[16] *SFE*, May 12, 1886, p. 3; *SFC*, June 6, 1879, p. 2.

[17] *Gloucester County Democrat*, Aug. 26, 1880, p. 3; Sept. 9, 1880, p. 2; Oct. 14, 1880, p. 2. Republicans followed a similar format on a different schedule, Sept. 23, 1886, p. 2.

[18] *NEN*, Oct. 3, 1886, p. 1; *NA*, Sept. 15, 1883, p. 1; *NSC*, Sept. 9, 1883, p. 1.

[19] Contemporary usage employed the terms "primary" and "caucus" interchangeably. For purposes of clarity, this text will label as a "caucus" assemblies of voters that function as a meeting, and will use "primary" to refer to instances where the only activity is voting by ballot.

congressional, county, and legislative conventions as well as candidates for city offices. These meetings also appointed a three-member panel of election judges. Four days later, voters made their choices using ballots prepared by the party's election officials.[20] The brief interval between the day when would-be delegates and local nominees were enrolled on the primary ballot and the date when they were voted on allowed little room for electioneering by candidates or their friends. Voters presumably were already familiar with their choices and in no need of edification or persuasion.

In small towns and rural areas, it was the custom to select county delegates in afternoon or evening meetings. Records of these rural caucuses, assuming any were kept, are hard to come by.[21] Town halls or schools housed the sessions, or sometimes a local law office or store, suggesting that no large turnout was expected. The terse reports in the local party organ described brief, highly informal and altogether harmonious proceedings. The close of the session afforded an opportunity to form a political club for the coming campaign. In 1880, the Republicans who convened in South Orange, New Jersey, listened to some stirring speeches, selected a state delegate and an alternate, formed a political club of sixty members, and adjourned.[22]

So little competition, controversy or interest attended the nominating process that rural areas sometimes dispensed with caucuses and county conventions entirely. Too many farmers were busy with their crops during the summer to travel all the way to town for a meeting.[23] In California the *Marin County Journal* urged the Republican County Committee to appoint the state delegates rather than call a county convention in 1882. The summer was a busy time of year, and it was too early to nominate for county offices. Moreover, the paper pointed out, "We have no special fight on the state ticket, that is our party is not committed to any aspirant for governor or any other office. All we want is a delegation of clear

---

[20] *Burlington Gazette*, Sept. 11, 1880, p. 2. In this case, the Democratic voters selected their local nominees directly.

[21] For one of the rare such collections, see Box 299, Warren T. Sexton Papers, California State Library, Sacramento.

[22] *NA*, Aug. 17, 1880, p. 1; *Gloucester County Democrat*, Aug. 19, 1880, p. 2; *Penns Grove Record*, Sept. 25, 1886, p. 3.

[23] *SFE*, Mar. 16, 1882, p. 3; *DFP*, June 25, 1900, p. 1. In years with a presidential election, some rural areas might select their delegates to all pending conventions (state, congressional, legislative, etc.) at one county convention in the early spring when they had to appoint delegates for the state convention that would be choosing delegates for the national nominating conventions.

headed, honest Republicans, who will go unpledged, and do the best that
the situation offers." Sometimes a county committee called for delegates
to be selected in a "mass meeting" that could hardly have been any larger
than the committee itself. When Colorado's Gunnison County Republican
Committee assembled in 1880 the many absentees induced it to allow
anyone in attendance to vote. (This "mass meeting," in a county that
would cast over one thousand Republican ballots for president later that
year, managed to squeeze itself into a drugstore.) The local Democratic
newspaper claimed that the selection of delegates was only accomplished,
"after a great deal of wrangling and quarling [*sic*]." Perhaps this is why, at
the end of the meeting, the assembly appointed a committee of three "to
draw up rules for the government of the Republican Party in Gunnison
County."[24]

Voters in the larger cities choose their delegates in a more formal process that more nearly resembled an election. A preliminary step was an
informal meeting to come up with a set of names of delegates to be voted
on. Responding to a newspaper announcement, 146 men attended a mass
meeting to compile a list of potential delegates the day before the 1882
Republican primary in Los Angeles. The more usual practice was for a
local party club to present a slate. The president of the Democratic club in
Denver's fashionable Third Ward convened just such a meeting in 1890.
After appointing a permanent chair, each precinct sent a representative to
a committee instructed to come up with a slate of delegates. After a "short
consultation" the committee returned with a roster that included the most
prominent Democrats of the city. The club promptly approved the selections and appointed another committee to prepare the necessary ballots.[25]
The number of names offered up in these initial "parlor caucuses" often
equaled the number of seats allotted, precluding any competition at the
primary. In Trenton, New Jersey, Republicans resorted to a primary only
if more names surfaced for a place on the delegation than were provided
for in the convention call, which usually did not happen.[26] The formality
of the process was tempered by the choice of polling place, which was
most likely to be a private residence, firehouse, livery stable, hardware or
cigar store, or some other male domain.

The absence of competition in the selection of delegates was not necessarily an indication of indifference or mere happenstance. Politicians

---

[24] *Marin County Journal*, June 15, 1882, p. 3; *Gunnison News*, Aug. 21, 1880, p. 1.
[25] *LAT*, Aug. 19, 1882, p. 4; *RMN*, Sept. 19, 1890, p. 6.
[26] *TTA*, Sept. 9, 1884, p. 3; *DSG*, Sept. 13, 1888, p. 5.

regarded a competitive contest for delegate seats as detrimental to party unity. Local leaders and factions endeavored to agree on a delegate slate in the primaries and caucuses. The *Los Angeles Times* congratulated local Republicans for having pulled off a primary in 1882 practically devoid of contests; this was accomplished in "cruel disregard" of the Democrats who knew that it insured their defeat. Likewise, the *Rocky Mountain News* praised Denver's Democratic factions for resolving their differences in advance of the primaries of 1902. "The Democrats in district C have set a splendid example for their brethren in the other districts of Arapahoe County. The various elements which have been contending for control of the district caucused yesterday and in a few hours agreed upon a ticket [of county delegates] which will be elected unanimously at the primaries."[27]

Even when a primary afforded the voter some choice in his representative at the county convention, it was rarely clear where any prospective delegate stood with respect to candidacies or causes. "The voting on Saturday was blind," observed the *San Francisco Call* of the primaries of 1886. "Not one voter in ten knew what he was trying to accomplish or knew if he was voting in a way to accomplish any purpose he might entertain. . . . [N]o one knew how his voting one way or another would affect the senatorial ambitions of [Morris M.] Estee or [George C.] Perkins, or any of the gubernatorial aspirants."[28] Discussion or even identification of the men seeking party honors did not get much play in the press. An assumption of the convention system was that the voters need not trouble themselves speculating about the nominees. It was sufficient for the party's mass base to send reputable citizens to their nominating bodies. It was the duty of the delegates to consider the array of candidates available for multiple offices and fashion a ticket of able men behind whom the party could unite.

Some voters were not happy with the limited scope and influence afforded them in a system of indirect nominations. Many citizens registered little enthusiasm for an electoral process with no clear options. A Republican who boycotted his party's Denver primaries in 1888 expressed his frustration with a process that so swiftly swept conflict under the rug. "I confess, Mr. Editor, that when I vote I would like to know whom I vote for and to have some means of knowing what the consequences of my voting will be." This was impossible in the recent primary, where not one man in fifty "would have known or could have made a reasonable

---

[27] *LAT*, Aug. 22, 1882, p. 4; *RMN*, Aug. 30, 1902, p. 2.
[28] Quoted from *LAT*, Aug. 18, 1886, p. 2.

guess as to what any of those thirty-five men would do in the county convention.... But so long as the present system of making nominations continues only a limited and favored few will know, and just so long will it be idle to expect that the members of the party generally will or can take part in our primary elections." The partisan press's policy of silence on prospective nominees was not well suited to a booming city like Denver, brimming with newcomers. A letter from "Tenderfoot" to the *Denver Times* in 1880 complained of the dearth of candidate coverage. "Some of us Republicans from the East, who expect to have our voice in the selection of Republican candidates, would like to have some of the older citizenship mention the special or peculiar claims of the candidates whom they befriend, that we might vote more intelligently." The *Times* responded by listing the men thought to be candidates for each office, but the paper demurred when it came to commenting on their qualifications or fitness. "A partisan newspaper can hardly be expected to furnish such information before the party convention is held, and if it does undertake to do so it renders itself liable to the charge of advocating the claims of some one over some other one, and what is intended to be information imparted without bias is apt to be construed as invidious."[29] While many voters were probably keen to learn about the political ambitions of prominent politicos, the party-controlled press did not seek to satisfy their curiosity if doing so threatened to sow discord.

Given the lack of clear alternatives when voters showed up for a caucus or primary, voter participation was understandably low. Morton Keller estimates that only about 10 percent of the electorate took part in caucuses and primaries during the Gilded Age. Other scholars find even this figure too high.[30] Scattered newspaper reports of caucus or primary results do not offer an opportunity for a systematic analysis, but they certainly do not suggest a high rate of participation. A ratio of one in ten may be a bit low when it came to selecting state delegates in the four states under review, but it may not be very far off the mark. About 23 percent of California's rural El Dorado County Democratic voters participated in the 1882 primary, a figure the local party organ deemed deplorable. Nine precincts sent no delegates at all to the county convention.[31] The *San Francisco*

[29] *DR*, Aug. 29, 1888, p. 6; *DT*, Aug. 14, 1880, p. 4.
[30] Morton Keller, *Affairs of State: Public Life in Late Nineteenth Century America* (Cambridge, Mass., 1977), pp. 533–34; Robert W. Cherney, *American Politics in the Gilded Age* (Wheeling, Ill., 1997), pp. 6–7.
[31] *Mountain Democrat* (Placerville), June 24, 1882, p. 2. The paper reported the actual turnout as around three hundred and fifty. The percentile estimate is based on the

Examiner proudly reported that over one-third of the city's Democrats came out to the primaries in 1882, a figure that it regarded as unusually high.[32] Other clues point to low voter turnout at these partisan events. The accommodations provided at these party functions plainly anticipated a small attendance. Caucuses for an entire township or city ward, containing hundreds of voters, took place in small, modest dwellings such as homes, shops, or law offices. If a primary was called for, a two-hour time slot sufficed to vote an entire ward (whereas balloting on election day took up most of the day and might be done in one of several precincts).

Party organs issued recurrent laments that grassroots involvement was not what it should be. They pleaded with their readers to take the time to show up for a caucus or primary; good government and the party's well-being required it. "Good nominations cannot be expected from bad conventions," the *Denver Republican* explained in 1892, "and the only way to secure good conventions is for the Republican voters to attend their primary elections in a body, in order to insure the selection of honest, able and trustworthy delegates." Yet, these same party organs and leaders did all they could to ensure that there was little for the voters to do once they got to the polls other than to rubber stamp a previously negotiated slate. The desire for widespread voter participation was real enough, but it worked at cross-purposes with the more highly prized goal of consensus. The glaring inconsistency revealed a deeper purpose behind the caucuses and primaries beyond expressing the vox populi. The parties promoted high voter turnout as a means of winning the electorate's assent to decisions taken by the nominating bodies. Securing the early acquiescence of a party's electoral base helped suppress or isolate internal dissent. "There is no factionalism in a full vote and an honest count,"[33] the *Denver Republican* affirmed in 1888.

Democratic vote for president in 1880 and 1884. For the official returns, see Secretary of State, *State and County Governments, Executive, Judicial and Legislative Departments* (Sacramento, 1881, 1885). The nine precincts absent accounted for 20 out of 135 seats at the county convention. The paper also reported that only 76 delegates showed up for the convention. Presumably some carried proxies for the other 39 missing representatives.

[32] *SFE*, June 3, 1882, p. 2. Twelve years later, the paper estimated that voter turnout at primaries statewide generally fell within a 15 to 20% range. *SFE*, June 25, 1894, p. 6. Unless otherwise specified, my references to turnout refer to caucuses and primaries whereby voters directly or indirectly selected delegates to the state convention. Additional caucuses elected representatives to go to county, municipal, legislative, and congressional elections, rendering any overall assessment of voter participation in the nomination process problematic.

[33] *DR*, Sept. 3, 1892, p. 4; *DT*, Aug. 13, 1880, p. 8; *DR*, Aug. 21, 1888, p. 4.

The hierarchical character of the convention system did little to promote meaningful participation on the part of the citizenry. This observation became more true the further one moved up the political ladder. Voters were one or two steps removed from the decision on state, congressional, and sometimes legislative nominees; they selected delegates who attended county conventions that designated still other delegates to attend state, congressional, or legislative conventions. The voter was unlikely to encounter someone running for delegate who shared his top choices for the many offices up for consideration at a state convention. Little wonder, therefore, that one usually did not find references in the newspapers linking a delegate's preferences to any candidate or faction. It was a different matter when it came to local offices. Removing a layer or two from the nomination process made it so much the less indirect and magnified the importance of the initial primary or caucus. With more clearly at stake, politicking at the local level was more open and contentious. One of the givens of American politics affirms that competition invites participation. Hence, voter turnout may have been highest in primaries and caucuses bearing on local races.

The county convention was one more partisan event of the convention system that drew the party faithful together as delegates or lookers-on. A newspaper recounted the busy "pregame activities" at a Republican county convention in Port Huron, Michigan:

The clock in that antique city hall tower had hardly announced the hour of seven before the political war veterans, city and provincial, were perambulating our streets Monday morning, ready to buttonhole their more unsophisticated brother delegates as the morning trains brought them in. By nine o'clock [5 hours before the convention opened] the politicians had succeeded in pretty effectively barricading the side walk in front of the court house, as they discussed the merits and demerits of the numerous candidates . . . in language which, if not convincing, was vehement. And so the morning passed away with the usual wire pulling, and politics gave way to the demands of nature for a while, as the delegates partook of the good things to be had at the several hotels.[34]

When the delegates got around to official business, they followed a similar routine in whatever party or state. The chair of the county committee called the meeting to order, usually several minutes late, with an appeal for harmony and a prediction of an imminent electoral triumph. Following a prayer from the local clergy, the first item on the agenda was the selection of a temporary chair and secretary. (In Michigan the county

---

[34] Republican Party of Lapeer County, "Minutes, 1881–87," p. 8, Bentley Historical Library, University of Michigan, Ann Arbor.

committee usually appointed these officials.) The duties of organizing the convention then devolved on two or three committees. One committee received and verified each delegate's credentials. Another suggested a list of permanent officers and produced an agenda. In some of the larger county conventions, representing urban areas, a resolutions committee worked up a platform; smaller, rural bodies more likely dispensed with the document. Sometimes the convention's temporary chair appointed these committees; in other instances their names were offered from the floor of the convention, and in still others the political subdivisions (wards or townships) furnished a representative to each body. A recess for lunch might then be in order while the committees got down to work.

When the delegates reconvened they first needed to hear from the credentials committee. If that assemblage was not ready to report, the delegates might call for an impromptu speech from a prominent member of their body or from among the spectators. Unless a contesting delegation was on hand, the work of the credentials committee was largely pro forma. The report from the committee on organization and order of business was looked for next, and it rarely excited much comment. In some circumstances the only remaining task was to select delegates to the state or other conventions for congressional, judicial, or legislative districts. The same county convention might also be called upon to name the party's choices for sheriff, clerk, or other county officers. In urban areas, where there were municipal offices to fill, the body might stay in session more than one day. The more a convention was required to do, the more contentious the proceedings became and the greater the threat of crippling discord. New Jersey's major parties arranged for different conventions to take responsibility for selecting different portions of the ticket. This was one way to isolate controversy, though it made greater demands of the voters' time. Sometime during the county convention proceedings a resolutions committee might present a platform draft. Such documents were almost always approved "with a whoop" and without amendment or debate. Controversy might arise if the language instructed the state delegation on how to vote. Lastly the convention selected a new county committee charged with organizing for the fall campaign and arranging for future party conclaves. If all went smoothly, the body adjourned sine die amid warm partisan camaraderie and confident predictions for November.

County conventions contrived many procedures for appointing state delegates, and it seems as though every possible scheme was adopted somewhere. The most popular method was for the convention to devolve into its constituent parts and have each township or ward put forward a specified number of delegates.[35] Another device was to appoint a committee to make the selections. More rarely, the convention as a whole might vote on each delegate or empower an aspirant for office to come up with the list,[36] or leave the decision entirely to chance. The custom in Michigan's Hillsdale County was to put the names of potential state delegates in a box and then draw out one name after another until they filled the delegation.[37] The diverse and decentralized structure of the delegate selection process accorded with the diverse and decentralized character of the party organizations themselves. It also posed serious complications for those who hoped to control a delegation in the interests of any candidate, especially an outsider.

For the major parties, the delegate selection process laid the groundwork for a harmonious state convention to ensure a united front before "our friends the enemy." Much was done through consensus. Factions negotiated on a unified slate of delegates to present to the voters in the caucuses and primaries. The voters' input conferred legitimacy on the process and was therefore welcomed. Decentralization of decision making was another device to ensure that all major players found a place at the table and had a stake in the outcome. State committees and county conventions deferred to their political subdivisions in deciding when and how state delegates would be chosen. Candidates intruded on the process somewhat at the local level, but they did not command the center of attention. Preserving party cohesion was the rationale behind much that was done under the rubrics of the convention system, and it was this devotion to party welfare that most commended the system to a partisan-minded public.

III

Party organs customarily lavished praise on the men chosen to attend the state convention.[38] How the press chose to portray the state delegates

---

[35] This was done after a committee of apportionment assigned each political unit an allotment of seats on the state convention floor. *LAT*, Aug. 22, 1886, p. 6; *Buchanan Record* (Mich.), July 14, 1892, p. 2; *DT*, Aug. 18, 1880, p. 8.

[36] On the various procedures, see *RMN*, Aug. 31, 1884, p. 1; *Chaffee County Republican*, Aug. 25, 1898, p. 2; *The Mail* (Stockton, Calif.), Aug. 2, 1890, p. 1; *DP*, Sept. 9, 1904, p. 3; *DR*, Sept. 15, 1888, p. 1; *Big Rapids Pioneer* (Mich.), July 14, 1892, p. 3.

[37] *DFP*, July, 30, 1896, p. 1. See also *RMN*, Sept. 21, 1884, p. 8; *DFP*, Aug. 4, 1880, p. 1.

[38] This practice can be dated back to the earliest national conventions. See James S. Chase, *Emergence of the Presidential Nominating Convention, 1789–1832* (Urbana, Ill., 1973), p. 289.

exposed the anomalous status of convention delegates and the convention itself in American political culture. Did the convention epitomize democratic principles by bringing together a representative body of citizens whose decisions reflected public opinion? Or was deference democracy the operating principle, filling the assembly with the "better element" who would act in the public interest? Democratic and Republican mouthpieces argued it both ways. They assured the public that all interests would be represented and that the sterling status of the delegates insured that they could be trusted to do the right thing. The partisan press coined the term "best representative men" to express the dual character of the delegates. "It was truly representative," the *Newark Advertiser* noted of the G.O.P. State Convention in 1883, "and the representatives were the best samples of their kind." "They are probably the best looking body of men ever brought together for the purpose of officers since the organization of the state government," the *Rocky Mountain News* observed of the Democratic State Convention of 1882. "All classes worthy of representation are found to be represented among them, and that by men of the highest respectability and integrity." Extolling the virtues and sagacity of the delegates was a prelude to trumpeting their accomplishments in the days that followed. A rural Michigan newspaper informed its readers in 1892 that "Capt. J. A. McKay left here on Monday armed with his credentials as delegate to the state convention. Mr. McKay is well posted on the merits of the different candidates for state officers, and no doubt cast the ballots for Ontonagon County in a manner that made them count."[39]

A collective profile of delegates to the state conventions raises some skepticism regarding how truly representative these bodies were even among the white, adult male citizenry. Racial minority representation among the state delegations was minimal. There were a few references to African American delegates in Republican[40] and even in Democratic[41] conventions during the 1880s. Singled out as they were, their presence plainly was viewed as something of a curiosity, however much the press pretended otherwise. "Pueblo's colored delegate to the Democratic state convention took part in the proceedings of that body with the sang froid of a veteran," the *Rocky Mountain News* asserted in 1888. "His

---

[39] SFE, Apr. 15, 1880, p. 2; NA, Sept. 19, 1883, p. 1; RMN, Sept. 21, 1882, p. 8; *Portage Lake Gazette*, July 23, 1892, p. 3.
[40] RMN, Sept. 15, 1884, p. 4; DFP, Aug. 26, 1886, p. 4; SFE, Aug. 14, 1890, p. 3.
[41] DT, Aug. 19, 1880, p. 1; RMN, Sept. 22, 1882, p. 1; SFE, Aug. 15, 1890, p. 2.

FIGURE 2.2. Newspapers frequently illustrated their convention coverage with portraits of the party's leading figures, most of whom could be found on the convention floor. Even the opposition party's press portrayed the delegates in dignified poses and formal attire appropriate to their status as "best representative men." (*SFE*, Aug. 14, 1890, p. 3; *RMN*, Sept. 11, 1900, p. 12.)

presence considered a matter of course and creating but little comment." But northern blacks were not satisfied with tokenism. An angry letter to the *Rocky Mountain News* complained that only two African Americans sat in Arapahoe County's Republican convention (which encompassed Denver) in 1886, "and these delegates were far from being representative men." That convention neglected to send any blacks to the state convention, even though Republicans reaped seven hundred votes from the African American community. "This is a direct insult to the colored people of this state, and if they don't resent it they are unworthy of being citizens."[42]

Other minorities fared worse. The list of names to either party's state conventions in California fails to produce any name of Asian derivation. This hardly surprises given that the state constitution denied citizenship to persons of Chinese extraction.[43] It is more remarkable how few Hispanic politicians attended these partisan gatherings. Only one to three delegates with a Hispanic surname appeared at any one of three Democratic or Republican state conventions in the Golden State between 1882 and 1890.[44] In Colorado the Mexican American population fared slightly better. Four to ten Hispanic names show up on the delegate roster, all of them hailing from one of five southern counties.[45] Studies of local politics in California and Colorado stress the "personal dependence and mutual obligation" in relations between the poor and rural Hispanic population and the largely Anglo power structure.[46] Few of the "padrinos" who represented heavily Hispanic communities were themselves Hispanics.

Without much representation in conventions at any level, racial minorities lacked the clout to land a place on the ticket for one of their own. Here and there some "colored Republican clubs" attempted to secure a nomination for a local office for a member of their race, but without much success. When African Americans did manage to gain a nomination, the Republican organization allegedly knifed them on election day. As the president of one African American Republican club in Indianapolis, Indiana, lamented: "We may talk as we choose about the love of the

[42] *RMN*, Sept. 13, 1888, p. 2; Aug. 31, 1886, p. 2. The 700 African American voters in Denver in 1886 would have constituted about 13% of the Republican vote cast for governor that fall. Hence, African Americans might have expected to be awarded about 9 of the 72 seats apportioned to Arapahoe County at the Republican State Convention.

[43] Alexander Keyssar, *The Right to Vote: The Contested History of Democracy in the United States* (New York, 2000), p. 141. Asian Americans also played no part in Colorado politics at this time.

[44] *SFE*, June 17, 1882, p. 2; Aug. 31, 1886, p. 1; Aug. 12, 1890, p. 2; Aug. 19, 1890, p. 3; *LAT*, Aug. 24, 1886, p. 4. The number of delegates attending these state conventions ranged from 457 to 677.

[45] *RMN*, Sept. 14, 1882, p. 1; Oct. 5, 1886, p. 3; Sept. 5, 1888, p. 2; Sept. 11, 1888, p. 2; Sept. 19, 1890, p. 6; Sept. 25, 1890, p. 2. The conventions ranged in size from 311 to 648.

[46] Timothy J. Lukes, "Progressivism Off-Broadway: Reform Politics in San Jose, California, 1880–1920," *Southern California Quarterly* 76 (Winter 1994): 377–400; William B. Taylor and Elliott West, "Patron Leadership at the Crossroads: Southern Colorado in the Late Nineteenth Century," *Pacific Historical Review* 42 (Aug. 1973): 335–57.

republicans for the colored man, but we know he [*sic*] will not vote for him."⁴⁷ Here too Colorado's Hispanic population was slightly better off. Casimero Barela served in the state senate from Las Animas County for many years, first as a Democrat and later as a Republican. Democrats twice nominated him for a state elected post. Both party presses, however, confessed to a deep-seated prejudice against the "Spanish American race" among the electorate that deterred the major parties from nominating others.⁴⁸

Deprived of much access to the convention floor or a place on the ticket, minority politicians invested more effort at securing some share of the patronage. Here, the convention system appeared to be more responsive. A black delegate at California's Republican State Convention in 1894 offered a resolution "calling upon elected officers to recognize colored voters in their apportionment of subordinates." The chair ruled the resolution out of order, claiming it required unanimous consent. "I hear no objection," the delegate countered. His remark "brought cheers for his ready wit. Unanimous consent was granted, the resolution was read and immediately adopted." The Colored Republican State Committee in New Jersey demanded of its white counterpart "that recognition and representation which is due to our numbers and influence in the distribution of political patronage of the State and the civil service of the United States." Continued agitation on the subject eventually induced the Republican State Convention of 1892 to set aside a seat for a black representative on the state committee to help oversee the distribution of the spoils. "[T]he colored brother realizes that he is not in it with the G.O.P.," the independent *Newark Evening News* observed. "[I]n order to get his just dues he must organize and then get, by threats to desert the ranks, what there is not the slightest hope for him to get otherwise. He is no longer satisfied to have doled out to him from the political coop a lean and tough old setting hen, but,... demands that he be allowed to reach in and extract a plump, yellow-legged pullet from the roost."⁴⁹

⁴⁷ *Newark Morning Register*, Aug. 19, 1880, p. 1; *DR*, Aug. 30, 1888, p. 5; *The Freeman*, May 21, 1892, p. 4.
⁴⁸ *RMN*, Oct. 7, 1886, p. 1. The Populists nominated Barela for state treasurer in 1894. *RMN*, Sept. 5, 1894, p. 5. The defeat of the Republican candidate for governor in Colorado in 1886 was attributed in part to his marriage to a Mexican American woman, even though some Republicans insisted "she is not a greaser, but a fine looking lady of Spanish blood." *RMN*, Sept. 14, 1884, p. 4; *DT*, Aug. 12, 1880, p. 4; *Georgetown Courier*, Oct. 7, 1886, p. 2.
⁴⁹ *SFE*, June 21, 1894, p. 2; *NYT*, July 16, 1880, p. 1; *TTA*, Sept. 13, 1892, p. 5; *NEN*, Sept. 14, 1892, p. 1. See in particular the correspondence of T. B. Morton, head of the

If the convention system demonstrably did not furnish minorities with a fair share of the political pie, it did provide a forum for them to make their demands and dissatisfactions known – and to threaten reprisals. Representatives from minority groups openly condemned some potential candidates who had proven unfriendly to their race. At Colorado's 1890 Democratic State Convention, Senator Barela denounced the candidacy of one aspirant for the gubernatorial nomination because he had blocked Mexican Americans from serving on juries.[50] Barela warned that the would-be nominee would not be welcomed in Hispanic precincts, and the gubernatorial honors went elsewhere. Conventions dismissed these protests at their peril. California's African Americans neither forgot nor forgave Morris M. Estee for failing to endorse the Fourteenth and Fifteenth amendments when he was in the state legislature.[51] Estee was twice nominated for governor by the Republicans (in 1882 and 1894) – and twice defeated at the polls. The political system severely limited the opportunity of minorities to participate and to share in the spoils, but within the convention hall the rare minority delegate could be heard and might even be heeded.

The almost exclusively white delegations at state conventions mostly comprised men occupying the higher end of the social scale. This is the conclusion imparted by an analysis of 952 delegates from the largest city in each of the four states under review.[52] Figure 2.3 offers a statistical portrait of Republican delegates from two state conventions: those of 1882 and 1886 in California and 1880 and 1886 elsewhere. City directories furnished occupational information.[53] The largest bloc of "best representative men" (27.7%) hailed from the "Business Elite" of Newark, Detroit, Denver, and San Francisco. Most of these men ran their own manufacturing or wholesale-merchandising establishments. About one in five of this group included managers or superintendents of the same. The ranks of the many government officials divided evenly between persons in positions of prominence (city department heads, judges, or elected officials) and persons holding lesser official posts (clerks, inspectors, or policemen).

"Afro American League," Box 1, Folder 4, Daniel M. Burns Papers, Bancroft Library, University of California at Berkeley.

[50] *RMN*, Sept. 26, 1890, p. 1.

[51] C. N. Post to Burns, Sept. 23, 1894, Box 2, Folder 41, Burns Papers.

[52] The methodology is outlined in Appendix A.

[53] A small percentage of Republican delegates (8.2%) could not be found in the directories for reasons explained more fully in Appendix A. The directories identified only one delegate, a Detroit bricklayer, as "colored."

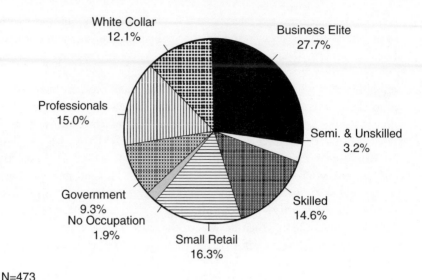

N=473

FIGURE 2.3. Delegates to Republican state conventions from four cities, 1880–1886.

Professionals accounted for about one in six delegates (15.0%), with lawyers outnumbering all others in this classification by almost two to one. In sum, about half the Republican delegates represented persons of minimally upper-middle-class status.

Republicans filled the ranks of their lower strata mainly from middle-class occupations of small-scale retailers (16.3%), skilled craftsmen (14.6%), and white-collar workers (12.1%). Small businesses were sometimes difficult to distinguish from larger enterprises or from skilled occupations, and they were a very mixed group. Contractors represented the largest single group in the small business category (one in five). Their presence was indicative of the close association between politicians and local developers in the burgeoning cities. Many other small establishments involved businesses catering to a male clientele (saloons and cigar shops), though there was also room for grocery and restaurant owners. White-collar workers were about evenly divided between clerks, book-keepers, and salesmen. Although manual workers (skilled, semiskilled, and unskilled) constituted about two-thirds of the adult male working population in the sampled cities, their proportion of Republican delegations was far less. (See Table A.2 in Appendix A for the overall distribution of occupations reported in the federal census of 1880.) The skilled workers

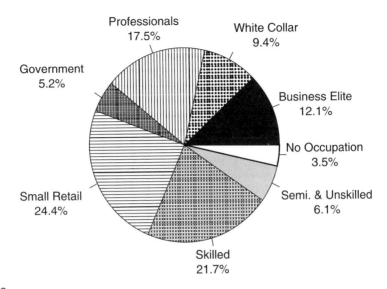

N=479

FIGURE 2.4. Delegates to Democratic state conventions from four cities, 1880–1886.

represented a broad array of crafts; the four most common occupations – foremen, carpenters, machinists, and janitors – constituted less than a third of the total. Only a dozen semi- or unskilled delegates appeared in the directories, half of them listed as teamsters.

Middle-class citizens found greater representation at Democratic state conventions, as indicated in Figure 2.4. Skilled workers and small retailers controlled almost half (46.1%) of the seats apportioned to the four major cities. The small retail category was more popular with Democrats due in part to the larger number of saloon keepers affiliated with the party of "personal liberty."[54] The proportion of seats held by members of the local business establishment (12.1%) was half of what it was among the G.O.P. The smaller percentage of government workers among the Democrats reflected the party's minority status in the North. The greater occupational diversity in the party of Jefferson and Jackson did not trickle down much below the shopkeepers and skilled workers. Only 6.1% of Democratic delegates fell into the semiskilled or unskilled category, most

---

[54] Saloon keepers constituted 31.6 percent of the small-retail category among the Democrats and 19.7 percent among the Republicans.

of them teamsters or bartenders. In sum, whether one speaks of Democrats or Republicans, during the 1880s the state delegations from the major cities contained many more of the "best" citizens than they did citizens of the truly "representative" variety.[55]

Lawyers far outnumbered all other professionals among Democratic and Republican delegates. The overrepresentation of attorneys on the floor of the convention (and on the ticket) was a sore point with some. Politicos with legal training and a practice preferred to pass themselves off as almost anything else. A speaker introduced himself as a farmer at Michigan's Democratic State Convention in 1900 and nominated a candidate for state office on behalf of the tillers of the soil. He stirred a ripple of laughter when he inadvertently addressed the convention delegates as "Gentlemen of the Jury." The chair of the convention "brought down the house" by interjecting that the verbal slip was "an extremely natural mistake for a farmer to make." Another orator, offering a member of the bar for state treasurer in 1884, assured his listeners that "Mr. [James] Blair is not so much of a lawyer as to affect his integrity."[56]

In keeping with its status as a deliberative body, most delegates to state conventions came uninstructed and unpledged to any candidate or course of action. The social status of the convention delegates explains in part why county conventions did not presume to tell them how to vote. Instructions violated the independent judgment that party representatives regarded as their prerogative. Many delegates took umbrage that anyone should "put a ring in their nose" (and lead them around like horse or oxen). The Los Angeles County Democratic Convention of 1882 affirmed that their delegates to the state convention went "unhampered, and without instructions." "[E]ach [delegate] singly and upon his own judgment shall act for the best interests of the party in accordance with the dictates of his own conscience." Even the local Republican press chimed in to

---

[55] The portrait of state delegates that emerges here largely resembles that of contemporary local party activists drawn by Glenn C. Altschuler and Stuart M. Blumin from an analysis that focused on small towns around the nation. See Altschuler and Blumin, *Rude Republic: Americans and Their Politics in the Nineteenth Century* (Princeton, N.J., 2000), pp. 237–46. The authors note some slight decline in the social status of party activists over the previous forty years. See also Ralph Mann, "National Party Fortunes and Local Political Structure: The Case of Two California Mining Towns, 1850–1870," *Southern California Quarterly* 57 (Fall 1975): 271–96. Mann finds that the majority of delegates from Grass Valley and Nevada City attending state conventions were professionals and merchants during the 1860s (see Table VIII).

[56] *DFP*, July 26, 1900, p. 3; *RMN*, Sept. 22, 1910, p. 2; *DFP*, Aug. 28, 1890, p. 4; Aug. 21, 1884, p. 6.

praise the convention's decision to respect the delegates' discretion: "This speaks well for liberty." Coverage of the actions of the county conventions or committees that selected the delegates commonly affirmed that no candidate's interests received any consideration. "No state candidates were named and no one knows who the delegates intend to support but themselves," noted the *Rocky Mountain News* of Hinsdale County's delegates to the Republican State Convention of 1884. Six years later the same paper characterized most of the delegates to the same body as "without any instructions whatever and . . . with plenary powers to act as judgment directs them."[57]

The time had long passed in the United States when politicians dared to openly endorse the principle of deference democracy, but the notion lay only half hidden in the tributes paid to the "best representative men." The occupational background of state delegates (from the major cities, at least) and the complimentary coverage they generated in the press suggest that the concept still carried some political force. The dearth of competition in the delegate selection process also enhanced the probability that only men of some social standing would attend the state convention. Minorities were rarely seen, though sometimes heard. The wide range of discretion afforded uninstructed delegates represented a vote of confidence in them as well as in the convention system. The participation of the best representative men enhanced the legitimacy of the convention, its nominees, and the parties themselves.

IV

County conventions typically convened within two weeks, often just two days, prior to the state convention. The hotels braced themselves for an invasion of thirsty, tobacco-chewing, agitated, and garrulous guests. Expensive carpets and fragile ornaments made way for cuspidors, cots, and refreshment stands. The first to arrive on the scene was the state committee. It met on the eve of the convention to set everything in place. The committee approved a preliminary roster of delegates, a delicate task if a set of contesting delegates appeared.[58] In New Jersey and Michigan the state committee also appointed the temporary officers – a chair and

---

[57] *LAT*, June 13, 1882, p. 2; *Gloucester County Democrat*, May 27, 1880, p. 2; *RMN*, Sept. 5, 1884, p. 1; Sept. 17, 1890, p. 2; *LAT*, Aug. 24, 1886, p. 4.

[58] The state committee could authorize a delegation to be seated on the convention floor – but delegates whose seats were in question were not supposed to vote on their case when it came before the full convention, a rule not always strictly enforced.

secretary – to preside until the convention got organized. During and after the state committee's deliberations, the party's luminaries had ample opportunity to discuss and negotiate matters bearing on candidates or the platform.

As the state committee finished up its work, the delegates arrived by train to liven things up around the railroad depot. The larger counties arrived en masse and marched grandly through the city streets to their hotel with a band leading the way. Reporters and party bigwigs greeted the visitors to pick up intelligence about a delegation's disposition on candidates or issues. Informal politicking and boisterous socializing went on well into the night, nourished by a generous supply of liquor and cigars. Delegates and onlookers jammed the streets and lobbies, or flocked to the hospitality suites sponsored by the many genial office seekers. In Michigan a visitor to a candidate's hotel room might be offered only cigars and ice water, a bill of fare that would have sorely disappointed a parched New Jersey or California delegate. A San Francisco reporter at a convention in San Jose commended the city's suspension of the ordinance barring the sale of liquor after midnight, but he judged the libations plainly inferior to what could be had back home. "The liquors dealt out are good enough, but the San Jose barkeeper lacks that skill in compounding which is essential to the happiness of those whose palates have been tickled with the marvelous drinks of the metropolitan saloons, where artists are employed. The local practice of making lemonade in a bath tub and ladling it out to customers in a dipper cannot be too strongly condemned, as it lessens the confidence of the average man in that seductive and harmless drink."[59] Upstairs, the "bosses" consulted among themselves, summoned their lieutenants, and bargained into the wee hours.

The next morning the groggy delegates caucused a final time. They chose a chair of their county delegation, or a representative to a party committee, or they might endorse a candidate or platform plank.[60] Thereafter they noisily made their way to the convention site. The representatives entered a theater or hall (with room for anywhere from 500 to 1,000 delegates and many more spectators) decked out with flags and bunting, flowers, cuspidors, and portraits of venerable party leaders. Sawdust often covered the floor – to lessen the noise and protect the wood from the poor marksmanship of the ubiquitous tobacco chewers. A sizable crowd looked on from the galleries and balconies. Women, often occupying a special

---

[59] *SFE*, June 22, 1882, p. 2.
[60] In Michigan the counties then met together in their respective congressional districts to appoint officers for the convention.

THE DEMOCRATIC CONVENTION AS IT APPEARED DURING THE SESSION OF YESTERDAY AFTERNOON.

FIGURE 2.5. Images of conventions that circulated in the popular press during the Gilded Age commonly adopted a panoramic view as achieved here with California's Democratic State Convention of 1894. The reader's attention was drawn to the well-dressed and well-mannered delegates in the foreground. San Francisco's Baldwin Theater could not easily accommodate the 661 delegates, and many had to mill about the aisles and foyer. The stage is reserved for convention officials, reporters, and dignitaries from both parties. Note the many women spectators in the "dress circles" in the boxes and balconies. (*SFE*, Aug. 22, 1894, p. 2.)

section, constituted a large share of the audience. A state convention had an irresistible appeal for politicians from around the state. Leaders of the opposition party not only attended but might even be assigned a place of honor on the stage. "Every prominent Republican in the state was present either as a delegate or a spectator," the *Rocky Mountain News* observed at the opening of the Republican State Convention of 1882, "and not a few Democrats of note also filled seats on the stage, silent but amused spectators of the Republican circus."[61]

As with the county convention, the preliminaries of the state convention followed a standard routine. The chair of the state committee opened

[61] *RMN*, Sept. 15, 1882, p. 1; *DFP*, Aug. 21, 1884, p. 6.

the proceedings by complimenting the delegates on their appearance. "I wish you could all see how you look!" gushed the presiding officer of New Jersey's Republican State Convention in 1883.[62] Party organs dutifully made similar remarks about the respectable and serious demeanor of the assembly. After a religious invocation by a local minister the party secretary read the call of the convention. A short speech by the chair of the state committee appealed for "fair play " and loyalty, all variations on a single theme: "Let us have harmony."[63] At this point, in New Jersey and Michigan, the head of the state committee introduced its choice for the convention's temporary chair and secretary. In Colorado and California, the selection of temporary officers was left to the full convention. However appointed, the temporary chair was supposed to be impartial and thoroughly familiar with the rules governing deliberative bodies. Usually, the decision on temporary officers did not require a full vote of the convention. Instead, the friends of the major candidates sought consensus on a choice to preserve the convention's reputation for honest dealings.

With the temporary organization in place, the convention proceeded to appoint the body's three key committees. If there was a contesting delegation, which was usually the case during the 1880s, the credentials committee had an important and delicate role to play. A committee on resolutions disappeared to draft the platform. A committee on organization and order of business took up the matter of the permanent officers, agenda, and rules. In New Jersey and Michigan caucuses of county or congressional districts appointed their committee representatives before entering the convention hall. In Colorado and California the full convention usually passed the appointing power over to the temporary chair, endowing him with considerable influence. With the appointment of the committees the convention took a break for dinner. Meanwhile, in the luxurious suites housing the party elite upstairs, negotiations over the composition of the ticket dragged on.

When the delegates returned, logic dictated that the first item of business was the report of the credentials committee. It was a good bet that the committee was still tied up processing paperwork or hearing testimony when the time for their report rolled around. The convention took these delays with good humor. Calls arose for impromptu addresses from prominent politicians, who discoursed on pressing issues of the day and derided the opposition. When at last the credentials committee appeared

[62] *NA*, Sept. 19, 1883, p. 1.
[63] *DT*, Aug. 26, 1880, p. 4.

with its report, an unresolved squabble over a contested delegation might be left for the full convention to decide. The delegates would impatiently hear one faction verbally abuse the other with charges of fraud or irregularities in the primaries or county conventions. Then it was the committee on organization's turn. In all but a handful of instances, the committee recommended that the temporary officers become permanent. Next, the committee framed an agenda that stipulated first the adoption of a platform and then the order of the nominations. Rarely did these motions elicit much controversy.

Because parties insisted that they represented "principles, not men," it was appropriate that their conventions first agree on a platform. Ideally, the resolutions trumpeted the party's enduring values and specific policy prescriptions. In Michigan, the *Niles Democrat* insisted that the choice of nominees "is and must be secondary" to a consideration of the issues of the day. The document had to speak boldly and clearly: "No mamby-pamby utterances will do at all, no conciliatory mouthings will answer. Every word must contain a truth, boldly declared – the language of the platform must be capable of but one construction." In Placerville, California, the *Mountain Democrat* offered extensive coverage of the adoption of the party's 1892 platform and was predictably effusive in praise. "Its ring is clear and unmistakable as to every subject it touches, and it grasps with a firm and masterful hand every subject of absorbing interest to our people." A copy of the state party platform appeared in every issue of the *Mountain Democrat* leading up to election day. "Party conventions and their platforms are the mouthpieces of the people," the chair of the New Jersey Republican meeting reminded the delegates in 1880. "Without them and what is called the machinery of politics there is no way for the utterances of those principles which guide the people and in time they would be absolutely lost."[64]

Nonpartisan observers took a more jaded view of Democratic and Republican manifestos. The *Newark Sunday Call* judged both parties' platforms in 1883 "such worthless rubbish that they scarcely merit the criticism of intelligent people. If all the political rubbish of this description of ten or twenty years past were collected together and examined, what a mess of 'promises made and never kept,' of bare faced lying and elaborate deceits would be developed!" The opposition press was even more dismissive of declarations likened to flypaper set out to catch unwary voters.

[64] *Niles Democrat*, Aug. 14, 1886, p. 2; *Mountain Democrat* (Placerville, Calif.), July 1, 1892, p. 2; *NA*, Aug. 19, 1880, p. 2.

A Republican editor in Michigan skewered the Democratic platform of 1882 for its "twinings and turnings . . . its total lack of principles, its capacity to eat dirt and its willingness to bow before copperhead, confederate or communist so that it may again have an opportunity to plunder, defile and destroy."[65] Historians and political scientists likewise tend to overlook, if they do not explicitly dismiss, the major parties' statements of principles.[66]

Party edicts did get the respect and attention of those on and off the platform committee. Many worried over the document's potentially deleterious effect on party unity. Those involved in the management of the campaign counseled a cautious course in framing party policy. They espoused a "big tent" philosophy that made room for varying and even conflicting opinions within their ranks. Political leaders were acutely aware that both parties contained disparate elements at the local and especially the state levels that sharply disagreed on many of the major issues of the day. The regulation of alcohol, the protective tariff, and the money supply aroused passionate debate among Democrats and Republicans and an imprudent stance could prove fatal in November. It was far easier to alienate the party's own followers than to attract votes from the opposition or from the thin ranks of the independents. Republicans feared that endorsing temperance legislation would lose them the German vote in such places as Denver, Detroit, and Newark. A speaker at New Jersey's Republican State Convention in 1889 urged the party to tread warily around the temperance issue. "We are a party of principle and not of policy," he explained. Years later, the *Trenton True American* advised the coming Democratic State Convention to be similarly circumspect:

There are many Democrats who believe in local option on the question of the sale and prohibition of liquors, but the party is not a unit on this question, and it should not be touched in the State platform. . . . [T]he opinions of the majority ought not to be attempted to be forced on the minority. There are a thousand other questions on which Democrats divide. None of them is fundamental. None of them has any place in the state platform.

[65] *NSC*, Sept. 16, 1883, p. 1; *Detroit Post and Tribune*, Aug. 24, 1882, p. 4.
[66] See, for example, James Edward Wright, *The Politics of Populism: Dissent in Colorado* (New Haven, Conn., 1974), pp. 51–84. A notable exception in the recent scholarly literature that draws heavily from party platforms is Richard Franklin Bensel's *The Political Economy of Industrialization, 1877–1900* (Cambridge, U.K., 2000), pp. 101–204. See also Ralph S. Boots, "Party Platforms in State Politics," *Annals of the American Academy of Political and Social Science* 106 (Mar. 1923): 72–82.

Democrats did stand in agreement regarding "certain essentials," the editor continued, without defining just what these "certain essentials" were.
"Unity on these is necessary. On all other questions Democrats should be
tolerant with one another." The tariff was a prime example. "There are
Democrats who believe in free trade; there are others who believe in moderate protection; but all are agreed that the tariff should be levied for the
benefit of the people, and not for the benefit of the trusts." Another New
Jersey politico suggested a three-word platform for his party in 1898: "We
are Democrats."[67] Party leaders who attempted to dilute or derail platform language implicitly conceded that partisan propaganda did matter,
even if it could only hurt rather than help.

Unlike the state party leadership, many delegates demanded more
explicit and uncompromising language in the platform. They cared mainly
about electoral prospects back home where an omission or evasion on a
locally important issue would not sit well with their constituents. In the
great majority of the state conventions of the 1880s surveyed, the platform sparked a lengthy, lively, and sometimes heated debate. In Colorado
the Democratic State Convention of 1880 consumed most of a full day
arguing whether to condemn the Republican governor's recent actions
in suppressing a strike in Leadville. Some Democrats left the convention warning that the harsh language adopted would lose the party many
votes among the state's "respectable element." In Michigan the Republican Party's platform committee in 1884 wrangled over whether to pledge
to put the issue of prohibition to a statewide referendum. Opponents
charged that similar language in the 1882 platform was responsible for
the defeat handed the incumbent Republican governor that year. After
a four-hour debate, the platform committee recommended wording that
merely committed the party to promote temperance. "The studied attempt
to gloss over the labor and temperance questions without saying anything
definite was met with approving nods by the politicians." But the drys
would not tolerate any backsliding; they offered the full convention a substitute plank that reiterated the language of two years before. Delegates
from the Upper Peninsula and the state's urban areas defended the platform committee's noncommittal stance. "This is a dangerous question
that is now discussed," one delegate warned. A speaker from Lenawee
countered that his county always sent pro-temperance men to the state
legislature; a congressman retorted that "his county [Houghton] did not

[67] *DEN*, Aug. 15, 1884, p. 3; *NEN*, Oct. 6, 1886, p. 1; *RMN*, Sept. 20, 1884, p. 8; *DSG*, Sept. 18, 1889, p. 5; *TTA*, Sept. 3, 1907, p. 7; *NA*, Sept. 13, 1898, p. 4.

think such laws proper, and declined to have its opinion on that point governed by Lenawee." When finally put to a vote, the convention adopted the language of the drys by a wide margin, putting the party once more firmly behind a state referendum.[68] Defining party doctrine at the outset of a political campaign had its risks. But by forcing conventions into going on the record on vital public subjects, the delegates reaffirmed that it was principles, rather than mere office seeking, that brought them together.

With the platform behind them, the tension in the convention hall became more palpable as the agenda moved to the nomination of candidates. Attention turned first to the top of the ticket. For days past, the gubernatorial horse race was probably the preeminent topic of conversation.[69] The delegates savored the hours of oratory expounding on the virtues of numerous individuals seeking party favor. By the time nominating speeches for governor had commenced, the delegates had already sat through a number of extemporaneous speeches made to fill in the time while they awaited the action of some committee or the chair. Yet the delegates' appetite for oratory was not satiated. Several hours, perhaps a full day, passed in displays of rhetorical fireworks as one candidate's name and then another's was offered for their consideration. Numerous briefer and less accomplished seconding speeches followed. "A nominating speech is really the most trying ordeal of the orator," the sympathetic political reporter of the *San Francisco Examiner* remarked. "The speaker who climbs the rocky road whereon 'a man who' pursues his devious crescendo in front of a steaming audience with the thermometer climbing the roof is a political martyr, helplessly adrift on a tide of adjectives."[70]

Nomination speakers introduced their subjects in a set of conventional guises: the statesman, the soldier, the enterprising businessman, the son of illustrious ancestors. They rarely associated their favorites with a particular issue, dwelt on their accomplishments in office, or hinted at their plans for the future. The newspapers, correspondence, and nominating speeches concur that the most important selling point for any candidate was what he could do for the rest of the ticket. Almost everybody on the floor of the convention, even if they were not expecting to be on the ballot

[68] *DT*, Aug. 19, 1880, p. 1; *DFP*, Aug. 14, 1884, p. 1.
[69] In California and Colorado the nomination of judges for the states' supreme courts sometimes preceded that for governor, and these too attracted considerable attention.
[70] *SFE*, Aug. 19, 1898, p. 1.

themselves in the fall, had a vested interest in the outcome. The delegates gravitated toward men who could help them "get there." Nevada City Democrat J. D. Carr bluntly put the question uppermost in the minds of most delegates to Stephen M. White, California's future U.S. senator: "I want to see the one selected who will be most likely to win. Who is it?" "Who's the strongest man?" was the question heard on every side as the delegates congregated around the hotels on the eve of California's Democratic State Convention of 1886. Nominating speeches endeavored to answer this question by dwelling on a candidate's potential to draw votes to the whole ticket: he was popular, offended no faction, habitually hustled for votes, and had a track record of running ahead of the party slate in past elections. California's Republican delegates were urged in 1886 to turn to William H. Dimond as "the safest man to nominate because he will carry more votes and will do better work in the campaign." "This is no time for mistakes," a speaker admonished Michigan Republicans two years earlier. "We want the man who will poll the last possible vote of the Republican party."[71]

At no time was the chair's skill, patience, and stamina as sorely tried as when the convention began balloting. The animated, noisy, contentious, impassioned, and sometimes inebriated delegates cheered, jeered, applauded, and demanded recognition as they reacted to the changing vote totals. A Republican newspaper characterized New Jersey's Democratic State Convention of 1880 as an "informal row," during which one delegate threw another through a window. "When the fourth ballot began Chairman [Leon] Abbett was pacing up and down the platform waving a stick and shouting for order, the delegates and audience were mixed up in inextricable confusion, and everybody was screaming." "They didn't call it a deliberative body yesterday," the *Rocky Mountain News* observed of Colorado's 1888 G.O.P. State Convention, "it was a mob." The stress was too much for the chair of that body, who complained that "the element predominating in this convention is that upon which the Savior rode to Jerusalem." The climax came when it became clear that a winner had emerged; the hall exploded in enthusiasm. Hats, fans, and canes were tossed wildly into the air. Delegates cheered, sang, shook hands, or hugged in an outpouring of congratulatory salutations. "The thunders of the applause, wild shrieking of men thrilled

---

[71] J. D. Carr to White, July 14, 1890, Box 20, Folder 14, Stephen Mallory White Papers, Stanford University, Palo Alto, Calif.; *SFE*, Sept. 1, 1886, p. 1; *LAT*, Aug. 27, 1886, p. 4; *DFP*, Aug. 14, 1884, p. 6.

FIGURE 2.6. More conventional scenes. (a) The chair of Colorado's Populist Party State Convention in 1894 trying to maintain order with a club. (*RMN*, Sept. 5, 1894, p. 5.) (b) A badge, as might be worn by a delegate, bearing the likeness of California gubernatorial candidate Henry H. Markham. Aside from the occasional ribbon or badge, delegates did not feel it necessary to adorn themselves with political or patently silly paraphernalia. (*SFE*, Aug. 12, 1890, p. 4.) (c) Markham emerges from among the delegates to mount the podium after securing the gubernatorial nomination. Conventions did not invest a lot of time or effort at stagecraft to showcase their nominees. Candidates were assigned only modest roles in the proceedings if they were present at all. (*SFE*, Aug. 14, 1890, p. 3.) (d) A California Republican convention celebrates after nominating their gubernatorial candidate in 1894. (*San Francisco Chronicle*, June 22, 1894, p. 1.)

to the verge of frenzy through delirious joy and the other sounds that made the uproar that followed the announcement that Judge [George T.] Werts' friends had won the great battle cannot truthfully be described as the loosening of pent-up enthusiasm. There was not an individual in that

TABLE 2.2. *Competition in Roll Call Balloting for Governor by State and Party, 1880–1892*

	Acclamation	Noncompetitive	Competitive	Multiballot
California				
Democratic	0	0	0	3
Republican	0	0	2	1
Colorado				
Democratic*	5	1	0	0
Republican	2	0	0	5
Michigan				
Democratic†	3	1	0	0
Republican	2	2	2	1
New Jersey				
Democratic	1	0	2	2
Republican	1	1	1	2
TOTAL	14	5	7	14
PERCENTAGE	35.0%	12.5%	17.5%	35.0%

* Does not include 1892 election when the Democratic Party split over fusing with the Populists.
† Does not include three gubernatorial nominations assigned to the Greenbackers (1882–1886) as part of a fusion agreement.

mighty assemblage who would permit his feelings to become pent up at any time."[72]

Most conventions offered an uncertain and exciting contest for governor, especially when there were promising prospects for victory in the general election. Table 2.2 documents the competitive character of state conventions by recapitulating the balloting on governor for each party in each of the states under investigation.[73] It estimates the level of competition by determining whether a gubernatorial nominee between 1880 and 1892

[72] *NA*, Sept. 2, 1880, p. 2; *RMN*, Sept. 7, 1888, p. 2; *NEN*, Sept. 15, 1892, p. 1.
[73] Technically, almost all nominations at state conventions were unanimous. The losing side usually offered a motion to such an effect after a winner had emerged on the roll call. Another motion at the end of any roll call allowed delegations to switch their votes, which often happened when one candidate's total stood close to a majority. The vote totals recorded here do not reflect changes made after the completion of the roll call. In a few cases the Democratic Party fused with Greenbackers, Populists, and Silver Republicans. In doing so, Democrats agreed to endorse whomever the third party nominated for specified offices in exchange for third party support for other Democratic nominees. Candidates first nominated by third parties under the terms of such agreements are not included in the tables. In Michigan, the Democrats fused with the Greenback Party and did not nominate a candidate of their own for governor in 1882, 1884, or 1886. It was impossible to establish which of two Democratic state organizations in Colorado in 1890 through

was selected: (1) by "Acclamation" (on a voice vote and without an opponent); (2) in a "Noncompetitive" race where the winner secured more than 60 percent of the votes on the first roll call; (3) in a "Competitive" race where the winner emerged on the first ballot but with less than 60 percent of the votes; (4) after a "Multiballot" contest that required two to nineteen roll calls before settling on a nominee.[74] Lumping the first two categories together as noncompetitive contests and the latter two as competitive produces a roughly equal number in each grouping: 19 to 21 respectively.

The level of competition for gubernatorial honors in a state convention was a function of two factors. A spirited contest could be anticipated when election prospects looked propitious. In New Jersey and California, where elections were closely contested, competitive gubernatorial nominations outnumbered the noncompetitive variety 13 to 3. Most of the candidates selected by acclamation (8 of 14) did so in Democratic conventions in Colorado and Michigan. The bleak outlook for Democratic candidates in these states in presidential years daunted all but the foolhardy or true party stalwart. Instances can be cited of men turning down unsought nominations that carried hidden costs. The practice of levying assessments on candidates to fund a hopeless campaign scared off some potential nominees. The disruption to one's business entailed by a fall campaign dissuaded others. Colorado's Democrats presented a sorry picture in 1880 when three men in the convention hall spurned the gubernatorial nomination despite the pleas of prominent party leaders. The convention adjourned for the evening, as telegrams went out to men around the state until a sacrificial lamb came forward. One Colorado Democrat sought to put the best light on the situation in 1890: "It is to the honor and glory of Colorado Democracy that the office solicits the man and not the man the office."[75] Incumbency was another factor suppressing competition, up to a point. Most of the votes by acclamation in Republican conventions in Michigan and Colorado went to governors securing renomination; party usage assured a second (but not a third) two-year term for state officials who displayed minimal competency.[76] Competition to head the state ticket was keen in those instances

1894 was the genuine article, so neither state convention made it into the database. The same situation obtained with Colorado's Republicans from 1896 through 1898.

[74] Incompleted ballots for office – where all but one candidate withdrew before all the counties were polled – are treated as "Noncompetitive."

[75] *DT*, Aug. 20, 1880, p. 1; *RMN*, Sept. 23, 1884, p. 4; Sept. 26, 1890, p. 1.

[76] *DEN*, July 30, 1894, p. 4.

where victory in the fall was plausible and the second-term rule did not apply.

The gubernatorial choice made, the convention moved quickly to bind up or at least conceal any wounds. The threat posed by disgruntled candidates or factions, who might bolt the ticket or at least not render it wholehearted support, was rarely acknowledged. To do so would impugn the character of the party and its leaders. As the Colorado Republican State Convention opened in 1888 the *Denver Republican* predicted that, "The nominees will have no more ardent supporters in the campaign than the candidates they defeated in the convention." Acceding to the will of the majority was the surer path to political preferment, the party press reminded its readers.[77] Yet the words and actions of the newspapers and the conventions betrayed anxiety that disappointment might succumb to revenge. A delegate representing one of the losing candidates was expected to move that the final ballot on governor be recorded as unanimous. Following this, the defeated candidates frequently addressed the convention to express their full support for the ticket. The press heaped praise on the "manly" stance of also-rans who reaffirmed their loyalty. Magnanimous losers received a warm and even enthusiastic reception that rivaled that accorded the victor. When Cyrus Luce stood before the 1884 Republican State Convention in Michigan "the delegates fairly split their throats in cheering him." Displaying a churlish attitude unbecoming in a defeated candidate, the grim-faced Luce asked the assembly how it was possible that he had lost "after such a demonstration." The appearance of the magnanimous loser was sufficiently engrained in the convention's proceedings that his failure to put in an appearance was duly noted by the opposition press.[78] Defeated candidates had an important lesson to convey to the faithful: it was the party and its principles that mattered – not any one man's ambition.

Before or after his rivals spoke the winning candidate might also address the convocation. This was the standard practice in California and Michigan, but not in New Jersey. Both parties required that all candidates for California's chief executive address the convention to endorse the platform before the balloting. By contrast, both parties in the Garden State, up to 1889, appointed a committee to formally inform the gubernatorial nominee of his selection. This was done even when, in a few instances, the nominee attended the convention. Immediately after the

77 *DR*, Sept. 6, 1888, p. 4; *RMN*, Sept. 16, 1900, p. 16.
78 *DR*, Sept. 7, 1888, p. 1; *DFP*, Aug. 14, 1884, p. 1; *NA*, Sept. 14, 1883, p. 2.

G.O.P. endorsed his candidacy in 1886, Benjamin F. Howey boarded a train for home, allegedly responding to a family illness. In Colorado, Republicans had to make a thorough search for their nominee in 1888 and almost drag him to the podium.[79]

The acceptance speech did not occupy the prominent place on the convention program that it would in later years. When winners did speak to the assemblage prior to 1900 their remarks were brief, typically less than a paragraph, and confined to expressions of thanks. The delegates were eager to get on with the balloting for several lesser offices. "I am no speech maker," Colorado's Republican nominee confessed to the convention of 1884 in an address that amounted to sixty-one words. "I don't intend to make a speech," candidate George Stoneman assured California's Democratic Convention of 1882. "My experience in life is that four politicians out of five ruin themselves by talking or writing." As if to prove his point, Stoneman then burdened his long-suffering audience with a short but rambling oration. Stoneman "is not a man of great personal magnetism," one Democratic paper confessed. "When he makes a speech he talks slowly and deliberately like an orthodox parson." "About four such efforts as he made on his nomination at San Jose would rupture the party," another Democratic newspaper groaned.[80] The brief attention doted on the standard-bearer was one more illustration of how the convention system promoted party-centered rather than candidate-centered politics.

The pace of the work picked up when it came time to nominate candidates for other state offices.[81] Once again the delegates subjected themselves to round after round of nominating speeches. At this point the convention commonly set limits of five or ten minutes to all further oratory. Delegates had numerous means of making their displeasure known when orators overstayed their welcome. As with the gubernatorial race, the speeches highlighted the contribution a potential nominee could make to the party's margin of victory. Speakers sought to close the sale by convincing the convention that their county could be relied upon to furnish more votes for the whole ticket if their favorite son appeared on it. Although there was less competition for these lesser offices than for the top of the slate, balloting was far more likely to occur in the majority party.

---

[79] *NEN*, Oct. 6, 1886, p. 1; *DR*, Sept. 6, 1888, p. 1.

[80] *RMN*, Sept. 13, 1884, p. 1; *LAT*, June 24, 1882, p. 3; *Redwood City Times and Gazette*, July 1, 1882, p. 4; Aug. 5, 1882, p. 4.

[81] In New Jersey the convention concluded its labors after selecting its gubernatorial nominee, the only state official on the ballot.

TABLE 2.3. *Competition in Roll Call Balloting for Minor State Offices by State and Party, 1880–1892*

	Acclamation	Noncompetitive	Competitive	Multiballot
California				
Democratic	4	7	6	7
Republican	5	7	10	2
Colorado				
Democratic*	26	6	2	0
Republican	12	7	3	13
Michigan				
Democratic*	25	4	3	2
Republican	24	2	4	6
TOTAL	96	33	28	30
PERCENTAGE	51.3%	17.6%	15.0%	16.0%

Note: The six minor state offices elected in each state include lieutenant governor, secretary of state, treasurer, attorney general, controller or auditor, and superintendent of instruction. Other state offices voted on in the conventions were either judicial in character or – like California's state surveyor – not elected elsewhere.
* Does not include nominations assigned to third parties as part of fusion arrangements.

Table 2.3 classifies the actions of the conventions in selecting their nominees on the same continuum of competition as found in Table 2.2. About half the time lieutenant governors, treasurers, attorneys general, and the like won their place on the ticket without opposition. This was, unsurprisingly, the primary method among hard-pressed Democrats in Michigan and Colorado. The greater tendency to rush a nomination through with little or no competition was also a product of the demands for a geographically balanced ticket. When a county or region received "recognition" for a favorite son, it ended the political prospects of any other candidate hailing from the same locality. Conventions fielded an electoral team that satisfied as many constituencies as possible. Hence, the pool of available candidates shrank as the slate took shape. Time permitting, the nominee for comptroller or superintendent of public instruction might offer his thanks to the convention – on behalf of his county as well as himself – in a very short speech.[82]

The quick work accomplished in the conclaves' closing hours reflected the delegates' growing restlessness. As the aspirations of a favorite son were realized or passed by, delegates scanned the railroad schedule for the next train home. Absenteeism began to increase, with departing delegates

[82] *DT*, Aug. 28, 1880, p. 1.

bestowing proxies on those who remained. The last significant decision left to the convention was the selection of a state committee to handle the coming campaign. Thereafter, custom dictated a set of resolutions thanking the convention's officers, the spectators, and perhaps the host city. The chair announced the convention closed sine die as delegates raced for the door.

A grand "ratification meeting" marked the transition from the nominating stage to the general election. Days or even hours after state, national, or local conventions had made their choices an assembly of voters met to register their approval. The rallies offered an opportunity for the nominees to make an address and for the losers to again urge everyone to close ranks. Speaking for himself and his supporters, a disappointed office seeker assured a Detroit audience in 1880: "We throw down the gauntlet to the friends of the other candidates to vie with us in a friendly contest to see who shall now be found casting their lances furthest into the ranks of the enemy." The format of the meetings sometimes resembled a deliberative body. A chair put motions and resolutions to the gathering to endorse the convention's choices. A half dozen speakers extolled the virtues of the Republican national ticket in 1872 before a San Francisco ratification meeting featuring stirring musical interludes by a band and glee club. At its close the meeting adopted a resolution by a rising vote and three enthusiastic cheers: "That we, the Republicans of San Francisco, in mass meeting assembled, do ratify the ticket nominated at Philadelphia; that we endorse it unanimously and unitedly, and that we will go into this campaign, and then into the election, with a determination to give a larger majority than we did four years ago." The ratification meeting closed the circle of the convention system by once again soliciting the input of voters. It manifested the importance attached to vox populi in bestowing legitimacy on the work of the conventions and thereby draw any disaffected elements back into the fold. "The great council of the Democracy has spoken," a Detroit speaker reminded another such gathering in 1896. "It has written its platform, and this is hereafter both the law and gospel for all true Democrats."[83]

The state party convention was a businesslike proceeding for men who were mostly businessmen themselves. The ritual and pageantry that we

---

[83] *NYT*, June 19, 1880, p. 5; Republican Party of San Francisco, California, "Proceedings of a Meeting Held at Platt's Hall, San Francisco, June 11th, 1872...to Ratify the Nominations of U. S. Grant and Henry Wilson," Bancroft Library; *DFP*, July 21, 1896, p. 1.

associate with Gilded Age politics were not so apparent when the delegates got down to work. Lengthy and noisy demonstrations on the floor, balloon drops, and even placards with the names and images of a favored candidate belonged to a later era. There was no need to manufacture enthusiasm when a close roll call loomed. Too many decisions had to be made, and, of course, there was no need to impress a viewing audience outside the hall. The convention's curt and prosaic proceedings burnished its reputation as a deliberative, decision-making body rather than as a campaign backdrop. The platform elicited discussion of the major issues, even if leaders often managed to water down much of the language. There usually was a contest for the top spot on the ticket – at least when there was a reasonable prospect of victory. The candidates might be granted space on the program, but they did not dominate the proceedings. Last and certainly not least, the state convention preserved the peace by observing "fair play" and settling on candidates best able to unify the party.

V

The major parties of the Gilded Age put their faith in outcomes rather than in procedures. Democrats and Republicans nominated their candidates in a highly decentralized process that accorded local affiliates considerable latitude in fulfilling their duties. Informality reigned in a process that relied on satisfying geographically based factional interests rather than written rules. The parties sought in their convocations at various levels for the major players to come to an agreement on a slate that all could support. They turned to candidates who could marshal the full party vote, and this was not always the man with the largest following. A party could not expect to poll its full vote if one faction hogged all the offices, even if it played strictly by the rules. "It is the fervent wish of nine-tenths of the rank and file of the [Democratic] party," the *Rocky Mountain News* affirmed in 1900, "that the sensible, levelheaded, independent delegates, who are under no man's thumb, shall take care that no mere factional victory in the convention shall pave the way for party defeat outside the convention."[84]

The convention system nurtured the deep partisan roots that underlay nineteenth-century politics. The sheer number of conventions and the apportionment ensured that many partisans could take part in the deliberations at some level. New Jersey's Democrats in 1880 reserved a seat

[84] *RMN*, Sept. 7, 1900, p. 4.

in the state convention for one in every one hundred Democratic voters, and the proportion for congressional and legislative conventions dropped to one in fifty and one in twenty-five respectively. Voter participation was anemic, but the prodigious numbers needed to fill the conventions helped Democrats and Republicans maintain a cadre of party stalwarts. The caucuses and conventions brought like-minded men together to renew a common bond and reaffirm their fealty to the organization. They provided an opportunity to organize many of the political clubs responsible for the mobilization campaigns that characterized elections of the era. In their platforms and speeches, the conventions affirmed that it was party principles that mattered and not the mere ambitions of any man. The obsession with harmony dictated that all potentially disruptive influences be cast aside. Extensive newspaper coverage of the proceedings transmitted these values to the rest of the body politic.

Even as it promoted partisanship, the convention played a significant role in preserving aspects of a republican political culture dating back to the nation's birth.[85] Although the maturation of political parties in the Jacksonian Era contravened one of the central tenets of good government as it was understood among the generation of the founders, their grandchildren and great-grandchildren reconciled these organizations to the older ideological framework. Federalists and Democratic Republicans rationalized political parties in the 1790s as necessary evils to offset the pernicious influence of the self-interested factions and special interests they associated with the opposition. Democrats and Whigs were more ready to tolerate and even embrace parties as inevitable if not benign. Party conventions played a useful role in facilitating the transition to a party system by drawing on republican ideology. Partisans looked upon their own parties as faithful custodians of the nation's political traditions. Both major parties insisted they were the only political entity representing the people and promoting the public interest in the true spirit of republicanism. The convention, ostensibly filled with delegates "fresh from the people" in Andrew Jackson's phrase, allowed the parties to wrap themselves in the mantle of public opinion. Democrats and Republicans affirmed that demagogues, greedy office seekers, and corrupt

---

[85] Although historians had thought hoary republican principles had been snuffed out by the partisan spirit of the Jacksonian Era, more recent works have found key concepts still resonating with the public well into the nineteenth century, though slowly losing their potency. See Altschuler and Blumin, *Rude Republic*, p. 151; Ethington, *The Public City*, pp. 55–58; and Thomas Goebel, *A Government by the People: Direct Democracy in America, 1890–1940* (Chapel Hill, N.C., 2002), pp. 14–16.

special interests gravitated to the opposition party. Deference democracy, another holdover from classic republicanism, also survived in the persons of "the best representative men." Not only were delegates drawn disproportionately from society's upper crust, but they attended conventions as free agents required to do only what they thought best for the party and the public interest. Above all, by insisting that the office (or convention) should seek the man, nineteenth-century American parties expressed a time-honored disdain for political ambition.

As reporter Annie Laurie learned at the state convention, the parties had to struggle some to maintain their public façade. They fashioned a "politics as they seem" that aimed to foster unity by suppressing all evidence of competition in the selection of delegates or in the race for a place on the ticket. They functioned with a "politics as they are" that left critical decisions to insiders and secret negotiations often carried on outside the convention hall. The convention system also labored under significant handicaps. Lack of grassroots participation in the primaries and caucuses mocked the parties' efforts to endow their partisan functions with a public mandate. A complicated, informally administered nominating process with too many working parts produced frequent breakdowns. Procedures varied from place to place, rules were rarely committed to paper, and authority was diffused. More importantly, the incessant hankering after public office was increasingly difficult to deny or conceal. It was possible, even in Laurie's day, to glimpse "politics as they are" behind the curtains, and they would soon spill out onto the stage.

3

The Emergence of the Hustling Candidate

I

After his name was presented to California's Republican State Convention as a candidate for governor in 1861, Leland Stanford mounted the podium. He was acutely conscious that this was not the first time he stood in line for party favor. Conventions past had nominated Stanford for state treasurer and governor, but he wanted it clearly understood that ambition had nothing to do with it. "I never was a candidate for the nomination upon my own motion. . . . I did not solicit those nominations, but I submitted because I was devoted to the principles of our party. (Applause.) I felt it was my duty, as it was the duty of every man, to serve when called upon in times of trial." Stanford assured the assembly that this was no less true in 1861. "No gentleman in this convention has ever received a letter in regard to this gubernatorial contest, [*sic*] from me during my absence from the State. There is not to-day, in this convention, a gentleman who ever received a letter from me in regard to it." The impetus for his candidacy originated elsewhere. "My friends insisted that my name should come before the people, and so I have consented." He closed by reminding his listeners that "This is not a struggle between men, we are here to-day for the purpose of sustaining principles."[1]

Raw political ambition was still a vice in the eyes of many nineteenth-century Americans. They continued to honor republican precepts that envisioned a civic-minded citizenry and an even more virtuous elite. It was

[1] Republican Party of California, "Proceedings of the Republican State Convention, Sacramento, June 18th to June 19th, 1861," p. 25, Bancroft Library, University of California at Berkeley.

Two Schools of Good Government.

FIGURE 3.1. Voting in primaries in urban areas often took place in small businesses or private residences. A competitive contest might draw a small but lively crowd to watch or perhaps dispute the actions of the election officials, hence the police presence. The crowded and contentious atmosphere of the primaries allegedly kept many "respectable" citizens away. (*NEN*, Sept. 10, 1907, p. 1.)

unseemly for candidates for major offices – representative, governor, and certainly president – to explicitly solicit support from the public. "[T]he cardinal principle of true reform in politics," California's Workingmen's Party affirmed in its state platform of 1879, "is that the office shall seek the man and not the man the office." Ideally, it was the convention's function to recruit worthy men to public service. It deliberated over the qualifications of prospective officeholders and called upon the ones deemed most fit. An avid pursuit of public office was interpreted as evidence of a lack of public virtue. In Michigan the editor of the *Grange Visitor* put all such candidates on notice in 1880: "Our state conventions will do a good thing for the people by following the example of the national conventions in ignoring every candidate for official position, who has spent time and money, and had their [*sic*] agents perambulating the state to pack delegations in their behalf."[2]

---

[2] *SFC*, June 5, 1879, p. 4; *Grange Visitor* quoted in *DFP*, July 31, 1880, p. 4.

As the century drew to a close, the gap between republican ideology and political reality widened. Aspirants for more prestigious political offices tried to appear indifferent and aloof. However, few candidates for Congress or for the governorship or for other state offices in the 1880s could make so sweeping a declaration of noncandidacy as California's Governor Stanford. While some office seekers stood by (their lightning rods pointed to the sky), the more successful ones acted on the principle that party honors usually did not come unbidden. In the weeks before the state convention, candidates of the Gilded Age employed coy flirtations and outright subterfuges to bring their names to the attention of the delegates. Over time, ever more assertive candidates dispensed with much of the pretense. In the 1890s, candidates for statewide offices became more forthright about their aspirations and far more open and aggressive in amassing support before the convention. Candidates for local offices in particular were unabashed about asking for support. "Hustling" candidates aroused more admiration than indignation. Reconciling what was practiced with what was preached would ultimately require reclassifying political ambition as a virtue instead of a vice. It would also put some strain on a convention system that affected to be oblivious to self-promotion and intrigue.

II

During the 1880s, the amount of effort a candidate had to exert to win a place on the party ticket, and the type of tactics required, varied by the office sought. It did not pay to be diffident when the object of desire was a seat in the state legislature or in the county courthouse. The would-be county treasurer or state assemblyman announced his intentions and then devoted days or even weeks to meeting with the voters. Even advertising came into sporadic use. But the men who hoped to secure a place on the ticket at the state convention avoided the limelight. They had to rely on their friends to make their case and cut the deals. One might suppose that the prejudice against openly campaigning for a party nomination for a major office made few demands on a candidate's time or money. But the ordeal of conspicuously not running for office presented complications of its own. If a man was too virtuous to ask for an elected post, for example, how was he to make his availability known? Candidates grappled with this and other conundrums of a convention system that officially had no use for them. The tribulations of chasing after a state office most fully revealed the convention system's shortcomings from the standpoint of elective office seekers.

Competition for a nomination at a state convention was a two-stage process. The first step required aspirants to win the endorsement of their home county convention and perhaps that of other conventions in their congressional district or region. Especially when it came to lesser state offices, the appeal to nominate a particular candidate was often made at the behest of his home delegation. And no county, no matter how large, could expect, much less demand, more than one place on the state ticket. Only a delegation fully committed to a single candidate could strike deals with other delegations by promising to back their favorite sons for other offices. "Trading delegations" had to be ready to align their votes for various offices in whatever manner would advance the interests of their local choice. A prospective gubernatorial nominee put the plans of other politicians in his home territory on hold. The candidate for a state office could not assume that all his neighbors would be eager to climb on his bandwagon. At county conventions he vied against men who likely were after different offices but who also hoped to control the delegation. Only after a candidate had his home delegation solidly behind him could he proceed to "try conclusions" at the state convention.

The process by which an individual's name appeared on the short list of "available men" for a given office was a mysterious one. Editors, politicians, and county conventions prepared editorials, statements, and resolutions praising one candidate and – every so often – damning another. This was ostensibly a job for the candidate's friends. Newspapers circulated these press releases as commentary or political gossip in the weeks or days before a state convention. Thus was a man "boomed" for office. "Perhaps one of the best known and most popular names mentioned in connection with the Democratic nomination for congress in the Second District is that of William H. Waldby, of Adrian," the *Detroit Free Press* announced in 1880. "Mr. Waldby is not an aspirant, but his friends insist that in this campaign the office should seek the man." That same year the *Rocky Mountain News* reported "a strong movement on foot in various portions of the state to bring out Hon. William A. Hamill as candidate for the [Republican] gubernatorial nomination."[3] Rarely was there any suggestion in these announcements that the candidate had any hand in the business. The party's call came unbidden and was perhaps

[3] *DFP*, July 8, 1880, p. 4; *RMN*, July 17, 1880, p. 4.

unwelcome in a few cases. Candidates engaged in a "still hunt" for delegates had to contend with rumors launched by their rivals that they were not interested in public office and would not even accept a nomination if tendered.[4]

Some office seekers considered a favorable reception in the press too important to be left entirely to others. Job Adams Cooper, a Denver banker with limited office-holding experience, hired "Fitz-Mac" in 1888, "to secure a little newspaper influence wherever Fitz could do it with the appliances with which he had been furnished." Fitz-Mac wrote newspaper articles purporting to be interviews between himself and a fictitious reporter inquiring about the men currently boomed for governor. One man's Methodist ties would offend the Catholic vote, Fitz-Mac quoted himself observing, while another had accumulated too many enemies. This left only Cooper as a viable choice. "[F]riends say that he would make the race if the nomination were offered him, although he is in no sense an office seeker," Fitz-Mac affirmed. "A quiet citizen standing in the front rank of the state's successful businessmen, Mr. Cooper does not appear to have devoted any time to gaining attention as a politician; yet he has always given loyal support to the Republican cause in this state, and has strong friends among the men of greatest weight in the party councils."[5] While evidence points to pecuniary considerations in the favorable notices of some newspapers, one could hardly accuse Cooper's public relations man with corrupting the press. Small partisan newspapers targeted aspirants for public office and appealed for funds to tide the publishers over during some looming financial crisis. Usually, it was unnecessary to link this subsidy to an endorsement; other times it was.[6]

While maintaining a public veneer of indifference to his fate, a candidate for a statewide office made frequent trips to the post office. "Campaigning for the governorship in the seventies entailed an enormous amount of letter writing," notes the biographer of one Iowa governor

---

[4] John E. Mapes to Beal, July 27, 1880, Box 1, Folder "Correspondence July 1880," Rice Aner Beal Papers, Bentley Historical Library, University of Michigan, Ann Arbor.

[5] *Colorado Graphic*, Sept. 22, 1888; *Colorado Springs Gazette*, Aug. 12, 1888. Both are found in the Job Adams Cooper Papers, vol. 3, Colorado Historical Society, Denver. The name "Fitz-Mac" is evidently a nom de plume. He revealed – after the election – that he had been under some obligation to Cooper for his assistance with past financial difficulties.

[6] Alf D. Bowen to Burns, Feb. 27, 1892, Box 1, Folder 5, Daniel M. Burns Papers, Bancroft Library; James M. McMillan to Dexter M. Ferry, May 2, 1896, Box 5, Folder "Politics, Correspondence, 1896–1900," Ferry Family Papers, Bentley Historical Library; G. H. Baker to Hamill, Aug. 24, 1878, Folder 4, William A. Hamill Papers, Denver Public Library.

elected in 1871. Cyrus Clay Carpenter began sending letters out months in advance of the Iowa Republican State Convention. Like other aspirants for major party honors, Carpenter viewed the letter writing as a necessary if distasteful task. He assured his readers that he was only acting in response to the entreaties of his friends. "[W]hile I did not originate my own candidacy, and in fact, at the first suggestion of my name in connection with it, shrank from its mention as a candidate, yet now that I have come to be regarded as in the field, I would like to succeed."[7] Letters came back identifying other likely competitors for state honors and the names of influential local party leaders or possible delegates to contact. A candidate might hope his supporters would take up a letter-writing campaign of their own on his behalf. T. J. O'Donnell of Colorado received words of encouragement regarding his gubernatorial plans from one correspondent who tempered his remarks with this admonition in 1900: "Remember Wolsey's advice. 'Cromwell, I charge thee fling away ambition; by that sin fell the angels.'"[8]

Political decorum required that candidates not blatantly interfere in the delegate selection process. When voters met in their caucuses and primaries, the main issue was supposed to be the qualifications of the men running as delegates, not the suitability of prospective candidates. "The first requisite is to elect honest, intelligent and public spirited delegates to our county, state and district conventions. Let these delegates take counsel together to select the best and most available candidate for every office." In New Jersey, the *Burlington Gazette* urged the friends of various candidates to refrain from meddling with the delegate selection process at the 1883 county convention:

> Enough good men may be found in the Democratic Party of Burlington County who may be sent to the State Convention entrusted with the duty of selecting a candidate that shall not only command the vote of every Democrat but shall also gather in those of many Republicans. . . . Men have tried to make [the convention] hew wood and draw water for them, but the time, we hope, has passed forever. . . . The individual is nothing; party, in a true sense, is everything.[9]

An outright scramble for delegates undermined the image of the convention as a deliberative body seeking the most qualified candidate. The press

---

7 Mildred Throne, "Electing an Iowa Governor, 1871: Cyrus Clay Carpenter," *Iowa Journal of History* 48 (Oct. 1950): 342.
8 R. F. Weithrec to O'Donnell, July 25, 1900, Box 9, Folder 15, T. J. O'Donnell Papers, Archives at the University of Colorado at Boulder Libraries.
9 *RMN*, Aug. 28, 1884, p. 4; *Burlington Gazette*, Sept. 1, 1883, p. 2.

delighted in portraying the opposition party's powwows as anything but a meeting of minds. "The Republican party has become so depraved and demoralized that the state convention, which should be a calm council to select the fittest men for the various places within its gift, will be a howling mob of unscrupulous office seekers and their purchased retainers, all engaged in a gigantic grab game."[10] The candidate who "hired men to sound his praises" was an object of censure. A truly worthy candidate would not need to advertise himself and would not stoop to manipulate the process in his interest. A fight broke out on the floor of Michigan's Republican State Convention in 1884 after one delegate accused another of traveling the state and "manipulating things and fixing caucuses for [eventual gubernatorial nominee Russell A.] Alger." That year the *Rocky Mountain News* editorialized: "It is a safe rule that the man who seeks by devious and dishonorable means to pack primaries and control conventions in order to secure a place on any ticket, is unfit and unworthy to be elected, and no decent voter can be expected to vote for such a candidate."[11]

The gubernatorial candidate who was not content to let the nominating process run its course had to recruit others to sing his praises and organize a following. Rice Aner Beal, an Ann Arbor merchant and newspaper publisher, was just such a man. In 1880 he hired at least three men to travel around the rural parts of Michigan sounding out his gubernatorial prospects and lining up support. All was done with the utmost secrecy and subterfuge. "C. Mosher" described his canvassing routine in some detail. Upon arriving in a locality, he first visited the county clerk and the local clergy to learn the identity of the leading Republicans in the area who were Methodists and pro-temperance. Posing as a temperance proselytizer, he visited these "strong men of the county" in their homes. At some point Mosher would direct the conversation to a discussion of politics and the coming state convention (concealing his relationship with Beal). Very few of his interviewees were aware that Beal was a candidate for governor; Mosher's job was to bring Beal's name to their attention. He assured them that Beal was willing to serve and could be trusted on temperance matters. Mosher urged his listeners to write to his patron. He passed on to Beal lists of men who might be friendly to his candidacy, especially those expected to attend the state convention. Mosher complained that he could accomplish more if he did not have to travel under false pretenses,

---

[10] *RMN*, Sept. 9, 1884, p. 4.
[11] *DFP*, June 27, 1900, p. 2; *DEN*, Aug. 13, 1884, p. 4; *RMN*, Sept. 15, 1884, p. 4.

but, presumably at Beal's insistence, Mosher maintained his temperance cover.[12]

By the standards of a later decade, Beal's tactics appear amateurish and halfhearted. The correspondence does not suggest that Mosher or Beal's other emissaries were professionals in this line of work or that they were reaping much reward for their efforts. Beal paid Mosher three dollars a day, plus expenses. After a couple of months on the road, Mosher reported that he needed to return to his peach orchard. Thereafter, Beal carried on a correspondence with his supporters, urging them to do what they could to attend the state convention as delegates. "It has been *fixed* so that myself, Geo. B. Walken and Edward Harrett are to represent this Township," one letter writer assured him, "and I can easily control Harrett and Walker on the question of Governor." Beal received many communications from supporters who contrived to fill delegations with friendly proxies. A. C. Dutton warned Beal that the delegate from his district, Tyler Hull, was supporting one of Beal's rivals, but Dutton had a solution. "It is very possible that I may be his proxy. If you can send a woman down there to be confined about 6 o'clock a.m. Aug. 5 you can secure one vote in the convention. Hull is an M.D."[13] Beal's candidacy at the state convention collapsed after several ballots. Evidently, his stealth candidacy did not go unnoticed. The *Detroit Evening News* interpreted the convention's verdict as "a reminder to Mr. Beal that mere wire-pulling, however skillful, cannot make a man governor of Michigan in a few weeks."[14]

Attendance at the state convention was not mandatory for the successful gubernatorial candidate in the early 1880s. Most of the men nominated for governor in New Jersey, Colorado, and Michigan between 1880 and 1886 did not show up at the proceedings. A candidate was an unsettling presence at a convention. After a convention in Shiawassee County, Michigan endorsed one man for Congress in 1880, it was announced that their favorite "just happened to be in town." When a delegate offered a motion to invite the candidate to address the body, the ayes and nays of the voice vote were so evenly divided that the chair could not

---

[12] C. Mosher to Beal, Apr. 10, 15, 17, 30, June 11, 1880, Folders "Correspondence Apr. 1880" and "Correspondence June 1880," Box 1, Beal Papers. Another canvasser was paid $100 for four weeks work; see W. Judson to Beal, June 10, 1880. Judson then returned to his wool business.

[13] W. G. Terry to Beal, July 16, 1880; A. C. Dutton to Beal, July 26, 1880, both in Box 1, Folder "July 1880," Beal Papers. See also J. D. Ronan to Beal, Aug. 2, 1880, Folder "Aug.-Dec., 1880," Beal Papers.

[14] *DEN*, Aug. 6, 1880, p. 2.

discern the convention's will.[15] Only California's major parties expected all candidates to come before the full state convention and make a brief address endorsing the platform just prior to the balloting. The candidates, and even some delegates, found the exercise somewhat awkward. One waggish delegate proposed in 1886 that the candidates "be required to sing a song and dance a jig."[16] Appealing for votes or even making themselves conspicuous was disagreeable to many budding statesmen. On arriving at the California Democratic State Convention in 1882, gubernatorial candidate George Stoneman elected to spend the evening drinking brandy with a friend "whilst the 'boys' were waiting for him." George Hearst, one of Stoneman's opponents, hosted a fine reception for the delegates, with cigars and liquor, but it was Stoneman who secured the nomination.[17]

The desultory and surreptitious manner by which gubernatorial candidates solicited support usually ensured uncertainty about the identity of the eventual standard-bearer when the convention at last met. While bands of supporters circulated in the lobbies loudly extolling their favorites, the decisive deliberations took place in the famous "smoke-filled rooms" upstairs. Room 100 of the Trenton House served this purpose for both of New Jersey's major parties. Custom assigned the room to the parties' designated leaders: William Sewell for the Republicans and James Smith, Jr., for the Democrats. Every three years the hotel staff removed the room's carpet and expensive furnishings and added some extra cuspidors to accommodate the many politicos who would surely stop by.[18] Uppermost in the considerations of those who met behind closed doors was a prospective nominee's electability. In the party period, a successful candidate was one who could leave the convention with the full support of the party behind him. George L. Record, who participated in some of these conferences in Room 100, summarized the discussions thusly: "The average set of politicians who run a convention sit down in a room and they say, 'Shall we nominate So and So?' 'Oh, he has got too many enemies.' And one after another the names are checked off because they have got some personality and individuality, as a rule, and finally they select some dummy who is not known, who has created no antagonism and is

---

[15] Eventually, it was decided in the affirmative. *DFP*, Aug. 1, 1880, p. 4.
[16] *LAT*, Aug. 27, 1886, p. 4. Judicial candidates were not invited to make a similar appearance because it violated notions of judicial dignity and independence. *SFE*, Sept. 2, 1886, p. 5.
[17] *Redwood City Times and Gazette*, July 1, 1882, p. 4.
[18] *NEN*, Sept. 27, 1886, p. 2; Sept. 17, 1889, p. 1; Sept. 12, 1904, p. 8.

just a negative character."[19] Record's indictment of the system exaggerates its tendency to pluck out political nonentities, and treats a candidate's qualifications as the only issue. For those who insisted it was party rather than personalities that mattered, the "lowest common denominator" was a logical choice.

The presence of aspirants after other spots on the state ticket complicated discussions over gubernatorial choices.[20] Many delegations arrived at conventions widely publicized as "trading delegations," eager to work a deal with any candidate who could deliver votes for their own favorites.[21] All such deals remained secret since they interfered with efforts to recruit support from rival office seekers. Some candidates may well have avoided making bargains for just this reason. And the practice itself came under recurrent criticism for undermining the convention's reputation as a deliberative body.[22] When rumors of too many such deals gained credence, losers and the opposition party began decrying a "programme" that had "fixed" the proceedings in the interests of a faction or boss. "It is possible to have too much management in a state convention," one Colorado delegate complained.[23]

In popular parlance, a man's candidacy was "in the hands of his friends."[24] "All appears to be spontaneous," the British observer James Bryce noted, "but in reality both the choice of particular men as delegates, and the instructions given, are usually the result of untiring underground work among local politicians, directed, or even personally conducted, by two or three skillful agents and emissaries of a leading aspirant, or of the knot which seeks to run him."[25] Few candidates could afford to stand by and await the call of their friends or anyone else. Would-be governors, attorneys general, congressmen, or aldermen wrote letters, doled out "swag," and negotiated alliances. Candidates preferred to appear

[19] National Conference on Practical Reform of Primary Elections, *Proceedings of the National Conference on Practical Reform of Primary Elections, January 20 and 21, 1898* (Chicago, 1898), p. 89.
[20] This was not an issue in New Jersey where the governor was the only official elected statewide.
[21] *SFE*, Aug. 13, 1890, p. 2; *RMN*, Sept. 30, 1886, p. 2.
[22] John S. Hopkins, "Direct Nomination of Candidates by the People," *The Arena* 19 (June, 1898): 736; *DFP*, Aug. 28, 1886, p. 4.
[23] *RMN*, Sept. 30, 1886, p. 2; *Daily Alta California*, Aug. 28, 1886, p. 1; *LAT*, June 19, 1894, p. 1.
[24] *RMN*, Oct. 5, 1886, p. 3; *SFE*, Sept. 2, 1886, p. 1; *NYT*, July 3, 1894, p. 1.
[25] James Bryce, *The American Commonwealth*, edited and abridged by Louis M. Hacker, (New York, 1959), vol. 1, p. 245.

unconcerned about their political prospects, even if the masquerade was becoming a bit thin. California's Morris M. Estee professed ignorance regarding the circumstances surrounding his gubernatorial candidacy in 1894. "So far as I know, it was brought about by my friends in the country, . . . I did not seek to be a candidate of our party at this time nor have I endeavored in the slightest degree, directly or indirectly, to influence the Republicans of any county in this state to select delegates in my favor. . . . I shall do nothing to secure the nomination."[26] Estee delivered these remarks to a reporter while standing in the foyer of the convention's main hotel where he devoted a full day to shaking hands with attentive delegates.

III

As was so often the case when a partisan newspaper turned its attention to the opposition, the *San Francisco Examiner* claimed by turns to be amazed, amused, and appalled by the proceedings of the Republican State Convention of 1886. The paper particularly objected to the doings of one gubernatorial aspirant. "[John F.] Swift left his rooms last night and for hours made his canvass in the hall and doorways of the Neadeau House. His eagerness for the coveted nomination is so marked, and his way of canvassing for votes so unprecedented that old time Republicans, who prefer to see a candidate for the governorship act with some dignity, are openly expressing disgust."[27] It turned out that there were not enough disgusted Republicans to deny Swift the nomination on the eighth ballot.

Complaints of violations of the norms of appropriate political behavior reverberated in campaign coverage during the last two decades of the nineteenth century. Candidates cautiously became more assertive in staking their claims to party honors. Office seekers made themselves ever more conspicuous outside and inside the convention hall. During the 1890s, the competition spread to the primaries and county conventions as prospective nominees worked openly to elect friendly delegations to the state convention. The success that often crowned the efforts of "hustling" candidates ensured that what was daring, innovative, and successful one year was standard practice the next. Political decorum increasingly made allowances for self-promotion. By 1900 it was expected that persons desirous of a nomination had to expend extra time, money, and energy to

[26] *SFE*, June 18, 1894, p. 1.
[27] *SFE*, Aug. 26, 1886, p. 5.

win it. Although many candidates, and perhaps even some voters, found the electioneering distasteful, an aloof posture was less and less viable. As the friend of one political aspirant explained in 1898, "A man who lays back and waits for a convention to hand him a nomination generally spends his time laying back and waiting." The lesson was not lost on the men hoping to land a nomination at the state convention. Announcing his candidacy for state treasurer in 1894, a Michigan Republican allowed that "while the office should seek the man, . . . [the] man should be around where the office can find him."[28]

The more aggressive mode of electioneering first appeared in races for local offices. Candidates for sheriff or assemblyman met with no indignation when they mounted an open, all-out effort to secure a nomination. The *Detroit Free Press* took note of the year-long campaign of one local alderman for election as Wayne County sheriff. "He appears at all Sunday school excursions, at all concerts, at all social gatherings to which he has the entree. At all times his pockets are crowded with cigars and a flush wallet is depleted many times a day by treating groups of party friends and foes."[29] The newspaper considered the candidate's rigorous schedule as "remarkable" in 1886, but similar efforts soon became the norm. Newspaper advertising, virtually unheard of when it came to statewide offices, was widely utilized for county posts in California. There were fifteen ads by Democratic candidates seeking the party's endorsement for such offices as auditor, sheriff, assemblyman, and superintendent of schools in California's *Tulare County Times* in 1886.[30] Candidates for county or local offices had to work a lot harder making the rounds with the voters than did individuals eyeing a state or even a congressional post. Candidates for assemblyman and county assessor were "compelled to be in their buggies almost day and night" the week preceding California's Orange County primary of 1902. Like the emergence of mass culture around 1900, the candidate-centered campaign was another example of "contagion from below."

There were multiple reasons why candidates for local offices were more proactive in furthering their political careers. The lesser prestige associated with a city or county post diminished the social distance separating candidates from the electorate. This surely made it easier for office seekers to rub elbows with the voters and solicit their support. A prospective county

[28] *DEN*, Aug. 18, 1898, p. 1; *DFP*, June 20, 1894, p. 5.
[29] *DFP*, Aug. 2, 1886, p. 5.
[30] *Tulare County Times*, Aug. 5, 1886.

clerk or member of the state legislature was not expected to maintain the same statesmanlike indifference to his political fate. Simple logistics was another factor making the personal canvass more critical in local contests; it was far easier to reach a substantial percentage of the voters in a city or county than across the state. But most importantly, voters had a more decisive impact on the selection of local candidates than they did on congressional or statewide races. Voters themselves selected some local nominees in caucuses and primaries or at least sent delegates to county or municipal conventions to make the choice. When it came to state offices, electors were a further step removed in the decision-making process. They usually selected delegates to county conventions who appointed other delegates to state conventions. The electorate's influence was diluted as it filtered through two conventions instead of one. The average voter might have been interested in who was going to sit in the governor's chair, but his ability to influence the state convention was remote. Gubernatorial candidates had to convert the delegate selection process into a personal plebiscite if they hoped to mobilize support at the electoral level that could translate into votes at the state convention.

The political career of Michigan governor Hazen S. Pingree epitomized the transition to a more candidate-centered campaign. Like other political aspirants of the 1890s, Pingree relied mainly on surrogates to make his case and marshal support around the state. No candidate for state office during that decade made more effective use of his "friends" (many of them on the city payroll) than did the Detroit mayor. He built a formidable organizational network over the course of four runs for governor between 1892 and 1898. His agents tapped grassroots support by organizing Pingree clubs and used these to recruit delegates. The Republican gubernatorial nominee of 1890 drew a stark contrast between his campaign and that of Pingree and his rival in 1892. "I never left my office on a political mission; neither did I write a letter to a solitary individual in Michigan asking him to favor my candidacy." And he did not hire anybody to do these things. "The masses of the people believed at one time that they were competent to select men for high office like that of governor ... without instruction. They did not believe that it was necessary to have a literary bureau, and to have paid agents working in every part of the state to urge his candidacy."[31]

With the assistance of his many supporters, Pingree made his candidacy the focus of primaries, caucuses, and county conventions around the state.

[31] *DEN*, July 15, 1892, p. 1; *DFP*, June 15, 1894, p. 5.

Pingree "manipulators" were an unwelcome presence in many places. His followers and paid agents disrupted a network run by local notables who used the state nomination process to advance their own political agendas. Ren Barker, an Osceola County politico, encountered one of Pingree's heelers from Detroit at the local Grand Army of the Republic encampment in 1896. "You can form all the clubs you want to up in my county," Barker snapped, "but I'll form the delegation that helps nominate a governor, and it will be for Col. [Aaron T.] Bliss. Just paste that in your hat." Months later at the state convention, Pingree controlled three of the county's five delegates.[32] Pingree's tactics forced his competitors to respond in kind. "We are receiving letters from all parts of the state which indicate that the people who are at work for Mr. Pingree are getting their work in pretty effectively," one letter warned a lieutenant to Pingree rival John T. Rich in 1892. "They are making inroads in the western part of the state and good politicians express the fear that he will be nominated. Mr. Rich *must* have some effective work done at once." The letter writer advised hiring more political operatives to travel that portion of the state on Rich's behalf.[33] "[N]ever before has there been such an assault upon a state convention," the *Grand Rapids Evening Press* observed of the 1896 contest. Pingree and his opponent "did not even pretend that they were in the hands of their friends. They openly organized armies of paid emissaries to go through the state and commit highway robbery upon the county conventions and township caucuses." Pingree was more methodical than his contemporaries, but his competitors were not far behind.[34]

Still in the future was the day when a candidate for nomination toured the state making several speeches daily, but as the new century dawned more and more aspirants put in appearances at a limited number of party and public functions. A tent perched on "Politicians Hill" at the annual New Jersey state fair provided one such forum. Here, political leaders from around the state congregated to consult and meet with potential gubernatorial candidates. Democrats and Republicans held court on different days.[35] The annual meeting of the Michigan Club served a similar

[32] *DEN*, Aug. 8, 1896, p. 5; *DFP*, Aug. 15, 1896, p. 2.
[33] W. R. Bates to Greer, May 13, 1892, Harrison Greer Papers, Bentley Historical Library. The correspondence indicates that Rich was doing some traveling around the state at this time, but it is not evident here or from the press just what he was up to. See E. R. Phinney to Greer, May 11, 1892, Greer Papers.
[34] *Evening Press* (Grand Rapids), Aug. 7, 1896, p. 2. On Pingree's success, see *DFP*, June 21, 1902, p. 4.
[35] *NA*, Sept. 8, 1898, p. 1; Sept. 9, 1898, p. 5.

purpose. Attendance at the dinner became a prerequisite for G.O.P. gubernatorial candidates. This required them to roll out their campaigns so
much the earlier, as the *Detroit Evening News* noted in 1900. "It has
seldom if ever happened before that at a time so early as the banquet –
from four to six months in advance of the [state] convention – the booms
of the several candidates have been so well developed and the prospective candidates have come here, taken private rooms and mingled with
the crowd like common mortals." As in New Jersey, the small talk and
glad handing that took place did not expand very far outside the circle of
political notables and their minions. Those office seekers who showed up
at "Politicians Hill" in New Jersey did not appear to use the occasion to
press the flesh among the many voters attending the fair. Likewise, gubernatorial candidates did not have a place on the program at the Michigan
Club's dinner. It was enough to be seen and to converse with the crowd
of roughly six hundred. Even this amount of exposure was too much
for one prominent Detroit businessman in 1900. "Mr. [Dexter M.] Ferry
made his appearance during the evening and stood in the lobby for a
time surrounded by a circle of his local workers and some of the fellows
from the outside. He went home early though, and left his backers to take
care of the crowd for the rest of the evening." A Wayne County politico
correctly predicted that Ferry's gubernatorial ambitions would come to
naught. The successful candidate, he explained, "gets around and gets
acquainted with the people.... Voters do not warm up to a man whom
they never see and never hear."[36] Ferry's fate reflected an important shift
in public expectations of elective office seekers by 1900. The candidate
who did not make himself accessible was more likely to be criticized as
cold and aloof than be lauded for his statesmanlike demeanor.

No longer content to rely on their hired emissaries or letter-writing
skills, would-be nominees hit the road after 1890. "Candidates for state
offices on the different tickets prospective and otherwise are jostling each
other all over [Colorado]," the *Rocky Mountain News* noted in 1896.[37]
A candidate's itinerary during the 1890s little resembled a modern-day
campaign stop. He generally showed up in a town unannounced to meet
with local leaders and to offer his backers moral and material support. A
visit with the editor of the local party organ was almost certainly on the

---

[36] *DEN,* Feb. 21, 1900; Nov. 28, 1899, in "Political Scrapbook," Box 5, Vol. 1, Ferry
Family Papers. A shy gubernatorial candidate in New Jersey suffered a similar fate. See
NEN, Sept. 22, 1901, p. 1.
[37] *RMN,* Aug. 17, 1896, p. 5.

to-do list. The candidate usually made no speeches and did little to make his presence widely known. If confronted by a reporter, he was often at a loss to explain himself. The cornered candidate would insist he was in town for some other business than corralling votes. Chase S. Osborn, another Michigan gubernatorial aspirant in 1900, was bolder than most. "Hon. Chase S. Osborn was in the city Saturday," one paper reported, "and though he was not here on a political mission he frankly discussed his chances of obtaining the nomination for governor with those of his friends whom he happened to meet during his brief stay." Osborn confined his travels to his political base in the Upper Peninsula and maintained an air of informality. It was still important that the candidate not appear too eager or devious. "Mr. Osborn is not making an aggressive campaign in the sense of trying to secure the election of delegates pledged to him by working up support through the employment of professional manipulators of caucuses and conventions." Osborn's hopes were not realized in 1900, but his time would come.[38]

Candidates ratcheted up the competition another notch when they organized and elected slates of committed delegates. Care was taken that the name of one – and no more than one – delegate endorsing a particular candidate was offered in each electoral unit. Ballots had to be made available at the polling places, along with a number of challengers and watchers. This happened mainly in the urban counties, where a rich load of delegates was up for grabs. The former governor and frequent stump speaker Leon Abbett was perhaps the first gubernatorial candidate in New Jersey to parlay his name recognition into delegates at the primaries. In 1889 he organized an assault on the Essex County Democratic primary, supplying voters with printed ballots that linked an individual running for delegate with his candidacy. "In almost every instance where printed tickets were used the names of the candidates were preceded by the words: 'For Governor, Leon Abbett.' In every instance Abbett candidates were elected. Personal popularity or prestige availed opponents of Abbett little in the primaries"[39] In New Jersey and Colorado, pledged delegations rarely materialized outside a candidate's home base. Only in Michigan and California were aspirants for state offices openly mounting

---

[38] *Pioneer Tribune* (Manistique, Mich.), June 1, 1900, p. 1; June 8, 1900, p. 2. A decade later, Osborn secured the governorship using the state's new direct primary law. For examples of other gubernatorial candidates "caught in the act," see *DFP*, June 20, 1894, p. 5; June 12, 1902, p. 4; *DR*, Aug. 29, 1888, p. 4.

[39] *NEN*, Sept. 7, 1889, p. 1. What makes Abbett's action the more bold – or perhaps necessary – was that his political base resided next door, in Hudson County.

and electing slates of delegates around the state. Populous Kent County, Michigan, encompassing Grand Rapids, proved a decisive battleground in several gubernatorial races between 1892 and 1902. The contests injected new life into otherwise cut-and-dried primaries and caucuses. "Rarely in the history of politics in this county has such activity been shown in the caucuses for the selection of delegates to the state convention," remarked the *Detroit Free Press* of the effort to capture the delegation in 1900. In California, Governor Henry T. Gage arranged for a series of such slates when he was up for reelection in 1902; he was sufficiently active promoting his candidacy to come under criticism for neglecting his official duties.[40] It was still a rare thing to see a gubernatorial candidate appear in town to urge the election of his slate,[41] but aspirants now cast a far larger shadow over the proceedings.

The appearance of slates of delegates openly tied to the political aspirations of specific candidates had important consequences for the nominating system. Competition in the primaries of the major cities was becoming the norm. Efforts to avert a donnybrook by working out a consensus slate, as was often done in the past, now met with condemnation. A proposal to arrange a single fusion slate in Denver's Democratic primaries in 1900 drew a rebuke from at least one prominent Democrat. No person or organization, he insisted, "has the right or power (inherent or otherwise) to dictate for whom the Democratic voters of the precincts shall cast their ballots.... The voters of each precinct have a right to vote for candidates of their own choosing.... Any attempt to interfere with this right, or in any manner to dictate the action that shall be taken, will only serve to further confuse, mystify and disgust the people." More voters appeared at the polls, drawn by the opportunity to register an opinion on the man to head the state ticket. The question of whom a prospective delegate endorsed for governor dictated whether he would attend the

---

[40] *DFP*, May 27, 1900, in "Political Scrapbook," Box 5, Vol. 1, Ferry Family Papers; *LAT*, Aug. 5, 1902, p. 10; Aug. 9, 1902, p. 1. Gage had also been very active hunting up votes in the previous campaign. See *LAT*, July 22, 1898, p. 15.

[41] In Denver, gubernatorial candidate Benjamin Lindsey took the unusual step of addressing a rally on the eve of the primaries in 1906. It was, in the words of one newspaper reporter (and Lindsey supporter), "one of the most exquisitely effective political meetings ever held in Denver." The large turnout was a testimony to the new "power of personality" in American politics. The stage held only Lindsey and was "eloquent in its emptiness"; *DP*, Sept. 1, 1906, p. 14; Sept. 2, 1906, p. 4; Sept. 10, 1906, p. 1. Essex County's Democratic sheriff managed to attend thirteen rallies in Newark on behalf of his gubernatorial aspirations in 1910. *NEN*, Sept. 9, 1910, p. 2. Neither candidate was successful even in gaining control of his home delegation.

state convention. Would-be delegates who expected to be elected on the strength of their social standing now encountered competition. Prominent candidates gained ownership over the delegates as they eventually would over the process itself. "[E]veryone has known that I am an aspirant for Governor," California state treasurer J. R. McDonald averred in 1894. "I have made my canvas in the San Joaquin Valley and the southern portion of the State. In some of the counties I know that entire delegations could not have been elected had they not been pledged to me."[42]

Seekers after lesser state offices were lost sight of as the gubernatorial race monopolized the attention of the press and public. Candidates for attorney general or comptroller could not hope to elect their own delegates if voters were casting their ballots for slates drawn up in the interests of a gubernatorial candidate. With ten days to go before the G.O.P. State Convention in 1896, the *Detroit Free Press* noted that the six-man race for governor "seems to have absorbed all interest in the remainder of the state ticket.... The situation is unprecedented as to the scarcity of candidates and as to the spiritlessness of the contest." Gubernatorial candidates would not share the limelight. Hazen S. Pingree's supporters at the Wayne County Republican Convention in 1896 squashed the candidacies of other Detroit politicians hunting up other state offices. "This time no small fry will be permitted to have ambitions. This time Pingree's ninety-seven votes will be traded right and left for votes for Pingree."[43]

As active canvassing for a nomination became the norm, conventional expressions of indifference to political advancement lost credibility. One Republican gubernatorial candidate's disavowals of political ambitions drew the sarcastic scorn of Michigan's *Genesee Democrat* in 1892. "We sincerely pity Mr. [John T.] Rich, as it is said by his friends that although he never was a candidate for office and preferred to live in contentment on his farm, he could not do so because so many dear people always wanted him to hold some sort of office or other and he could not find it in his heart to refuse." The paper enumerated the many public offices Rich had occupied over the past thirty years. Noting that Rich's name had been voted on for governor at most state conventions since 1880, the paper concluded: "[H]e must have assuredly been the most unhappy man in the United States during the last thirty years."[44] A candidate

---

[42] *RMN*, Aug, 30, 1900, p. 7; *SFE*, June 18, 1894, p. 1.

[43] *DFP*, July 26, 1896, p. 16; July 21, 1896, p. 4. Two years earlier, Pingree supporters charged that a Wayne County delegate had flirted with Pingree's opponents in an effort secure his own nomination for state office, thereby undermining the mayor's candidacy.

[44] *Genesee Democrat*, July 16, 1892, p. 4.

professing unconcern about a political office ran the risk of ridicule or, worse yet, the risk of being believed. Republican Frank Goudy circulated about the hotel lobby at Colorado's state convention in 1902 issuing a "stereotypical" reply to all inquiries about his gubernatorial intentions: "I am not a candidate, but if the convention should name me, I shall not decline to run." The backer of a rival candidate scoffed at Goudy's strategy of playing hard to get. "We have a man who is not playing hide-and-seek. He is not going around shaking hands and claiming that he cannot afford to accept the nomination, and at the same time in his heart, secretly longing for it.... We fully expect that a man who wants the place and is willing to work for it will get it." Goudy did not "get there." Another unsuccessful Colorado candidate for state treasurer was perhaps even a bit too forthright in 1896: "I'm not playing the 'my friends are urging me' racket a little bit; I want to be state treasurer if I can get it. I need it in my business, for times have been awful tight, and I'm not as flush as I used to be."[45]

The decades spanning the new century witnessed a shift in the types of activities candidates engaged in to lay the groundwork for a state nomination. The hustling candidates entered the political arena through the lively contests for the more local offices. Here they learned to greet voters, make speeches, and even employ advertising on their own behalf. They put the electioneering skills they mastered in running for lesser offices to use as they sought higher positions. They worked hard at getting themselves or at least their names before the public. Gubernatorial candidates put in some public appearances at least with the party cadre. Elective office seekers even took to the road to quietly visit with small groups of supporters and men of influence. Jeremiads deploring the ever more blatant forms of self-promotion died away. Candidates for state offices still remained one step removed from the nomination process in certain important respects. They relied heavily on their surrogates to organize support, and, unlike during the general election, they rarely took to the hustings. But, especially as they arranged for the election of friendly delegates around the state, they assumed a dominating presence. Gubernatorial aspirants crowded lesser political figures to the margins. The local politician who arranged the state delegation and used it to negotiate some plum for himself and, perhaps, for his home constituency, lost influence. Candidates for state treasurer or superintendent of public instruction were almost entirely lost sight of.

[45] *RMN*, Sept. 12, 1902, p. 1; Sept. 11, 1902, p. 6; Aug. 10, 1896, p. 1.

IN CANDIDATE FERRY'S HEADQUARTERS.

FIGURE 3.2. Gubernatorial candidates at state conventions generally stayed confined to their hospitality suites where they greeted delegates and offered them refreshments. Here, political newcomer Dexter M. Ferry holds court at Michigan's 1900 Republican State Convention. Ferry was described as stiff and aloof, which is how he appears in this drawing, even under the tutelage of some of the party's leading lights. (*DEN*, June 28, 1900, p. 4.)

The contours of a candidate-centered campaign were taking shape while the convention system was still in place.

IV

The state convention offers an especially good vantage point to appreciate the greater visibility and influence of the parties' elective office seekers. Attendance at the state convention was becoming a prerequisite for the nominee. State conventions in Colorado, New Jersey, and Michigan had nominated a number of men for governor and other state offices during the 1880s who were conspicuously absent. Only New Jersey's Democrats preserved this practice after 1890. The gubernatorial candidacies of two California congressmen received mortal blows when official business kept them in Washington, D.C., during the state conventions of 1890 and 1894. The supporter of one admitted that "the representative ought to be here to speak for himself." Mere proximity soon was not enough. Where once convention-going candidates had confined themselves to their rooms to consult with their lieutenants, increasingly they were called upon to make a good impression with the delegates. Michigan's gubernatorial rivals of 1884, Russell A. Alger and Cyrus G. Luce, had different comfort levels when it came to hobnobbing with strangers. Alger, in a stylish gray suit and white plug hat, welcomed visiting delegates to his convention head-quarters. "He manifested so much affability and good humor, and made himself so much at home with all sorts of people, that his friends took new pride in him, and those who met him for the first time and might have been prejudiced against him, were quite charmed at his pleasing manner." Luce, the eventual runner-up, "kept himself secluded in his room . . . [where] he was inclined to complain of the tactics of his opponents."[46]

In time, candidates ventured outside their hospitality suites to mingle with the delegates off the convention floor. The *San Francisco Examiner* had chastised the Republican gubernatorial nominee of 1886 for circu-lating freely among the delegates. Eight years later, a reporter from the same Democratic paper could express only admiration for how smoothly and efficiently eventual gubernatorial nominee Morris M. Estee greeted delegates one by one at the foot of the stairs of the Golden Eagle Hotel:

That experienced shaker has gone through so much of that sort of pump-handling that he has developed a method of saving himself. Extending his right hand and grasping that of a rural delegate he at the same time grips with his left hand the delegate's right arm. Then, just as the countrymen [*sic*] is ready to give one of his haypress squeezes, Estee throws his force into his left hand, gives the too exuberant shaker a reassuring squeeze, and at the same time by a deft pinch paralyzes the muscles which threaten to damage his oft-shaken palm. In this way he is able to shake around the circle without special pain or digital fatigue.[47]

Some office seekers were unschooled in the art of charming delegates. A Denver reporter overheard a conversation in 1886 in the Ladies Wait-ing Room at a Republican convention hotel between anxious gubernato-rial candidate Frederick D. Wight and his manager, E. B. Sopris. Wight

[46] *SFE*, Aug. 14, 1890, p. 3; Aug. 22, 1894, p. 1; *DFP*, Aug. 13, 1884, p. 1.
[47] *SFE*, Aug. 26, 1886, p. 5; Sept. 19, 1894, p. 1.

complained that he was "green in this business," and wanted to know how to converse with the delegates. "[C]onfine your talk to monosyllables or to the weather or the Cleveland administration or something of that sort," Sopris advised. "Don't give your views on anything else. . . . Look wise and be a good listener." "Well," Wight interjected, "suppose I am asked for my views on railway legislation?"

Be evasive; don't answer positively pro or con. Say the family is the foundation of the state. Ask your questioner how many children he has, and express the hope that some one of them will live to be president. Then look off very earnestly and find someone whom you must talk with at once, and excuse yourself. . . . If pressed take a violent fit of coughing and rush off for a glass of water. Some friend will stop you on your return and introduce you to a new delegate.[48]

Office seekers lacking in affability like Wight got left behind. One gubernatorial candidate's social skills failed to impress a San Francisco delegate to the 1890 Republican gathering: "I've seen him blow into a dozen saloons, look around to find if he knew anyone, take a drink all by himself and blow out again. I'm for [William M.] Morrow myself, but if there's a break I'll go for anybody but that old solitaire."[49]

Candidate domination over the nomination process altered the format of the convention itself. As the competition for delegates moved to the primaries, the state convention lost some of its salience. By the time the state delegates assembled, the gubernatorial candidates had already fought the key battles in the more heavily populated counties. The convention served mainly to ratify and acclaim that choice. After 1892, state conventions usually settled on a choice for state chief executive with little or no opposition, as indicated in Figure 3.3. The chart tracks the level of competition associated with a nomination as evidenced by convention votes on governor for both major parties in all four surveyed states (as was done in Table 2.2). The results for the first years of the "Fourth Party System" (1894–1910) are paired against those of the waning years of the "Third Party System" (1880–92). The least competitive scenario had the

<hr />

48 *RMN*, Sept. 29, 1886, p. 1. If a delegate were to ask for "something substantial," Wight was to get his name and room number and pass them on to Sopris.
49 *SFE*, Aug. 12, 1890, p. 4. It was still possible for a candidate to appear too self-seeking, even in California. Ira G. Holt, a candidate for superintendent of public instruction on the Republican ticket in 1890, stood up on the convention floor to read a telegram from a textbook publisher saying Holt had to be beaten at all costs. One delegate interrupted to raise a point of order as to whether candidates could speak for themselves from the floor and his objection was sustained by the convention. Holt withdrew his name before the balloting commenced. *SFE*, Aug. 15, 1890, p. 2.

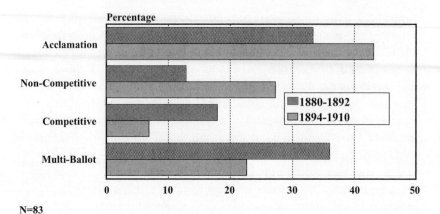

N=83

FIGURE 3.3. Competition in gubernatorial nominations.

nominee selected by "acclamation" with no other name offered to the convention. The proportion of such nominations increased from 34.1% to 43.2%. Noncompetitive ballots (where the nominee took 60% or more of the vote on the first ballot) also became more common after 1892: up from 14.6% to 27.3%. Lumping together the two remaining categories as competitive shrinks the proportion of truly contested nominations from 51.2% to 29.5%. The pattern is evident in majority parties as well as in the minority variety, so it is not merely a reflection of the less competitive electoral environment associated with the "system of 1896."[50] Rather, the trend reveals how gubernatorial candidates had been amassing their majorities well before the convention was gaveled to order.

The pattern for gubernatorial contests applied to lesser offices as well, though it was less marked (see Figure 3.4). Instances where a candidate for lieutenant governor or treasurer won without opposition had been the norm prior to 1894 and remained so. Nominations by acclamation rose slightly from 51.3% of all such ballots prior to 1894 to 56.9% thereafter. Instances where a candidate emerged with less than 60% of the vote on the first ballot became the more rare: going from 31.0% to 19.7%. The pattern applied almost everywhere. Colorado's Democrats stand out as

[50] Consider the situation of two states where Republicans remained firmly in control during the latter time period. In five state conventions in New Jersey between 1898 and 1910 the delegates selected their nominee by acclamation three times and in a noncompetitive ballot in the remaining two. Michigan Republicans witnessed their last competitive roll call for governor in 1900.

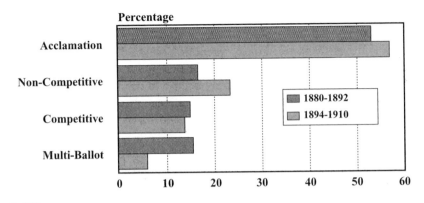

N=363

FIGURE 3.4. Competition in minor state office nominations.

the exception because the party's electoral fortunes improved markedly after 1896.[51] When the results for minor offices (in Figure 3.4) are combined with those for governor (from Figure 3.3) the decline in competition over time proves to be statistically significant ($p = .02$). The reputation of the convention as a deliberative body suffered as decisions on gubernatorial nominees were made elsewhere. The swift votes by acclamation, accomplished without even a hint of opposition, made some observers skeptical. "Where there is freedom of action, there must be divergence of opinion," one New York Democrat opined. "No thousand men can get together and think the same. If they did you and I would suspect them."[52]

State conventions came under tighter management by their gubernatorial nominees and achieved a dubious reputation for efficiency after 1900. Once the credentials of the delegates had been established,[53] division inside the convention often failed to manifest itself. Lengthy and acrimonious battles over the platform, for example, became more rare. New

[51] Unlike Democrats elsewhere in the North, those of Colorado and other Mountain and Great Plains states saw their political prospects improve markedly after the party wholeheartedly embraced silver in 1896. The more favorable odds on victory attracted more applicants for office. Democrats nominated their gubernatorial candidate by acclamation in five out of six conventions during the Third Party System and in only three out of eight in the Fourth.

[52] *DFP*, Aug. 4, 1904, p. 7; Daniel S. Remsen, *Primary Elections: A Study of Methods for Improving the Basis of Party Organization* (New York, 1895), p. 29.

[53] Disputes over credentials did become a bigger problem for later conventions. (See Figures 4.4 and 4.5.)

Jersey Democrats adopted a rule in 1898 prohibiting any amendments to the platform as submitted to the convention. It was merely to be voted up or down. The relevance of these documents in an increasingly candidate-centered campaign was in question. "Better by far than the platform of the Democratic convention was the speech of Woodrow Wilson accepting the gubernatorial nomination," the *Newark Evening News* editorialized in 1910. A Democratic politician echoed this sentiment: "A party platform was hardly necessary for the candidate is a platform in himself. If anyone asks you what the Democratic platform is, just tell him 'Wilson.'"[54] With less to vote on and little to argue about, state conventions became shorter in duration. Michigan's Republicans concluded their labors in record time in 1902. A convention that formerly required two or three days convened at 10:30 A.M. and adjourned sine die at 5:30 P.M. – with time out for lunch. In that time, they enacted a platform and nominated thirteen men for state office.[55] Faced with roughly similar duties, Colorado's Republicans concluded their labors in 1908 in four hours and fifteen minutes. An efficiency expert might marvel at the state convention's ability to transact business in record time, but others complained that the whole exercise had been fully scripted.

The candidates' more visible presence at the convention allowed them to steal the show. Instead of celebrating Democratic or Republican principles or organization, the convention served to showcase the parties' candidates. The gubernatorial nominee's acceptance speech, largely unheard of in most conventions in the 1880s, assumed its place as the convention's climax around 1900. In 1889, E. Burd Grubb broke tradition among New Jersey's G.O.P. by coming before the convention to thank them for the gubernatorial nomination.[56] From that date on, every Republican nominee addressed the convention immediately after his selection with speeches that became longer and more detailed. Only New Jersey's Democrats failed to capitalize on the state convention to introduce their new standard-bearer. But Garden State Democrats were becoming impatient with a tradition everywhere falling out of favor. When the 1907 state convention nominated Trenton's mayor as the state's chief executive, there were loud calls for him to appear on the podium – but he stayed away. The delegates had to content themselves with marching to his nearby headquarters and serenading him. Three years later, Woodrow Wilson finally

---

[54] *NA*, Sept. 27, 1898, p. 4; *NEN*, Sept. 16, 1910, p. 6; Sept. 18, 1910, p. 1.
[55] *DFP*, June 27, 1902, p. 1.
[56] *DFP*, June 27, 1902, p. 1; *NEN*, Sept. 18, 1889, p. 1.

broke the mold by traveling to the convention from his home in nearby Princeton immediately after his nomination. Wilson used his oratorical skills to work up enthusiasm even among delegates who had just voted against him.[57]

In no state under review did gubernatorial candidates fully metamorphose into the outgoing and indefatigable "happy warriors" found campaigning for local offices. Capturing a nomination to a state office under the convention system was still a less taxing activity than what would soon be required under the direct primary. However much more active California's gubernatorial candidates had become by 1906 they worked at a leisurely pace by twentieth-century standards. Two months before the Republican State Convention, Congressman James N. Gillett visited local Republican leaders across the state. Traveling unaccompanied by rail, he carried letters of introduction from his campaign manager, George F. Hatton. "This will introduce you to Congressman J. N. Gillett.... [T]ell him who he should see and what he should do." There is no evidence in the correspondence or the press that Gillett was doing much more than meeting quietly with local notables. Hatton advised Gillett to impress on his hosts that his nomination was inevitable, and that they had best get on the bandwagon. Gillett even told his listeners that Governor George C. Pardee was not interested in another term. Informal press releases that Hatton mailed to friendly newspapers warned that Pardee's renomination effort was faltering and that the governor would lose in November in any case.[58]

While Gillett endeavored to make himself known to the party organization, Governor Pardee was busy with his correspondence. Late in July he mailed hundreds of form letters appealing for support or at least for some intelligence on the local situation. "If the Napa County Republicans, including yourself, think the present governor of California has done well enough to warrant his renomination at the coming Republican state convention (and I hope they do think so), do they think hard enough to say so at their county convention? And will they send a delegation to

[57] *DSG*, Sept. 18, 1907, p. 1; Sept. 16, 1910, p. 2. This pattern represents one of the rare instances wherein the Democratic and Republican organizations in the same state operated under different sets of rules or customs.

[58] Hatton to Gillett, July 24, 1906, and Hatton to J. L. Armstrong, July 10, 1906, Box 1097, Folder 17, James N. Gillett Papers, California State Library, Sacramento. The collection includes letters of introduction to twenty-one individuals in ten cities across the state. Fortunately, Gillett neglected to follow one of Hatton's instructions, "Please destroy my letters carefully after reading."

the state convention to help renominate him?" Pardee's diffident tone and use of the third person suggests some discomfort with the task of soliciting support. Canvassing by mail from the state capital, however, plainly appealed to him over pressing the flesh. His friends in Los Angeles urged him to pay a visit, but the governor did not relish the opportunity. "[I]t may be possible for me to get down there by the end of the week. But just what I would do when I get there, I don't quite see. If there were a 'doing' of some kind, such as a club dinner, or something or other to give me a chance to show myself, I could see something to do."[59] Pardee supporters eventually arranged a barbecue, and he made a poorly publicized visit to the city that apparently did not do much to burnish his image.

Most damaging to the governor's prospects for renomination was his neglect at organizing support around the state. Pardee's private assessment was that his rival was "not a bad fellow at all," but he did not take Gillett's candidacy seriously. The governor organized slates of delegates to enter a few primaries around the state, but he did little to help get them elected. Pardee and his rival avoided an open clash or anything resembling "negative campaigning." Three weeks before the primaries in the major cities that would elect the bulk of delegates to the state body, the governor took his family to Pacific Grove for a week's vacation. Pardee's unhurried pace in pursuit of renomination reflected a fatal overconfidence. "I think that I can say," he confided to one correspondent, "without any great degree of egotism, that if the people of the State were given a perfectly fair chance to express their preference for a governor, I would stand a mighty fine chance to win." The political reporter of the *San Francisco Examiner* concurred: "I have always felt that Pardee was strong before the people if he could ever get by the politicians."[60]

The problem for Pardee – as for other candidates – was in getting past the politicians. He did not mount a campaign that presented the voter with a simple choice between himself and the challenger. In many counties, especially San Francisco and Los Angeles, Pardee did not put up a slate to challenge the one organized locally. If a Pardee delegate faced

[59] Pardee to John Zolner, July 20, 1906, and Pardee to P. A. Stanton, July 23, 1906, Box 34, Folder "July 20–26," George Cooper Pardee Papers, Bancroft Library. The governor's secretary was also busy mailing pamphlets on "Governor Pardee and His Administration." See Nye to H. B. Palkington, July 27, 1906, Box 34, Folder "July 27 to 31," Pardee Papers.
[60] Pardee to P. A. Stanton, July 23, 1906, and Pardee to M. L. Ward, July 21, 1906, Box 34, Folder "July 20–26," Pardee Papers; Pardee to Harold T. Power, Aug. 1, 1906, Box 34, Folder "August 1–11"; and Pardee to John Wasson, Aug. 14, 1906, Box 34, Folder "Aug. 12–19," Pardee Papers; SFE, Aug. 28, 1906, p. 5.

any competition it was usually against a slate drawn up in the interests of a candidate running for some other office.[61] As was so often the case in the past, the gubernatorial prize in 1906 was a product of negotiation. From his office in Oakland, Gillett's campaign manager concentrated on working out trades or "combinations" with local leaders. "Strain advises me from Red Bluff that Matlock there wants the nomination for State Senator and they think they could get the delegation for you if they could offer it to Matlock for what he wants. Of course this is impossible in view of Rolly's candidacy, so I am answering it along lines that will get matters in the best shape for us."[62] Historians claim that Gillett's candidacy was materially aided by the political arm of the Southern Pacific Railroad, an association only hinted at in the correspondence.[63] If the Southern Pacific was pulling the strings, it was only because it faced an indolent incumbent. Pardee did not make a determined effort to convert whatever support he had among the public into delegates at the convention. A political reporter expressed surprise at the governor's passive stance that doomed his renomination prospects. "When Governor Pardee made his campaign before the people, he succeeded. Why he did not make a direct campaign in every district in the state is one of the mysteries of politics. He permitted the [William F.] Herrin organization to capture a majority of the delegates without putting up a fight at all."[64]

The men who sought public offices around 1900 had each foot planted uncomfortably in a different political era. They knew what to expect if they remained aloof and waited for lightning to strike, but many still flinched at the prospect of waging an all out campaign for a nomination. No one better illustrated this ambivalent attitude toward electioneering than Michigan's Hazen S. Pingree. During the 1890s, he developed an extensive network of supporters to carry the primaries and caucuses in communities all around the state. He and his agents exercised unprecedented control over his delegates at state conventions. When traveling the state by train, Pingree made a point of disembarking and introducing himself to the locals. As a public speaker, however, Pingree was a disappointment. He also did not have much use for the press; a reporter complained that trying to get a statement out of the Detroit mayor was

---

[61] John L. McNab to George F. Hatton, July 19, 1906, and Hatton to Gillett, July 23, 1906, Box 1097, Folder 17, Gillett Papers.
[62] Hatton to Gillett, July 23, 1906, Box 1097, Folder 17, Gillett Papers.
[63] George L. Mowry, *The California Progressives* (Berkeley, Calif., 1951), p. 51.
[64] *SFE*, Sept. 7, 1906, p. 2. Herrin was the political director of the Southern Pacific Railroad. See Mowry, *California Progressives*, p. 9.

like trying to grab a bone from a dog. And, when it came time for him to attend the 1896 Republican State Convention, Pingree confessed to a hearty distaste for the exercise:

If I could consult my own convictions, I wouldn't go at all. It is the hight [*sic*] of arrogance for a candidate to put in an appearance at a convention and circulate among the delegates trying to pull them his way. My view is that the candidates ought to keep away. It would be more dignified and not degrade our politics to the level we now find them.... Those conventions ought to be conducted by the delegates and not by the candidates.... The presence of a candidate at a convention ought to be stopped. What are you going to do when the other fellows are there, though?"[65]

Pingree's successors would refine his tactics without worrying much about the propriety of their behavior.

V

Candidates for office and the delegates who nominated them occupied opposite ends of a political seesaw. As the visibility and influence of the candidates rose, the authority and stature of the delegates sank. At an earlier time, men of prominence in a community were readily accorded a place on the state delegation. As candidates began fielding friendly delegate slates in the primaries, however, even men of local standing met with unaccustomed opposition. Who a would-be delegate was became less important than whom he was supporting for office. Where once voters expected delegates to exercise some judgment in the selection of nominees, now delegates were supposed to register the will of the voters (or candidate) who sent them to the convention. Competition opened the way for men and (in Colorado) women of more modest social standing to take their place among "the best representative men." As the nomination process became more candidate-centered, the profile, duties, and image of the convention delegate changed.

The more circumscribed influence of state delegates was evident in the growing tendency of county conventions to instruct delegates on how to vote and to tie them to the "unit rule."[66] Some delegates objected to the

---

[65] *DFP*, July 26, 1894, p. 2; July 29, 1896, p. 5. For more on Pingree's campaign skills, see Charles R. Starring, "Hazen S. Pingree: Another Forgotten Eagle," *Michigan History* 32 (June 1948): 129–49.

[66] The unit rule required that all the delegates from a county vote alike, either for the candidates endorsed by the county convention or in accordance with the will of the majority of the delegation. The national Republican Party officially did not recognize the unit rule, but this was not always true of its state affiliates.

imposition of a "yoke," but their protests grew fainter as time passed. Wayne County's Republicans instructed their state delegation to loyally stand by Pingree for governor in 1896, a motion one state delegate denounced as an "insult" and "unnecessary humiliation." Pingree's managers, however, wanted word to go out across the state that the mayor had the full backing of his home county.[67] Instructions from county conventions could not always guarantee that a delegation obeyed. After Justus S. Stearns carried the Republican primaries in Lansing, Michigan, in 1900, the Ingham County Convention told its delegates to support him in the hotly contested gubernatorial race. Yet, some delegates ignored their instructions, and Stearns garnered only 14 of 19 votes in the early roll calls at the state convention.[68] The insubordinate delegates were primarily interested in promoting an Ingham County politician for another state office, and on his behalf they traded their votes on governor. The episode illustrates why gubernatorial candidates "sat on" all such competing ambitions when they could. It also explains why candidates who expended considerable money and effort to win control of a county convention might feel cheated under the multistage nomination process.

Loyalty, rather than notability, emerged as the overarching consideration for candidates working up slates of delegates to elect at the primaries. The James M. Seymour Association took responsibility for ensuring that one – and no more than one – Seymour supporter was running as a delegate in each of Essex County's 168 precincts in 1901. "Care was taken in making the selections to take up only men who are known to be favorable to the nomination of the mayor and who are believed to be unapproachable with influence or money." Candidates looked for delegates who would do their bidding not only on the roll call for governor but also on procedural matters and trades. "In regard to the delegates to the state convention," California governor Pardee confided in one of his political lieutenants in 1906, "It might be well to get together lists of reliable men in each district, who will 'make good' and 'stay put.' ... [E]verybody who goes on the delegation should understand that he must 'programme' for the head of the ticket clear down the line."[69]

Not everyone viewed a delegate's steadfast support for the candidate or faction that elected him as a virtue. Increasingly the press characterized

---

[67] *DFP*, July 20, 1896, p. 1. For other examples of delegate "outrage," see *DSG*, Sept. 18, 1907, p. 5; *RMN*, Sept. 5, 1908, p. 1; Sept. 6, 1910, p. 7.

[68] *DEN*, June 27, 1900, p. 4.

[69] *NA*, Sept. 16, 1901, p. 6; Pardee to J. Cal Ewing, July 20, 1906, Box 34, Folder "July 20–26," Pardee Papers.

delegates to conventions at all levels (state, county, congressional, etc.) as puppets or pawns in the hands of a candidate or boss. A California newspaper charged in 1906 that Tulare County's delegates "had no more say about who the candidates were to be than the people of San Francisco had about the earthquake." A political commentator for the *San Francisco Examiner* likened delegates to humble foot soldiers. "The tactics of the modern politician are quite similar to those of the soldiers. He moves masses of men in the shortest time with the least apparent expenditure of force toward a determinate purpose of which the individual soldier, like the individual delegate, has no sort of comprehension. He only knows he is there in the ranks, firing his ballot when he is ordered to fire, and aiming at whatever object is designated." How was it possible, the writer asked, "for men of fair standing in the community, of independent judgment in their own affairs, men who would resent the slightest interference with individual rights, commercially or socially, nevertheless [to] attend a convention pledged to do whatever is marked out for them to perform, to vote without reference to their individual preferences, and to execute, with their fellows political, maneuvers, the extent or object of which they seem utterly unable to comprehend?"[70]

As the reporter's rhetorical query implied, the greater emphasis on loyalty had an impact on the types of people who served as state delegates. This becomes apparent when the occupational profiles of urban delegates are compared over time. As they had for the 1880s, city directories furnished occupational information on state delegates from four major cities covering the last two state conventions in three states: Detroit (1902/04); Denver (1908/10); and San Francisco (1902/06). No listing of Newark delegates appeared in 1907 and 1910, so it was necessary to use the last available rosters from 1898 and 1901. Women delegates appeared at Colorado's state conventions after women won the suffrage in 1894, and their social status will be analyzed separately. The data do not indicate that state delegations became any more racially diverse over time,[71] but the social class of the sample did shift in significant respects. The biggest change appeared among Republicans, as seen in Table 3.1. The

---

[70] *Tulare County Times*, May 24, 1906, p. 2; *SFE*, Aug. 23, 1898, p. 1. See also *LAT*, June 19, 1894, p. 1; *DP*, Sept. 15, 1906, p. 2; Issac M. Brickner, "Direct Primaries Versus Boss Rule," *Arena* 41 (Aug. 1909): 550–56.

[71] Three delegates were listed in the directories as "colored" during the 1898–1910 time frame (out of 1,871 sampled delegates from all four cities). The Hispanic presence in Colorado's and California's conventions, gauged by perusing surnames, also remained minimal.

TABLE 3.1. *Percentage of Male Delegates to Republican State Conventions by Occupational Grouping for Newark, Detroit, Denver, and San Francisco*

	1880–1886 (%)	1898–1910 (%)	Differential (%)
Business leaders	27.7	15.8	−11.9
Professionals	15.0	21.4	6.4
White collar	12.1	11.7	−0.3
Government	9.3	12.8	3.5
Small retail	16.3	17.6	1.3
Skilled	14.6	12.6	−2.0
Semi- and unskilled	3.2	5.3	2.1
No occupation	1.9	2.7	0.8
N of cases	473	1023	

TABLE 3.2. *Percentage of Male Delegates to Democratic State Conventions by Occupational Grouping for Newark, Detroit, Denver, and San Francisco*

	1880–1886 (%)	1898–1910 (%)	Differential (%)
Business leaders	12.1	12.3	.2
Professionals	17.5	20.9	3.3
White collar	9.4	12.7	3.3
Government	5.2	14.5	9.3
Small retail	24.4	16.6	−7.8
Skilled	21.7	12.4	−9.3
Semi- and unskilled	6.1	7.8	1.7
No occupation	3.5	2.8	−0.7
N of cases	479	848	

proportion of men representing the business elite fell from 27.7% in the 1880s to 15.8% just before the appearance of the direct primary. In their place came larger numbers of government employees and professionals (lawyers constituting 70% of the latter). There was virtually no change in the percentage of business executives and managers going to Demoratic state conventions (see Table 3.2), though their representation (12.3%) was less than it ever was among the G.O.P. Among Democrats, the biggest declines came among the small retailers and skilled workers and the biggest increase again came among government employees.

TABLE 3.3. *Percentage of Republican and Democratic Male Delegates by Condensed Occupational Groupings for Newark, Detroit, Denver, and San Francisco*

	Republicans		Democrats	
	1880–1886	1898–1910	1880–1886	1898–1910
Business and professional	33.6	22.9	18.4	18.3
Lawyers and government	19.4	28.5	17.7	30.7
Small retail, skilled, white collar	43.8	43.1	57.6	43.0
Semi- and unskilled	3.2	5.4	6.3	8.0
Sig.	.000		.000	
N of cases	1459		1286	

Appointed and elected government officials accounted for about half of the seats vacated by middle-class craftsmen and store owners. White-collar workers and professionals also evidenced gains. The increase among the latter owed entirely to the ubiquitous lawyers, who now outnumbered all other professionals by 3 to 1.

Two trends are evident in the changing occupational status of male state delegates from the major cities. First, the social standing of the delegates had fallen somewhat, especially in Republican losses among their business elite. The small increase in both parties in the proportion of seats held by semi- or unskilled workers was consistent with this pattern. (Table A.3 in Appendix A indicates that the social status of delegates to the later state conventions more nearly resembled that of the urban residents they represented than had been the case in the 1880s.) In addition, there was an increase in the percentage of delegates from both parties whose names could not be found in the city directories; here was more evidence that the delegates were not locally prominent.[72] A second development, clearer than the first, was the growing presence of a "political class" composed of lawyers and public officials. To better illustrate this point, Table 3.3 reshuffles and collapses the occupational categories.[73] The table lumps together the business elite and professionals (minus the lawyers) as well as middle-class occupations of small retailers, skilled

[72] Among Republicans, 4.3% could not be found in the directories of the 1880s versus 11.8% in the later time period. For Democrats, the respective figures are 7.7% versus 11.5%. See Table A.1 in Appendix A.
[73] Here the "no occupation" group is treated as a missing value.

workers, and white-collar employees. The decline in upper-class representation among Republicans was largely accounted for by an increase among the politically connected class of lawyers and men with a major or minor government job. This political class infiltrated the Democratic Party too. Here a wide swath of middle-class occupations made room for attorneys and public employees. Chi-square values establish that the change over time in each party was statistically significant.

Men on the public payroll or connected to the courthouse constituted a growing share of urban delegations in both parties. Table 3.3 finds that the percentage of delegates who were lawyers or government officials rose from 19.4% to 28.5% among the G.O.P. and jumped from 17.7% to 30.7% among Democrats. The growing presence of the political class in the state delegations may have reflected their greater activism and better political connections. Candidates and politicians organizing a slate may also have valued lawyers and government officials for their greater reliability – or vulnerability; they could be fired or lose important clients by displeasing political higher-ups. The greater presence of the political class in county and state conventions did not go unnoticed. By its own count, the *Rocky Mountain News* figured that public office holders or their relatives constituted a clear majority of the delegates attending Denver's Democratic County Convention in 1910. "It is by this system of selecting as delegates only those who are ready to take any dictates that may save their job, or those who are after new jobs, or the relatives dependent on the job holders, that the Democratic machine of Denver ... has run its county conventions in the past and built up its 'your vote or your job' pistol-at-the-head power." The *Detroit Free Press* explained that many local government workers got involved as a form of job security. "It is a well known political rule that the man who cannot have himself elected a delegate in his own precinct is not worth giving a job to."[74]

Political connections also played a role in the recruitment of Colorado's female delegates. Women represented a relatively small portion of the state conventions in either party, but their numbers increased over time. Between 1908 and 1910 women more than doubled their percentage of the Denver delegation in both parties: from 7.4% to 15.9%.[75] It is harder

[74] *RMN*, Sept. 14, 1910, p. 1; *DFP*, June 24, 1904, p. 4.
[75] Many delegates were listed using only the initials for a first and last name, and these have all been treated as men. Possibly they included a few women. In 1902 women constituted but 4.9% of the state delegates from Denver attending the Democratic State Convention and 5.1% of those attending the G.O.P. conclave. *RMN*, Sept. 7, 1902, p. 7; Sept. 9, 1902, p. 5.

to generalize about the backgrounds of Denver's women delegates; about one-third (35.1%) of the names of the Democratic and Republican female delegates of 1908 and 1910 failed to appear in the city directories.[76] Half of those women who were found in the directories (54.5%) were not recorded with an occupation. The 39 remaining women (out of a list of 127) followed one of 17 different occupations. The most common form of employment was clerical: clerks (5), stenographers (4), "computers" (3), and "copyists" (2). A reporter perhaps had these women in mind when he characterized the female contingent attending the Democratic State Convention of 1900 as "'shirt waist girls' – 'girls' they always are, even though it has been some few years since they passed the last mile stone in their teens. The type... that has made the equality of voters in Colorado a principle of aggression and this aggression is the very life of it." They hissed vociferously when anything in the proceedings incurred their displeasure and turned on their charm when a speaker or motion met with their approval. "A smile and a kiss, carelessly, nonchalantly, while the fans were flitting back and forth – but not to hide a blush – blushes out of vogue of a convention where women are delegates on an equality with men."[77] The most striking fact about the women delegates listed with an occupation was that nearly half (18) were on a government payroll. This included most of those with clerical posts (only the stenographers worked in the private sector) and some in white-collar positions: a police matron, factory inspector, teacher, principal, and superintendent of schools. As was true of their brothers, husbands, and fathers, women in government employment assumed certain additional political duties.

Many regarded the increasing influence of government officials in the nominating process as evidence of "machine politics." Complaints about the "interference" of federal or state officials in state and local politics had surfaced in the Gilded Age, and there had been halfhearted efforts to exclude them from conventions. A California law barred employees of San Francisco's fire department from serving as delegates, but it was flagrantly disregarded by those who plausibly claimed it violated their civil rights. Only the Populist parties in Colorado and California went so far as to prohibit persons on the public payroll from acting as delegates.[78] Deploring "the officious intermeddling of the office-holding

---

[76] This does not include married women, who were identified on the basis of their husband's name, as in "Mrs. Olin Johnson."

[77] *DT*, June 8, 1900, p. 1.

[78] *SFE*, Aug. 13, 1880, p. 4; Aug. 12, 1894, p. 12; *DEN*, July 31, 1894, p. 2; *SFC*, June 12, 1879, p. 3; On the Populists, see *RMN*, Aug. 22, 1894, p. 5; Sept. 2, 1894, p. 1.

class," the *Los Angeles Times* endorsed the ban in 1894: "There is a growing feeling of disgust at the manner in which conventions are too often manipulated by and in the interests of persons already in office." The *Rocky Mountain News* contended that the 1900 Republican State Convention "was composed largely of officeholders who sneezed vigorously whenever Senator [Edward O.] Wolcott took snuff." The *Detroit Free Press* dismissed the Republican State Convention of 1904 (the last to nominate a gubernatorial candidate) as "a convention of the office holders, by the office holders and for the office holders and their allies who are too well known to require introduction." Secretary of State Fred M. Warner captured the gubernatorial nomination that year by drawing heavily on the patronage afforded him by the state census; a speaker at the state convention jocularly greeted the delegates as "fellow census takers."[79]

The demand for loyalty sent many of the parties' "old wheelhorses" out to pasture when it came time to appoint state delegates. "One of the odd sights of the [Los Angeles] convention [of 1906] was the spectacle of one time Republican leaders wearing 'guest' badges, while the riff raff that once blacked their shoes and sold them drinks blossomed forth with the blue badges that admitted them as delegates to the convention floor."[80] In many cases, old-timers were turned down because they were on the losing side in the gubernatorial fight or because they were not regarded as sufficiently safe on the issue. Many shared the fate of O. A. Hale, "about the biggest store keeper in San Jose, California." "[I]n Santa Clara Valley when they are talking about first class Republicans they are very apt to have O. A. Hale in mind," the *San Francisco Examiner* opined in 1902. He was a recurring presence at state conventions for many years past. "Mr. Hale likes to go to Republican conventions. He likes to meet his friends and neighbors from different parts of the state there, and he thinks it is a good thing for a man with large business interests to take a hand in shaping the politics of the state." In 1902, however, the local Republican leader informed Hale that he must agree to abide by the unit rule, voting in accordance with the will of the majority of the delegation. "'In that case,' said Mr. Hale, 'you would better send a proxy instead of a man. If I go to the state convention I will vote for whom I please.'" Hale decided to run at the head of an independent slate of delegates;

[79] *LAT*, May 26, 1894, p. 4; *RMN*, Sept. 18, 1900, p. 12; *DFP*, July 1, 1904, p. 4; *DEN*, June 15, 1904, p. 3; July 1, 1904, p. 12.
[80] *LAT*, Sept. 9, 1906, p. 4.

AT THE CONVENTION

"Touchin' on an' appertainin' to—"

FIGURE 3.5. The cigar, spittoon, pinchbeck suit, and ample girth signify that the figure represented here is a politician rather than a true "gentleman." Derisive caricatures of convention delegates as political hacks became more common in text and image after 1900. "Respectable" upper-class or middle-class citizens constituted a smaller share of delegates representing urban areas at state conventions about this time. (*Harper's Weekly*, Oct. 4, 1902, p. 1440.)

he lost in the primaries to a ticket associated with a gubernatorial candidate.[81]

Press coverage of conventions both reflected and shaped the changing social status of the delegates in the Progressive Era. Attacks on the "unwashed humanity" attending the opposition party's convention occasionally appeared in the partisan press of the 1880s,[82] but the overall

---

[81] *SFE*, Aug. 9, 1902, p. 6; Aug. 13, 1902, p. 4; Aug. 16, 1902, p. 1. Hale later secured a proxy from a delegate from another county that allowed him to attend the convention that year.

[82] *RMN*, Sept. 28, 1886, p. 1; *Detroit Post and Tribune*, Aug. 28, 1882, p. 2; *SFC*, June 19, 1879, p. 2.

tone remained respectful. As urban newspapers became more independent around 1900, their portraits of the delegates became less flattering. References to the stately appearance of the convention throng disappeared. Instead, reporters bemoaned the dirty and slovenly appearance of some delegates.[83] The press delighted in drawing attention to the few citizens of humble social backgrounds on the convention floor. An anecdote in the *Detroit Free Press* related the unhappy experience of one local politico, John A. Grogan, at the Republican State Convention of 1898. Grogan had elected a delegation "with the promise of a free ride and meal tickets." They were a rough-looking crowd and encountered some difficulty finding lodgings when they got to the convention city. Some had to string up hammocks in a city park. This failed to satisfy the "out-of-doors" delegates very long, and at 4:00 A.M. they forced their way into Grogan's room and camped out on his floor. The next morning, the "rag-tag and bobtail ward politicians" stole his meal ticket and helped themselves to a hearty breakfast. The press portrayed conventions as beyond the pale for respectable citizens. The presence of women delegates at Denver's Democratic County Convention in 1902 offered a study in contrasts to an overwrought reporter from the *Denver Times*:

The women! whose high ideals and noble purposes soared through the rose tinted ether, while their petticoats dragged in unspeakable filth. Who, for the sake of suffrage, left the clean, sweet environment of their homes and spent an entire day, long into the night, in the reeking atmosphere of a political kennel, who squeezed and pushed and jammed through crowds of the "unwashed" to gain the ear of a ward boss; who gave the cordial clasp of friendship to the unregenerate and submitted to the leering patronage of the ungodly; who stood in puddles of expectoration, skirts gathered high around them, while they smiled conciliatingly [*sic*] in the faces of the powers that be.[84]

Convention delegates eventually came to personify the corruption said to be eating away inside the major parties. It is by no means clear that politics or politicians were becoming more corrupt, but the political culture certainly was changing. Allegations of bribery and corruption were not new, but, back in the Gilded Age, one man's "corruption fund" was another man's "legitimate campaign expenditures." Delegates and campaign managers saw nothing unethical about candidates or their

---

[83] *RMN*, Sept. 28, 1886, p. 1; *SFE*, June 15, 1894, p. 5. The *Los Angeles Times* referred to San Francisco's Democratic leader as "general manager Buckley ... [of the] Unwashed." See William A. Bullough, *The Blind Boss and His City: Christopher Augustine Buckley and Nineteenth Century San Francisco* (Berkeley, Calif., 1979), p. 200.

[84] *DFP*, June 24, 1898, p. 5; *DT*, Sept. 16, 1902, p. 1.

surrogates paying for the transportation, housing, and hospitality of men
who journeyed to the state convention on their behalf. Cash payments,
ostensibly to assist with the fall campaign, were not unheard of.[85] Toler-
ance for such favors waned as the Progressive Era dawned. A muckraking
spirit linked politicians with vices of all kinds, helping to undermine public faith in politics and in the convention system in particular. References
abound to a criminal element among county or state delegations.[86] In
Michigan, a highly competitive Republican gubernatorial contest in 1900
spawned numerous charges of flagrant vote buying in the state convention
and the county ones that preceded it. The 1909 Republican State Convention in Michigan felt called upon to respond to a rising chorus declaiming
corruption. "We repudiate the theory that the delegates of an honest people are less honest than the people they represent." The resolution fell
well short of a ringing denial of the charges and did not presume that
the delegates were more honest than their constituents.[87] The message
was evidently intended for the Michigan legislature, just then completing
work on the state's first comprehensive direct primary law.

The reputation of nominating conventions rested in part on the reputations of the men and women who attended them. Over time, the parties
recruited less heavily from the ranks of upper- or even middle-class citizens. Convention coverage by a more independent press exaggerated
the presence of persons from less respectable backgrounds, but statistical evidence lends some credence to their claims. On one level, there
was a drop in representation of small businessmen, white-collar workers, and skilled artisans among state delegates after 1900. Perhaps this
reflected what some historians see as a growing alienation of middle-class
Americans from the nominating process and from politics in general at this
time.[88] On another level, upper-class Democrats and Republicans, who

[85] Henry A. Haigh, "The Alger Movement of 1888," *Michigan History Magazine* 9 (1925):
173–214.
[86] *RMN*, Sept. 6, 1896, p. 5; *DP*, Sept. 5, 1906, p. 14; Ralph M. Easley, "The Sine Qua Non
of Caucus Reform," *Review of Reviews* 16 (Sept. 1897): 322; A. C. Bernheim, "Party
Organizations and Their Nominations to Public Office in New York City," *Political
Science Quarterly* 3 (Mar. 1888): 99–122.
[87] See *Detroit Tribune*, June 30, 1900, in "Political Scrapbook," Box 5, Vol. 3, Ferry Family
Papers; *DEN*, July 31, 1902, p. 1; *DFP*, July 15, 1900, p. 3; Stephen B. Sarasohn, "The
Regulation of Parties and Nominations in Michigan: The Politics of Election Reform,"
(Ph.D. diss., Columbia University, 1953), p. 130.
[88] Glenn C. Altschuler and Stuart M. Blumin employ the concept of "engaged disbelief" to
characterize popular attitudes toward politics during much of the nineteenth century. See
Altschuler and Blumin, *Rude Republic: Americans and Their Politics in the Nineteenth
Century* (Princeton, N.J., 2000), pp. 252–73. The breadth or depth of public alienation

formerly filled delegate seats as a matter of course, found their prerogatives and leadership challenged. Competitive primaries elected delegates
on the basis of their affiliation with a candidate. State delegates had to
"take programme" rather than exercise their own judgment. Politically
well-connected individuals (lawyers and public officials) constituted a
growing share of the state delegations and epitomized for many a sleazy
"machine politics" that had taken hold of the nominating process.

VI

One way to summarize the changes in nominating practices among the
northern states during the Gilded Age and Progressive Eras is to consider
a prototypical gubernatorial campaign from each era. During the 1880s,
prospective officeholders typically implored their friends to stand as delegates or to influence those who did, but beyond this candidates did little
to interfere in the nominating process. They might not even attend the
convention that put them in nomination. Often a local political club took
the initiative of organizing the proceedings and agreeing on the delegates.
Caucuses and primaries were poorly attended because the presence of a
single slate to be voted on rendered the exercise moot. The relevance of
the caucuses and primaries to the actions of subsequent county and state
conventions was unclear. If the delegates were pledged to advancing the
interests of any candidate it was most likely a local politico interested
in a state office. When they arrived at the state convention the delegates
might "trade" with other delegations in the interests of their favorite son,
or they might divide their votes among candidates thought most likely to
win or to do the most for the ticket back home.

   By the onset of the Progressive Era the autonomy invested in delegates and the local political establishment that elected them had been
considerably curtailed. Candidates for governor became more engaged
in the process as they sought to elect a delegation that would stand by
them to the bitter end. They often focused their efforts on delegate-rich
urban counties. Gubernatorial candidates turned first to their surrogates
to recruit a slate of loyal delegates and marshal support. In time, the candidate himself might make a brief local appearance to curry favor with

---

from or disillusionment with the nominating process appears limited for the Gilded Age,
but few historians doubt that these attitudes became more pervasive in the Progressive
Era. See Thomas C. Leonard, *The Power of the Press: The Birth of American Political
Reporting* (New York, 1986), pp. 193–221.

the local political establishment. Primaries and caucuses were now sometimes hotly contested, drawing out many more voters. The local politicos
who hoped to wrangle a political plum at the state convention found their
plans thrown to the winds as they battled with outsiders for control of the
delegation. When voters showed up at a caucus or primary they were more
interested in expressing an opinion on who should be at the head of the
ticket than in deciding who was to attend the conventions. Gubernatorial
candidates also emerged as the star attractions of state conventions that
increasingly served only to ratify a choice made in the primaries. All these
changes, it bears noting, occurred well before the enactment of the direct
primary.

The increasingly candidate-centered orientation of electoral campaigns
after the party era is a matter of historical record.[89] The trend appears
to be no less true for the contest leading up to the nomination. The local
political elite in Robert H. Wiebe's island communities were overwhelmed
by outside political pressures represented by the hustling candidate.[90]
What changes coursed through American society around the turn of the
century that allowed elective office seekers to carve out a larger role for
themselves in the nomination process? Certainly a candidate's ability to
make himself better known across the state improved during the period.
The telegraph and telephone, and a more independent press in the larger
cities, afforded greater coordination and much free publicity. An office
seeker could unobtrusively promote his cause by traveling by rail to all the
state's major towns and cities, and soon had access to the automobile to get
almost everywhere else. More important than these technological changes,
however, were political developments that heralded a restructuring of the
nation's major political parties.

The ability of local political networks to resist the encroachments
of candidates on the nominating system rested on three distinguishing

[89] Philip J. Ethington, "The Metropolis and Multicultural Ethics: Direct Democracy Versus
Deliberative Democracy in the Progressive Era," in *Progressivism and the New Democ-
racy*, ed. Sidney M. Milkis and Jerome M. Mileur (Amherst, Mass., 1999), pp. 195–96;
Richard Jensen, *The Winning of the Midwest: Social and Political Conflict, 1888–1896*
(Chicago, 1971), pp. 165–77; Michael E. McGerr, *The Decline of Popular Politics: The
American North, 1865–1928* (New York, 1986); John F. Reynolds, *Testing Democracy:
Electoral Behavior and Progressive Reform in New Jersey, 1880–1920* (Chapel Hill, N.C.,
1988), pp. 96–105; Thomas R. Pegram, *Partisans and Progressives: Private Interest and
Public Policy in Illinois, 1870–1922* (Urbana, Ill., 1992), p. 155.
[90] Robert H. Wiebe, *The Search for Order, 1877–1920* (New York, 1967); Robert D.
Marcus, *Grand Old Party: Political Structure in the Gilded Age, 1880–1896* (New York,
1971).

features of nineteenth-century party politics. The first was the widely shared rubric that the "office should seek the man." This republican principle left the convention with an important role in identifying suitable individuals for elective office. Prospective nominees plainly felt constrained not to appear politically ambitious and confined their activities to private communications with their many friends. Voters in a caucus or primary could not be expected to know who was available for any office or to trouble themselves with the makeup of the ticket; these were tasks better left to the "best men" whom they sent to the convention. Another key characteristic of nineteenth-century politics that prevented candidates from dominating the electoral process was the network of political clubs tied to the local party organization. Democrats and Republicans depended on their organizational bases to perform a variety of functions associated with the "mobilization campaign" of the Second and Third Party Systems (circa 1828–92). The clubs also furnished a party cadre that could reliably be expected to recruit delegates, turn up at the caucuses, and in other ways protect the interests of the local organization. Last among the bulwarks to the decentralized power structure of Gilded Age politics was the control the local organizations exercised over the mechanics of the nomination process itself. Ward or township committees decided when, where, and how the delegate selection process would take place, and they often did not seem especially interested in letting others know about it. The organization's influence vis-à-vis that of the elective office seekers was weaker when it came to local offices. A candidate openly and energetically amassing support in a contest for county clerk or state senator did not appear to pose a threat to the Republic. It was also far easier for a local candidate to stay posted on the date, time, and place of the caucuses and primaries, and to direct his friends to the same. Consequently, candidates for a nomination to a local office were more aggressive in hunting up votes by circulating among the electorate and even employing advertising. A candidate for a major office, however, had to contend with many more obstacles in getting his name before the voters in a caucus or primary and generally had to leave his fate "in the hands of his friends."

The diffidence displayed by candidates for governor or Congress gradually lifted as developments at the end of the nineteenth century undermined the influence of the local organization. The deference displayed by an earlier generation of statewide office seekers evaporated and with it the raison d'être of the best representative men. A candidate who threw his hat in the ring could expect to be complimented for his manly stance rather than chastised for his naked ambition. Once the names of the available men for any office were known, few dared to suggest that voters were not fully capable of ascertaining who among them was the most qualified. The appearance of new electioneering tactics during the 1890s was another blow to the local party organization. The popularity and influence of political clubs peaked during the Gilded Age, and the clubs' demise was a matter much commented on during the 1890s. They no longer could be relied upon to turn out to support the local organization's favorite over the claims of a gubernatorial aspirant. The "educational campaign" put aside the largely partisan functions performed by the party cadre and relied more heavily on literature and advertising to reach a more independent electorate. The greater competition that attended the nominating process revealed the hazards of a multilayered and loosely administered convention system and spurred calls for reform. Local organizations would surrender control over the caucuses and primaries to others further up the party hierarchy and still later to the state.

4

Coping with Competition

The Limitations of Party Self-Regulation

I

As the twice-elected chief executive of New Jersey's largest city, James M. Seymour was an obvious choice for governor in 1898. The Newark mayor never formally announced his candidacy for the Democratic nomination, but did admit that were it tendered him, "he would consider himself ... constrained to accept."[1] Seymour needed a friendly delegation from his home county of Essex to the state convention to make his candidacy viable.[2] The mayor's friends mounted a well-organized effort to carry the primaries, outdoing anything attempted by any previous gubernatorial aspirant. They had to be more aggressive because of the hostility of the local Democratic organization. Seymour's patronage practices had alienated many the party's leaders, a common source of strife that ended many an incumbent's political career. The turmoil that engulfed the ensuing primary revealed the deficiencies of the party-administered indirect primary when faced with a highly visible and contentious struggle for party supremacy.

Ostensibly, the Newark mayor's candidacy appeared formidable. His opponent, Elvin W. Crane, was an obscure politician who had served two terms in the state assembly a decade earlier. "[O]n his merits and popularity Mr. Crane would never have had a ghost of a chance of being nominated for governor," the *Newark Evening News* editorialized. But U.S. Senator James Smith, Jr., and the county's Democratic organization

---

[1] *NEN*, Sept. 24, 1898, p. 4; Sept. 23, 1898, p. 1.
[2] In Essex County at this time, state delegates were elected by the voters in their precincts, not by a county convention as in most other states.

FIGURE 4.1. An example of a Democratic ticket from the 1898 Newark primary prominently sporting Mayor James M. Seymour's likeness. Note the small billing for the name of the delegate who was actually up for election in the precinct. (*NEN*, Sept. 26, 1898, p. 9.)

endorsed Crane. In New Jersey as elsewhere in 1898, the administration of the primaries was in the hands of the party organization. This presented the Seymour forces with an almost insurmountable obstacle: "The county committeemen have the authority to locate primaries, appoint the officials at primaries and order other details. This gives to them an advantage in primary elections that is hard to overcome, even under ordinary circumstances, and when a serious fight is on the committeemen, if so disposed, can so arrange matters that it is almost impossible to defeat delegates of their choosing." The Democratic organization did indeed carry Crane to victory amid allegations of fraud and violence around the polls. "Democratic primaries cannot strictly be called elections," the local Republican mouthpiece sniffed. "Majorities polled have no other meaning than that one set of party workers has prevailed, by hook or crook, over another set of party workers. . . . The primary motto is 'get there,' and no scruples are entertained as to the methods of 'getting there.'"[3]

Three years later, Newark's mayor was again out to capture the county delegation. As in 1898, Seymour was doing little or no campaigning and instead relied on a network of supporters. And once again the local Democratic organization stood in his way, this time backing a slate of uncommitted delegates. "We'll elect the delegates and let them pick out the nominee," announced one local Democratic chieftain. The organization's control of the election machinery reemerged as a source of discord. Seymour supporters squawked when the county committee announced the primary's date, times, and polling places a mere three days in advance.[4] The organization's appointment of the election officials aroused further suspicion. In the past, the men who staffed the voting places included the two Democrats who served as election officials for the general election and a third person they appointed. In 1901 the organization appointed the third functionary, and it replaced about ninety election judges and clerks with persons who "will take orders from above." Some charged the machine with "colonization," or importing voters from New York and elsewhere. "I don't know how they are going to try to run things," said the mayor's campaign manager, "but I do know that we are going to have a fair primary, or the house will come down."[5]

[3] *NEN*, Sept. 29, 1898, p. 4; Sept. 23, 1898, p. 1; *NA*, Sept. 27, 1898, p. 4.
[4] *NEN*, Sept. 25, 1901, p. 1. Democratic officials had kept their promise to the Seymour forces that they would provide earlier notice in 1901 than they had in 1898, when the primary was held just two days after it was announced.
[5] *NEN*, Sept. 21, 1901, p. 1; Sept. 24, 1901, p. 4; Sept. 25, 1901, p. 1; Sept. 27, 1901, p. 1.

On primary day the house – or, to be more precise, the polling places – literally did come down in some areas. The mayor's friends and foes converged on the polls and sometimes engaged in hand-to-hand combat. In some precincts the election officials hunkered down behind wooden barriers and required voters to hand in their ballots through a narrow window. In a half dozen cases the Seymour forces stormed the premises after the officials refused to allow them to post a watcher inside the booths. The assaults induced the election officials to abandon their posts and set up shop elsewhere, while the Seymour supporters supervised the balloting at the original site. The Democratic County Committee received two sets of election returns from twelve precincts (out of 168) where Seymour's friends and enemies had established separate voting places. A standoff between the factions prevented any voting whatsoever in two other precincts.[6] Riots and fights broke out around at least six additional polling places. Reports of "repeaters" (men voting more than once) and Republicans taking part in the contest dominated press accounts. The *Newark Evening News* doled out blame on all sides.

The history of the Democratic Party in Newark abounds with narratives of exciting primary elections, but it is doubtful if any in the past equaled those of last night in the bitterness of opposing factions and unscrupulousness of methods. The air today is full of charges and counter-charges, claims and counter-claims, from out of the mass of which it is difficult to sift the truth. There seems no doubt, however, that neither side paid much attention to regularity or fairness, and that each was determined to secure a majority of the delegates by fair means or foul.[7]

The election results substantiated the *News*'s indictment of the process. Fifteen precincts reported a higher turnout in the primary than the number of votes that would be cast for the Democratic candidate for governor a month later.[8] Another fourteen precincts recorded turnouts in excess of 80% of the Democratic vote, a figure that surely could be achieved only with the help of Republican or fictitious voters. Combined, these twenty-nine cases represent more than one-third of the eighty-one

---

[6] In eight precincts, voters discovered that the polling place had been moved from the spot announced in the press, and they were not always able to locate it.

[7] *NEN*, Sept. 28, 1901, p. 6.

[8] In the Fifth District of Newark's Fourth Ward, for example, 65 votes were cast for the Seymour delegate, and 143 for his opponent. Six weeks later, the same precinct recorded only 158 votes for the Democratic candidate for governor (Seymour) in the general election. The Democratic vote for governor in Essex County in 1901 (29,824) exceeded that cast for president a year earlier (25,739), and represents the more accurate count of the number of Democratic voters in a given precinct.

precincts for which the newspapers printed election data. For once, the voters – not all of them Democrats – had heeded the call to participate in the primaries.

In the final analysis, Seymour's friends and foes each scored a Pyrrhic victory. Disputes over the vote count and the returns from irregular primaries left the outcome in doubt. The Smith faction claimed that the mayor had elected only about 30 delegates (out of 181), while Seymour's friends put the number at 107.[9] The county committee predictably decided the contests from fifteen election districts in the interest of the anti-Seymour slate. Then it was the Democratic State Convention's turn to sort things out. The Seymour forces contested every seat held by the Smith faction and brought affidavits alleging fraud in 140 precincts. The convention's credentials committee sought consensus through compromise. It sustained the decisions reached by the Essex County Committee, but prohibited the application of the unit rule, which would have delivered the county's full vote to the anti-Seymour faction. The peremptory actions of the Essex County Democratic Committee won sympathy and support for Seymour around the state, and he captured the gubernatorial nomination on the second ballot.[10] Seymour's triumph was short-lived. His loss in the general election a month later would be attributed to the treachery of the Smith forces in and out of Essex County. The *Newark Evening News* concluded that Democratic prospects for victory in the fall had been "deliberately destroyed" at the primaries when each faction set out to demolish the opposition at whatever cost.[11]

Newark's primary in 1901 was more raucous than most, but it was by no means an isolated incident. Similar contests and complaints arose in other cities as candidates and their surrogates battled for control over the party delegations. Disputes over the supervision of the primaries called into question the party organizations' stewardship over the nominating process. Ringing denunciations of "political machines" took aim at the dominant faction at the controls of a party's nominating machinery. A swelling chorus deriding "bossism" and "machine rule" reflected the appearance of a more competitive nomination process, particularly when it came to statewide offices. The machines and the party as a whole paid the penalty when the general election rolled around. Disgruntled elements urged voters to reprimand candidates who allegedly landed on the party

---

[9] *NEN*, Sept. 28, 1901, p. 3; *NSC*, Sept. 29, 1901, p. 3.
[10] *NEN*, Oct. 2, 1901, p. 6; Sept. 20, 1901, p. 6.
[11] *NEN*, Sept. 30, 1901, p. 6.

ticket through "dark lantern methods." Where competition was rife, in the major cities in particular, the parties undertook various initiatives to impose more rules and authority over the nominating process. Their efforts at reform met with only limited success. Two decades of controversy and Democratic and Republican party initiatives aimed at getting their houses in order set the stage for state intervention during the Progressive Era. A few months after the Democratic donnybrook of 1901, a bipartisan commission appointed by the New Jersey legislature set to work on the state's first direct primary law.

II

The decentralized and multilayered nomination process presented the parties with plenty of pitfalls. Primaries and caucuses needed to be supervised with care. County and state conventions had to conduct their business in a manner that all sides could regard as fair. When this was the case, harmony reigned; when controversy arose over the nomination process discord arose that the opposition was sure to exploit. Misunderstandings, incompetence, and outright duplicity all had a hand in disrupting the proceedings and endangering the ticket. The problems were bad enough before office seekers began meddling in matters. The appearance of hustling candidates exposed how poorly prepared the party organizations were to supervise a nomination process marked by competition instead of consensus.

The official "call" for local caucuses and conventions fired the starting gun in the competition for elective office. Sometimes the race got off on the wrong foot. Disagreements might surface over arrangements for soliciting voter input at the outset of the process. The death or departure of the chair of the county committee, or a meeting called on too short a notice, could result in rival county committees issuing conflicting orders to their local affiliates. More often, it was what was in the call that caused friction. County committees had a lot to say about the procedures for selecting the state delegates. Was this the duty of the county convention, the county committee, or the electorate? Would voters attend multiple caucuses and primaries to select different sets of delegates to attend state, county, legislative, congressional, and municipal conventions, or would a single county convention fill all the slots? Who would supervise the caucuses and primaries, and how was the voting to be conducted? What guidelines would determine who was a bona fide party member and who was an interloper at these functions? Local custom guided county committees on these and other matters, but tradition often proved inadequate to the task.

The most common source of discord triggered by a call involved insufficient notice about primaries and caucuses. The "snap" caucus, announced on very short notice and before any opposition could organize, was a popular tactic among party insiders. An early set of caucuses could boost the candidacy of a favorite son or the candidate preferred by the organization. The *Detroit Free Press* claimed that two-thirds of the Republican caucuses that had selected delegates backing Secretary of State Fred M. Warner for governor in 1904 "were called without proper notice and strenuous efforts were made to keep the knowledge of them from all but the members of the gang."[12] Voters could not always rely on their local party newspaper to tell them what to do. A call might report where and when the county convention was to meet, but say nothing about the primaries and caucuses that selected the delegates. Some observers suggested that keeping the electorate in the dark was no oversight. "In their anxiety to farm out Republicanism in such a manner to keep the 'Ring' in power, we are not called upon to publish the calls for local caucuses or conventions," complained the *Current* in Big Rapids, Michigan, in 1880. And since the paper was not asked (or paid?) to do so, it did not. The *Rocky Mountain News* could assure Denver's Democrats in 1902 that the primaries would be held the next day from 5:00 to 7:00 P.M., but little else. "Considerable complaint has been heard because of the failure to make public the places of holding the primaries. This matter has been left with the district leaders and they have manifested a disposition to keep their opponents in the dark as long as possible." Harmony was not well served when party members were deliberately kept uninformed, as happened to a large contingent of Denver Republicans in 1892. "Up to 10 o'clock last night they were totally unable to learn where officially the voting place [was located], though they had a tip on the outside that it would be at University Park.... Some one told them the poll would be open from 9 to 11 A.M., and even if notice appeared in the papers this morning they couldn't get their forces out to University Park in time. All those woes caused them to prance around in a wild eyed manner and vow vengeance on Miller and Babcock, who are leading the other faction."[13]

Those who did locate the voting places could not be fully confident that their ballots would be properly counted. Party primaries are our

---

[12] *DFP*, July 2, 1904, p. 4; *SFE*, Aug. 27, 1902, p. 3; *DP*, Sept. 12, 1906, p. 1; Frederick W. Dallinger, *Nominations for Elective Office in the United States* (New York, 1903), pp. 121–25; Frank B. Evans, "Wharton Barker and the Republican National Convention of 1880," *Pennsylvania History* 27 (Jan. 1960): 28–43; *DFP*, June 16, 1902, p. 4.

[13] *Big Rapids Current* (Mich.), July 8, 1880, p. 4; *RMN*, Sept. 3, 1902, p. 1; Sept. 3, 1892, p. 3.

chief source of a colorful political folklore detailing stuffed ballot boxes and individuals voting multiple times under different names. A healthy dose of scholarly skepticism would be in order if these charges emanated only from the opposition party. "But," as the *Rocky Mountain News* pointed out in 1884, "when the charges of corruption are made within the party, when party leader makes affidavit against party leader until none are left untouched, when the charges of corruption are left undenied and only met with countercharges of a like nature, what is the honest voter of that party to do?"[14] Investigations by credentials committees, judicial bodies, and an independent press furnish abundant evidence of a wide range of unethical (though not always illegal) activities.[15] A resolution passed by the Democratic Iroquois Club of Los Angeles in 1890 commended their party's local newspaper "for giving expression to the righteous indignation of respectable Democrats at the character of the late primaries.... Scenes of repeating... were unprecedented in their indecency and enormity, and were calculated to bring a blush of shame to the cheeks of all true Democrats." San Francisco's Republican Committee abruptly terminated its hearings into the "multitude of protests" filed in the wake of their 1886 primary. An exasperated member explained that "the committee could not remain in session until Christmas. There were so many affidavits of fraud and corruption on both sides that we could not see our way clear, and we gave it up as a bad job.... The Committee of Ten did everything in their [sic] power to have an honest election, but the safeguards we proposed to put up about the ballot boxes got lost on their way to the polls."[16]

Vote fraud was surely more copious in the primaries than in the general election. For one thing, election laws commonly stipulated a bipartisan election board for the November election, but the primary was often administered solely by "the machine." The political maneuvering and discord that accompanied the appointment of the election officials certainly did not instill confidence in the integrity of the process. Warring factions in San Francisco's Republican County Committee divided again and again, on a 5 to 2 vote, over the selection of judges, clerks, and inspectors for the 1894 primaries. A member of the losing faction charged that many of

---

[14] *RMN*, Sept. 11, 1884, p. 4.
[15] George Walton Green, "Facts About the Caucus and the Primary," *North American Review* 137 (Sept. 1883): 257–69; Charles Edward Merriam, Harold F. Gosnell, and Louise Overacker, *Primary Elections* (Chicago, 1928), pp. 5–7; *NEN*, Sept. 9, 1907, p. 7; *SFE*, Aug. 23, 1898, p. 1; *RMN*, Aug. 27, 1902, p. 9.
[16] *LAT*, July 30, 1890, p. 2; *SFE*, Aug. 21, 1886, p. 2.

the appointees were Democrats with a habit of stuffing ballot boxes. A committee member countered by asking if the accuser "had ever stuffed ballot boxes and if it was not his desire to control the machinery so as to do it again."[17] Sometimes the mere appointment of the election officials was enough to convince a faction to boycott the proceedings or to organize a primary of their own. "The men who are on the inside have the naming of the election officers who receive and count the ballots. With this advantage, it matters nothing to them who casts the ballots." The *Denver Republican* put little confidence in the party's 1894 preliminaries: "In fully 100 of 159 precincts of the city and county judges will be chosen for tomorrow's primaries with the express understanding that they shall return the slated lists of delegates selected by the machine as elected, no matter how the better elements of the party may vote." The most that a minority faction might expect was the opportunity to appoint a "watcher" to keep an eye on the vote counters. But the "watcher" could not always be sure of gaining entry when he showed up at the polling place.[18]

Vote fraud prevailed at the primaries because many perpetrators did not view the proceedings as equivalent to an election. The local party organization (like any other men's club) was a wholly private entity. The first statutes outlawing the most blatant forms of vote fraud only appeared in most states during the 1880s. The laws did not change the mindset of the ballot manipulators overnight. For some party workers, electoral chicanery in a primary represented an ethical lapse hardly more serious than cheating at cards or pulling a practical joke. The victim of one such "prank" in 1902 was a Republican ticket peddler handing out ballots marked for the Kelly faction outside a San Francisco polling place. The supporters of a rival slate treated him to some refreshment at a local bar and surreptitiously switched his wad of tickets with one of their own. "As he did not put on his spectacles he did not notice the substitution until hours had passed and he had induced numerous voters to vote his enemies' ticket." Theodore Roosevelt was appalled at the blasé attitude of many self-confessed ballot box stuffers and their victims when he investigated a Baltimore scandal in 1891. "Most of the witnesses spoke of the cheating in a matter of course way, as being too universal and too common in primaries generally to be worthy of notice, and a great

---

[17] SFE, May 27, 1894, p. 3; R. G. Dill, *The Political Campaigns of Colorado with Complete Tabulated Statements of the Official Vote* (Denver, 1895), p. 138.

[18] RMN, Aug. 26, 1886, p. 1; SFE, Aug. 4, 1898, p. 6; DR, Sept. 1, 1894, p. 4; RMN, Sept. 3, 1902, p. 1; SFE, Aug. 22, 1898, p. 3.

number of them did not seem to bear any special malice against their opponents for having cheated successfully – if anything rather admiring them for their shrewdness – and frankly testifying that it was only lack of opportunity that had hindered them from doing as much themselves."[19] The recurring rationalization that the "other side" would have done no less had they only had the opportunity stands as the most damning evidence of how thoroughly compromised and corrupted the system had become.

The widespread practice of vote buying occupied another gray area in the public mind. Some reformers (and some laws) claimed that it was wrong to offer a voter money, a drink, or even a ride to the polls. Many voters and politicians plainly thought otherwise. Vote buying was endemic in a privately managed nominating process that could function only if the men who ran the enterprise were sufficiently compensated for their efforts. Parties paid the judges, clerks, and inspectors who staffed the polls and counted the ballots. The ticket peddlers and heelers also drew a stipend. The voters who expected payment for their "services" felt that they were merely getting their fair share of the goods. They endorsed the political ethos of a generation of "spoilsmen" articulated by a San Francisco politician: "When men of wealth came to us for gifts which meant golden fortunes for themselves, does any fool suppose we didn't ask for a modest 'cut'? Of course we did. Was it not equitable and just?"[20]

Rewarding voters for their efforts ranks as one of the lesser corrupting influences at work in Gilded Age politics, if even that. The real problem was that neither the vote buyers nor the vote sellers were particularly concerned about restricting the practice to legitimate voters. The cash dispensed outside the polls encouraged other forms of fraud, such as repeating, impersonation, and voting by noncitizens or minors. Election boards appointed by one faction could not be relied upon to take notice of such infractions. "Votes were bought and sold on the public streets during the primaries yesterday as openly and shamelessly as though they were butter and eggs," a reporter for the *Los Angeles Times* averred in 1906. "Near the hobo corner on North Main Street," he was handed two dollars to impersonate a voter. The offer came from a prospective delegate, a prison guard, who assured the journalist that he had done business this way for the past twenty years. Thus far that day he had spent fifty dollars, and

---

[19] *SFE*, Aug. 13, 1902, p. 2; Dallinger, *Nominations for Elective Office*, p. 114.
[20] William Issel and Robert W. Cherney, *San Francisco, 1865–1932: Politics, Power and Urban Development* (Berkeley, Calif., 1986), p. 137.

FIGURE 4.2. The party-run primary was a highly informal affair. (*a*) Election officials converted a livery stable in Denver to a polling place in 1894. Voters walked up to the window and handed in their ballots. (*RMN*, Sept. 6, 1894, p. 2.) (*b*) Citizens' participation in primaries was notoriously low, as was the case for San Francisco's Republican primaries in 1898. (*c*) Just down the street, the election officials sit near the window with the ballot box at hand and refreshments on the way. (*d*) Staffing the polls was a major challenge, and the many irregularities perpetrated by inexperienced, incompetent, or indifferent election officials only exacerbated factional strife. (*SFE*, Aug. 19, 1898, p. 14.)

he expected to purchase another twenty votes.[21] Because it was so pervasive, complaints about bribing voters rarely appear in the litany of wrongs drawn up by losing factions in the aftermath of a disputed primary. Making voting profitable, however, encouraged other indisputably wrongful behavior.

A more vexing problem for party officials concerned the participation of nonparty members in their proceedings. As an abstract principle, everyone agreed that only party members should be admitted to caucuses and primaries. California's Republicans required their primary voters to affirm that they had supported the party's candidates for president or governor in the previous election.[22] Elsewhere the standards for determining who was a Democrat or Republican were less well-defined. Michigan's Democrats, lonely for company no doubt, were hardly troubled by the prospect of outsiders invading their turf. Their call for the primaries and caucuses did not specify Democrats but welcomed, "All citizens, irrespective of past party differences, who can unite with us in an effort for pure, economical, constitutional government and administrative reform."[23] The state's Republicans likewise made no effort to indicate who was and was not a member of the G.O.P.[24] No state in the 1880s required voters to register their party affiliation, so primary officials – if they bothered to ask – relied mainly on the voter's own testimony regarding his political proclivities.[25] While wary challengers and vigilant judges and inspectors occasionally staffed the polls, the system in most places and at most times functioned on the honor code.

---

[21] *LAT*, Aug. 15, 1906, p. 1; Aug. 16, 1906, p. 1.

[22] *LAT*, Aug. 13, 1882, p. 1; *SFE*, Apr. 24, 1890, p. 5. If they had not voted for whatever reason, electors had to swear that they would have voted for the G.O.P. nominees. Democrats asked only that the voter promise to support the ticket in the coming election. *SFE*, Aug. 9, 1890, p. 4; Winfield J. Davis, *History of Political Conventions in California, 1849–1892* (Sacramento, Calif., 1893), p. 431.

[23] *Niles Democrat*, July 17, 1880; Aug. 7, 1886, p. 5.

[24] *Big Rapids Current* (Mich.), July 1, 1880, p. 1; *Detroit Post and Tribune*, Aug. 8, 1882, p. 2; Aug. 11, 1884, p. 6. This was also the pattern for both parties in Colorado. *RMN*, Sept. 17, 1882, p. 4; *DR*, Aug. 20, 1884, p. 4; Aug. 31, 1892, p. 8. New Jersey was the same. *NA*, Aug. 11, 1880, p. 3; *Newark Morning Register*, Aug. 26, 1880, p. 1; *DSG*, Sept. 30, 1886, p. 3; Sept. 18, 1889, p. 5.

[25] To participate in their primaries, San Francisco's Democratic and Republican parties required the individual to hold a membership in a local political club, and there was even talk of striking persons from the rosters who participated in the opposition's primaries. *SFC*, Aug. 28, 1886, p. 8; *SFE*, Aug. 16, 1902, p. 8. But the system did not last long, and it certainly did not seem to inhibit partisans who wished to cross and recross party lines.

The flimsy barriers erected to protect the party from outside interference broke down when a highly competitive contest loomed. The *San Francisco Call* identified many Democrats coming out to vote in the city's Republican primaries in 1879. "The unterrified took as much if not more interest in the primary than if it was their own." Some feared that outsiders only wished to aid the candidate who would be easiest to beat in the general election, but there is not much evidence that this motivated many citizens.[26] Voters of whatever party commonly got caught up in the drama of an exciting primary contest. Rather than treating crossover voters as interlopers, contending factions locked in heated combat recruited voters with little attention to their partisan leanings. "It is charged on both sides that Democrats as well as Republicans were hired or bought to vote in the [Republican] primaries," the *Rocky Mountain News* noted with a tone of regret in 1882. "Unquestionably there is some truth in the allegation, but whose fault was it? Who tempted these men to sell their votes?" The election returns offer additional evidence of a largely open primary system. Turnout in Detroit's Republican primary in 1892 exceeded the vote cast for the party's candidate for governor two years earlier in four largely Democratic wards; it was only half this percentage in the wards where Republicans were in the majority. The figures might mean that "there has been a wonderful increase of republican votes in this town," the *News* speculated, "or that the friends of both the candidates for governor were wonderfully industrious in piloting people to the caucuses to vote, whether they were of the party or not." The presence of many Democratic workers recruited by the Republicans to help them in getting out the vote supported the latter hypothesis. San Francisco Republican leader Martin Kelly assured Democrats (and members of other parties) that they were welcome to participate in his party's 1894 primary. Voters needed to affirm only that "it is their intention to vote for the regular Republican nominee at the general election." The bemused *Examiner* considered Kelly's invitation a needless but "charming bit of hospitality.... Democrats in the 28th district have heretofore religiously participated at all primaries without a special invitation."[27]

---

[26] *SFC*, June 8, 1879, p. 4; *LAT*, June 3, 1894, p. 3; *NEN*, Sept. 14, 1895, p. 1; *DFP*, May 31, 1900, p. 1; *DR*, Aug. 28, 1888, p. 4; *DFP*, June 17, 1902, p. 4. On the motivation of primary voters, see James K. Pollock, *The Direct Primary in Michigan, 1909–1935* (Ann Arbor, Mich., 1943), pp. 60–61.

[27] *RMN*, Sept. 9, 1882, p. 4; *DEN*, July 9, 1892, p. 4; *LAT*, Aug. 13, 1902, p. 2; *SFE*, June 2, 1894, p. 9.

Given their complicity in the practice, party officials were understand-ably nonchalant about outsiders having a say in their deliberations. Few appeals to the party hierarchy to nullify the results of a primary or caucus based their case on crossover voting. Ultimately, only the losers could summon up much indignation at Democrats appearing at Repub-lican primaries or vice versa. One congressional candidate harangued the credentials committee at Michigan's 1898 Republican State Conven-tion with charges of Democrats voting in Marquette County's primary in the interest of his opponent. Significantly, his rival did not dispute the evidence but instead brought in numerous affidavits to prove that this was a case of "the pot calling the kettle black." The committee failed to see much merit in the matter and dismissed the contest. "The only kick the Stephenson men could have," a committee member shrugged, "was because [Carlos Douglas] Shelden had more democratic friends than [Samuel M.] Stephenson in the primary."[28]

The county convention represented another perilous stage in the nom-inating process that could sow dissension in the ranks. A faction that lost in the primaries but retained some influence in the party hierarchy was not without recourse if it was prepared to pursue a policy of rule or ruin. Many years after the fact, Colorado's U.S. senator Edward Keating recalled his role in derailing a Denver County Democratic Convention. Keating and his friends, who constituted a minority of the delegates, were aligned with the governor (who controlled the local police force) and the chair of the county committee. They made the most of these assets to gain mastery over the situation. Keating's faction first arranged for plainclothes police to ring the convention hall and hinder the opposi-tion's delegates from getting inside. While the delegates filtered into the auditorium, Keating and his confederates moved quickly to hijack the proceedings:

[Thomas J.] Maloney grabbed the gavel, gave the chairman's desk a few sharp blows, and declared the convention was ready for business. [Julius] Aichele nom-inated me for temporary chairman. Maloney walloped the desk once more and declared I was elected unanimously. I took over the gavel and Maloney nomi-nated Aichele for secretary. This time I walloped the desk and declared Aichele elected unanimously. Then Maloney presented the temporary roll call, which had been prepared by his county committee, and moved that it be made the perma-nent roll call of the convention. Once more I walloped the desk and declared the motion carried unanimously. Finally, Maloney moved that the temporary

[28] *DEN*, Sept. 22, 1898, p. 5; "Stephenson v. Board of Election Commissioners," 118 *Michigan Reports* (Oct. 1898): 396–417.

organization of the convention be made permanent and I announced that the motion had been carried. By this time our opponents had filled the theater and were shaking the rafters with their cries of "No!" Of course, I paid no attention to them.[29]

Members of the opposing faction rushed the stage and pushed Keating to the wall. They had to beat a hasty retreat when armed bodyguards surrounded the besieged chair. As was usually the case when a desperate faction resorted to heavy-handed methods, Keating's victory was incomplete. A large body of delegates walked out of the hall and put up their own slate of candidates for the coming election.

Critics of the nominating system related numerous incidents to prove that ruffian tactics were commonplace in conventions and caucuses.[30] A review of many hundreds of such meetings in the four surveyed states can document episodes of raw political tactics overpowering a more numerous opposition.[31] But wanton disregard for "fair play" or for rules marred but a tiny percentage of county conventions.[32] Keating's recollection of the Denver episode offers some clues as to why such tactics were not more common. First, it was essential that one control the party organization so as to be in charge of the proceedings from the outset. Second, the assistance of the local constabulary was critical to helping a minority faction keep the majority at bay. Third, and most important, a walkout by angry delegates would almost certainly have fatal repercussions for

[29] Edward Keating, *The Gentleman from Colorado* (Denver, 1961), p. 153.

[30] Dallinger, *Nominations for Elective Office*, pp. 115–21; National Conference on Practical Reform of Primary Elections, *Proceedings of the National Conference on Practical Reform of Primary Elections, January 20 and 21, 1898* (Chicago, 1898), p. 43; John W. Lederle and Rita Feiler Aid, "Michigan State Party Chairmen: 1882–1956," *Michigan History* 41 (Sept. 1957): 258.

[31] Now and then chairs of county or state committees violated their authority by keeping some delegates out of the hall or by using the police to remove their opponents. *RMN*, Sept. 12, 1884, p. 1. The power to make up the preliminary roster of delegates was another area open to abuse. *RMN*, Sept. 16, 1890, p. 1; Sept. 6, 1892, p. 1. Contested delegations were not supposed to vote on their own cases when these came before the full convention (a rule not always honored), but they could vote on other contests. Convention chairs could also manipulate matters by choosing not to recognize certain delegates, or by choosing to ignore calls for a ballot and instead ram decisions through on a voice vote. *SFE*, Jan. 29, 1882, p. 3. And convention chairs were not the only persons in a position to pervert the process. In a few instances, the vote tally reported by the chair of a county delegation varied considerably from what the delegates announced when it was demanded that they be individually polled: *SFE*, June 21, 1894, p. 1; *NEN*, Sept. 15, 1910, p. 2; *SFE*, Aug. 23, 1890, p. 2; *DP*, Sept. 15, 1904, p. 1.

[32] County conventions charged with nominating candidates for local offices proved more troublesome. There was less at stake when it came to selecting state delegates.

the general election. "We are beaten and I don't give a ———," growled
one delegate to a Republican County Convention in Denver. "I never saw
anything like [the temporary chair's] rulings. The result is the party is
split wide open. I wouldn't turn a hand to help the ticket."[33] It was never
enough merely to crush one's adversaries. One needed to win in such a
manner that all could unite for the general election. The men responsible
for organizing and officiating over conventions generally played by the
rules because of the consequences of doing otherwise.

Good intentions, however, did not always suffice. Unhappily for party
harmony there were too many instances when rules and customs were
open to dispute. Parties at the state and local levels usually functioned
without printed instructions, leaving many issues of governance unresolved. In Michigan, for example, the county or state committees sometimes appointed the convention's temporary chair to open the proceedings. This practice was not honored everywhere or every time,[34] hence its
status as a firm rule was in question. Most accounts of the conventions
refer to the county or state committee's choice merely as a "suggestion" or
"nomination." The delegates usually were entirely happy with the choice,
but some said or did things to indicate that they believed final approval
rested in their hands. From time to time whole delegations grabbed their
hats and headed for the door because the county committee's choice for
temporary chair was or was not installed in power.[35]

It did not help matters when parties waffled back and forth on crucial
regulations. Democrats vacillated in their application of the unit rule.[36]
Opposition to the proviso was strongest in New Jersey, where voters
directly elected the state delegates in most cases without the intervention

[33] *RMN*, Sept. 6, 1892, p. 1.
[34] *Big Rapids Pioneer* (Mich.), Aug. 6, 1886, p. 3; *DFP*, June 25, 1894, p. 4; *DEN*, June 11, 1898, p. 9.
[35] *DFP*, Aug. 17, 1884, p. 6; June 28, 1894, p. 1; Aug. 14, 1886, p. 4; Aug. 19, 1886, p. 1; Stephen B. Sarasohn, "The Regulation of Parties and Nominations in Michigan: The Politics of Election Reform" (Ph.D. diss., Columbia University, 1953), pp. 141–43; "Stephenson v. Board of Election Commissioners"; *DFP*, June 26, 1900, p. 6.
[36] Republicans were more hostile to the concept, but many county conventions imposed it just the same. As the state convention approached in Michigan, Hazen S. Pingree's campaign manager exuded confidence by noting the number of delegations tied to his candidate and the unit rule, "there is no getting away from those instructions." The chair of the state convention thought otherwise and asserted that the convention would allow each delegate's vote to be recorded. *DFP*, July 31, 1896, p. 10; Aug. 7, 1896, p. 2. The Republican National Convention went on the record in 1880 by refusing to recognize the authority of state conventions to bind their delegates, while the Democratic national body ruled just the opposite. See Austin Ranney, *Curing the Mischiefs of Faction: Party Reform in America* (Berkeley, Calif., 1975), pp. 174–79.

of a county convention. Essex County's Democratic delegates in 1895 "made it understood that they would not tolerate the unit rule and threatened to bolt if it were adopted." Three years later, the county's delegation implemented the rule over the protests of a minority of delegates who promptly walked out of the caucus. Called upon to settle the dispute, the state convention sided with the delegation's majority. When a nearly identical set of circumstances occurred in Essex County in 1901, the state convention reversed itself and now disallowed the unit rule.[37] Colorado's Democrats failed to maintain a consistent position on the issue. In 1892 the chair of the state convention imposed the rule over the protests of "kickers" in the Lake County delegation. Eight years later, the full convention abrogated the rule on a vote of 766 to 128. The written bylaws of the state Democratic Party, adopted around this time, required that the convention honor the wishes of county conventions when they chose to bind their delegates. In 1906, the Democratic State Committee, on a vote of 32 to 11, decided to repeal this clause because of "the trouble it has caused in the past."[38] California's Democrats likewise disregarded the unit rule in their state conventions of 1882 and 1890 and then adopted it in 1898. The suspicion lingers – then and now – that a state convention's position on the unit rule rested not on abstract principle but on its implications for an imminent roll call.

County and state conventions also increasingly squabbled over proxies. Absenteeism was surprisingly high at state conventions given that most of the delegates were elected just days in advance of the meetings. According to the official roster of California's 1882 Republican State Convention, about one in six delegates attended as proxies.[39] Well-to-do citizens could attend a state convention by purchasing the credentials of others, sometimes representing counties other than their own. During the 1880s

37 NA, Sept. 26, 1895, p. 2; NEN, Sept. 28, 1898, p. 1; NA, Sept. 30, 1901, p. 1. Both episodes relate to the Seymour candidacy alluded to at the start of the chapter.
38 RMN, Sept. 13, 1892, p. 1; DP, Aug. 16, 1906, p. 2; Democratic Party of Colorado, "Plan of Organization and By-Laws of the Democratic Party of Colorado," Box 3, Edward P. Costigan Papers, Archives at the University of Colorado at Boulder Libraries. There is no date on the document, but it appears to have been adopted around 1902.
39 Republican Party of California, "Roll Call of the Republican State Convention, 1882," Bancroft Library, University of California at Berkeley. The San Francisco Examiner reported a roughly similar percentage (13%) of substitutes attending the Republicans' 1894 state convention. SFE, June 20, 1894, p. 2. Another common practice, not accounted for here, was for delegates to hand their proxies over to others so they could leave the convention early. See DR, Sept. 7, 1888, p. 1; SFE, June 16, 1894, p. 6; DEN, June 29, 1900, p. 3. In some cases, an individual delegate might hold multiple proxies and cast as many as a dozen or more votes in a county or legislative convention. SFC, Aug. 24, 1886, p. 8; SFE, Aug. 18, 1898, p. 1.

the issue of proxies rarely surfaced, and many county conventions explicitly entrusted the individual delegate with authority to appoint someone in his place. State conventions were initially reluctant to address an issue that was viewed as a matter for their local affiliates.⁴⁰ The power to transfer their credentials to persons of their own choosing was one more illustration of the wide scope of prerogatives vested in "the best representative men."

The declining deference accorded delegates brought with it mounting criticism of the use of proxies. The practice of sending substitutes was denounced as "obnoxious to the people" as early as 1879.⁴¹ As years passed, long arguments erupted at county and state conventions over who was authorized to appoint proxies or whether proxies should be recognized at all. The Democratic and Republican organizations began setting limits on how credentials could be transferred. They insisted that any proxies reside in the county they were to represent or that they be handed over to individuals already attending as bona fide delegates.⁴² Eliminating proxies entirely became more common through the selection of alternates or by requiring that the full delegation cast the votes of missing members.⁴³ As with most party rules, enforcement proved problematic. Los Angeles Republicans went on record in their county convention of 1894 to deny their state delegates any authority to appoint substitutes, but the state delegates simply ignored the order.⁴⁴ With the rules in flux, the temptation to manipulate them proved too much for some politicians. The Republicans of Las Animas County in southern Colorado held forty-one of seventy-six seats in the Twenty-first Senatorial District's convention in 1910. They decided to send two delegates to the district convention with the authority to cast the county's full vote. The credentials committee at the senatorial convention, on which each of the three counties in

---

⁴⁰ *DT*, Aug. 17, 1880, p. 4; *Big Rapids Pioneer* (Mich.), Aug. 6, 1886, p. 3; *DFP*, Aug. 13, 1884, p. 8; Sept. 4, 1890, p. 5.

⁴¹ *SFC*, May, 29, 1879, p. 2.

⁴² *SFC*, June 20, 1879, p. 3; *RMN*, Sept. 6, 1896, p. 6; *LAT*, June 8, 1894, p. 8; *RMN*, Sept. 6, 1902, p. 2; Sept. 7, 1902, p. 2.

⁴³ *SFE*, Sept. 1, 1886, p. 1; June 18, 1894, p. 1; Sept. 3, 1902, p. 4; *RMN*, Sept, 6, 1896, p. 6; Sept. 3, 1898, p. 6; Sept. 11, 1910, p. 5; *LAT*, Sept. 13, 1906, p. 4.

⁴⁴ *SFE*, June 18, 1894, p. 1; *LAT*, June 19, 1894, p. 1. See also White to John Y. Gaffey, Aug. 1, 1890, Letterbook, "May 30–Sept. 13, 1890," Stephen Mallory White Papers, Department of Special Collections at the Stanford University Library, Palo Alto, Calif. White asked Gaffey for his proxy to the state Democratic convention. "An objection might be urged that a resolution passed by the convention prohibited certain proxies, but, of course, if the delegation has no objection to the proxy the convention will have none. That is certain."

the district had one vote, decided to admit no proxies.[45] The Las Animas representatives "kicked" and "howled," but the full convention endorsed the credential committee's decision by a vote of 35 to 2.

The vague rules of engagement that characterized the convention system accounted for much of the controversy and dissension that cropped up after a strenuous contest. Out of respect for local autonomy, county committees chose from a diverse set of practices for selecting delegates to county, state, or other conventions. The interference of outsiders in a party primary or caucus was deplored but hard to control without understandings on how to establish party identification. No fixed guidelines existed on such critical issues as the role of proxies or the unit rule. It is difficult to condemn politicians who manipulated the process when so many vital questions bearing on the outcome remained unresolved. Even when clear guidelines were in place, political machines sometimes demonstrated that they were determined to achieve their ends at whatever cost. The implications of a loosely administered nomination process became readily apparent on election day.

III

The men who directed the affairs of the Democratic and Republican parties understood how difficult it was to resolve disputes and heal political wounds in the highly charged atmosphere of a county or state convention. They also understood the consequences of failing to do so. "The leading men [at the California Republican State Convention of 1886] say that the convention, shall not, if it is possible to prevent it, involve itself in a fight that will leave ugly wounds behind to weaken the party at the polls."[46] Most of the time they succeeded. The convention fell in behind the slate, and the disappointed candidates pledged to work for the ticket as if they were on it themselves. On the stump and in the press party leaders beseeched voters to put aside any lingering animosities in the wake of the nominating process and cast a "straight" ticket. "Of all the unsatisfactory devices for getting political revenge, we know nothing that will make a man feel meaner or more contemptible than to knife his own party ticket," a New Jersey newspaper admonished in 1890.[47] "Don't

---

45 *RMN*, Sept. 21, 1910, p. 6. For similar episodes, see *DP*, Sept. 8, 1906, p. 3; Sept. 13, 1906, p. 7.
46 *SFC*, Aug. 24, 1886, p. 8.
47 *Hunterdon County Democrat*, Oct. 21, 1890, p. 2; *Cape May County Gazette*, Oct. 18, 1889, p. 2.

scratch. Don't pair. Don't swap votes with any Democrat on any part of the Republican ticket," pleaded a Colorado newspaper. "If you have prejudices against any nominee on the Republican ticket, bottle them up for future use."[48] Sometimes, reconciliation and solidarity proved impossible. In the aftermath of an especially close and bitter nomination contest the losing side might harbor resentment and even hostility. Losing a fair fight was hard enough; losing because the other side did not play fair was something else. The repercussions could affect every candidate on the ticket. Dissension in the ranks manifested itself in the election returns and spurred the parties to tinker first with the ballot and later with their nominating machinery.

Political observers often attributed electoral defeat to disaffection stemming from the nominating process. The most glaring example came in the form of "bolting" or maverick candidates. Conventions attended by too much controversy could lead to more than one candidate from the same party seeking the same office come November. Bolting candidates were mainly a feature of local politics, since it required a small army to make one's ballot available across an entire state. During the 1880s, at least twenty-one races for seats in New Jersey's sixty-seat assembly produced multiple candidates from the same party. These party mavericks on average amassed 12.7% of the vote that might otherwise have gone to the regular nominee.[49] Until the official ballot arrived on the scene it was not always obvious which of two candidates was a party's "official" nominee. Two Democratic candidates ran for Congress from New Jersey's Fourth Congressional District in 1886. Each claimed the mantle of "regular" after having been nominated by separate conventions. The dispute was left for the voters to resolve in the general election, but their decision might be rendered moot if, as often happened, the minority party squeezed through in a three-way vote. Fusion with the opposition or a minor party was another tactic by which a disappointed candidate could take vengeance on his party. Electoral reform became a means to deny access to the ballot for many such candidacies, or at least to prohibit them from passing themselves off as "regular."

Much of the ticket splitting that characterized elections in the Gilded Age can be linked to controversies stemming from contentious primaries

---

[48] *DR*, Nov. 4, 1888, p. 4. This was the same newspaper that encouraged its readers to vote against their gubernatorial nominee in 1882 and 1886, and would do so again in 1892.

[49] John F. Reynolds, *Testing Democracy: Electoral Behavior and Progressive Reform in New Jersey, 1880–1920* (Chapel Hill, N.C., 1988), p. 44.

and county conventions. "The defeat of two Republican candidates for alderman in this city meant that Republicans have made up their minds to run their own primaries or vote for whom they please," the *Denver Times* concluded after the 1880 election. "The rebuke was timely and effective." The *Colorado Springs Gazette* reminded Republican leaders in 1888 that the voters who flocked to their standard in presidential elections could not be taken for granted. Republican voters "have defeated the nominee of their party for governor twice [in 1882 and 1886], not by staying away from the polls, but by going deliberately to the polls and voting against him." The paper blamed "headstrong and blundering leaders [who] have said to themselves 'there is no danger' and have put up men just because they wanted to put them up, and not because the party wanted them." A Republican congressman from Michigan attributed the party's electoral setback in 1882 to the machinations of federally appointed office-holders. "Early in the campaign the seeds of dissension and disgust were planted promiscuously throughout the state by the systematic interference of custom house officials and revenue agents in primary meetings and conventions."[50]

Those who "cut" a portion of the ticket often denied that their actions represented any abandonment of party principles or even dissatisfaction with the candidates. They justified their apostasy as a response to unseemly actions taken during the nominating process, often accompanied by charges of "bossism." The *Denver Republican* bolted the G.O.P. in 1882 over the party's gubernatorial choice but refrained from mounting a personal attack. "The people have no objection to Mr. [Ernest L.] Campbell as a man. Personally, they may honor and respect him, but politically he represented the machine.... [H]e was the creature of an imported Bossism." The *Republican* denied that the voters who refused to back the full G.O.P. slate should be classified as disloyal. Their actions denoted a higher strain of Republicanism. Campbell's defeat allowed for a "purification" of the organization. "The party is better and stronger for it." Partisan newspapers sometimes urged their readers to cross party lines, while assuring them that they were not compromising their standing as loyal Democrats or Republicans. Numerous Colorado Republican newspapers advised their readers to scratch the party's gubernatorial candidate in 1886 out of concern for their party. "The men who are now

---

[50] *DT*, Nov. 5, 1880, p. 4; *Colorado Springs Gazette*, Aug. 12, 1888, in Vol. 3 of the "Scrapbooks," Job Adams Cooper Papers, Colorado Historical Society, Denver; *DR*, Aug. 22, 1888, p. 4; *Daily Morning Democrat* (Grand Rapids), Nov. 14, 1882, p. 2.

bolting the ticket are doing so not because they wish to leave the party, or because they do not expect to support the party in 1888, but because of the corrupt influence that has managed the state convention and the unrepresentative character of a portion of the men who have been placed on the ticket."[51]

Losing candidates took a dimmer and more conspiratorial view of these divisions within the ranks. James M. Turner well remembered how his rivals at Michigan's Republican State Convention in 1890 reacted to his gubernatorial nomination. One delegate "shook his fist in my face and shouted: 'You fellows beat us here, but now, damn you, let's see you get elected.'" Turner was convinced his defeat that year was owing to the treachery of the losing faction.[52] Like Turner, other election-day victims tended to blame not the voters but factional leaders who sabotaged the ticket out of revenge or in the interests of a local candidate. Perhaps it was simply easier for a losing candidate to believe he had been rejected not by "the people" but by a self-seeking and duplicitous cabal of politicians. Early initiatives bent on reforming the electoral system fixed much of their attention on these partisan intermediaries.

During the 1880s, the parties relied on the ballot's format and a small army of ticket peddlers to keep their voters in line. A party's official "ticket" listed only the names of its nominees for each office. To modify the ballot required penciling or "scratching" out the name of one candidate and writing or pasting in the name of another in the available space. The ticket peddlers, who lined up in front of the polling place, were also responsible for securing a full party vote from each elector. They watched out for their fellow Republicans, Democrats, or Prohibitionists as they approached the polls and supplied them with the appropriate ticket. The color and size of the ballots differentiated the respective parties so that a voter was under scrutiny to remain loyal. The rarer independent voter might be set upon by peddlers from all parties as they

[51] *DR*, Nov. 8, 1882, p. 4; Nov. 10, 1882, p. 4; *Greeley Tribune*, Oct. 27, 1886, p. 4.

[52] *DEN*, July 15, 1892, p. 1; *NYT*, Apr. 25, 1892, p. 3; *DFP*, June 17, 1894, p. 3; Aug. 15, 1896, p. 10. An analysis of the election returns does not lend much support to Turner's accusations. Although he trailed the rest of the state ticket by about six thousand votes, candidates for the other state offices also lost – though by smaller margins. In addition, the falloff in the Republican vote in 1890 from that in the previous off-year gubernatorial election (1886) was no heavier in counties that supported Turner's nomination than in those that backed one of his rivals. Turner's defeat in 1890 is best explained by the generally disastrous results Republicans experienced nationally that year. This is not how Turner and others chose to interpret the results, however, and in this context their perception of reality was what matters.

extolled their candidates and pressed a ballot into his hand. The model ticket peddler was a salesperson rather than a mere ballot dispenser. The major parties paid the peddlers from funds contributed by their candidates, and the latter expected the workers to proselytize on their behalf. The black woman hawking Republicans tickets outside a Denver polling place in 1890 fulfilled her duties: "She claimed to have brought out sixty voters, and to have changed the opinions of twenty-three to her side."[53]

Despite mechanisms designed to insure that only "straight" party votes made it into the ballot box, there were options for those who wished to exercise some independence. Because there were no official ballots in the 1880s, anyone could prepare and distribute "mixed" or "irregular" tickets. These might list persons running without their party's official endorsement or the nominees of another party. The candidates and the parties themselves were sometimes complicit in this business. They issued "pasters" to their ticket peddlers so they or the voters could alter a ballot by covering over the name of one or more candidates on the "regular" or straight ticket with the name of another. Ticket peddlers made pasters available in response to voter demand. They sacrificed a candidate or two on the regular slate for the benefit of the rest. The chair of Colorado's Republican State Committee in 1878 mailed fifty sheets of pasters to party officials around the state, noting cryptically, "You will of course fully understand their use and will dispose of them as you deem necessary."[54] In 1928 an elderly citizen recounted his experience running for Trenton's Common Council many years earlier. "In those days it was customary for a Republican candidate to have a supply of Democratic ballots with his name printed in and for a Democratic candidate to doctor Republican ballots in the same way. You see, partisans didn't vote a straight ticket then any more than now."[55] Sometimes ticket splitting took a more systematic form when party leaders, local peddlers, or voters agreed to swap votes. A Republican might agree to support the Democratic congressional candidate if a Democrat would support the Republican running for the state senate. Rumors of agreements by local politicians to "sell off" some

---

[53] *DR*, Nov. 5, 1890, p. 2. The ticket included a black candidate, which perhaps explains her presence at the polls.

[54] William A. Hamill to Orahood, Sept. 13, 1878, Box 1, Folder 48, Harper M. Orahood Papers, Archives at the University of Colorado at Boulder Libraries; H. Lueders to Hamill, Aug. 31, 1878, Folder 14, William A. Hamill Papers, Denver Public Library.

[55] *Sunday Times-Advertiser*, June 10, 1928, from the Trentonian Collection, Trenton Public Library; *Big Rapids Current* (Mich.), July 22, 1880, p. 4.

portion of the ticket in the interest of a local favorite or out of pure spite filled much of the political correspondence leading up to election day.[56] "Although frequently done before, [vote swapping] was never carried to such an extent as it was on Tuesday," an Elizabeth, New Jersey, newspaper noted in 1882. "It was thought the effect would be to largely impair the value of a regular nomination."[57]

Anecdotal evidence of rampant ticket splitting is abundant. It also finds ample support in the election data. Scholars have overlooked this phenomenon because it is buried deep within the election returns. Viewed at the aggregate level, the returns often appear to confirm partisan constancy by reporting very similar vote totals for different candidates of the same party across different offices. But the aggregate figures are deceptive, as they indicate only the net result of "scratching." Lost in the vote totals are all the canceled ballots where two voters split their tickets in opposite directions; one person votes for a Democratic congressional candidate and a Republican for governor while another individual endorses the Republican nominee for Congress and the Democratic one for governor. This was the pattern in Denver in 1880, as described by the *Denver Times*: "It may be said that while a great deal of scratching was done, it was done in all directions, and safely assumed that the average vote of each candidate will approximate the vote on the general ticket." In the Tenth Precinct, for example, "The name of Wolfe Londoner, Republican candidate for county commissioner, was scratched on about thirty [Republican] tickets, but was written in on about an equal number of Democratic tickets." The vote totals in Precinct Ten make it appear that all the Republican tickets listed Londoner and all the Democratic tickets named his opponent, when in fact sixty ballots were bipartisan. Taking account of all the other offices subject to scratching, the paper estimated that only about four hundred of the seven hundred votes cast in Precinct Ten could be

[56] N. H. Meldrum to Hamill, Sept. 7, 1878, Folder 4; L. P. O'Connor to Hamill, Aug. 19, 1878, Folder 21; and James Moynahan to Hamill, Sept. 1, 1878, Folder 22, Hamill Papers; James C. Harlan to Burns, Nov. 18, 1890, Box 1, Folder 18, Daniel M. Burns Papers, Bancroft Library, University of California at Berkeley; *DR*, Sept. 8, 1888, p. 5; Nov. 5, 1890, p. 2; *NSC*, Oct. 27, 1901, p. 3. It is also apparent that not all voters took their voting cues or their ballots from the peddlers. Some citizens acquired their preferred ticket prior to election day, modified it at home, and concealed it in their pockets on the way to the polls. Around some Denver polls in 1882, the *Republican* reported, "the men who dispensed tickets had little to do. Voters came to the polls, as a general thing, with their tickets prepared, and without any consultation deposited them." *DR*, Nov. 8, 1882, p. 8.

[57] *Elizabeth Daily Journal*, Nov. 8, 1882, p. 3; *TTA*, Oct. 15, 1890, p. 4.

classified as either "straight" Democratic or Republican.[58] Plainly, aggregate level election returns could conceal a great deal of nonpartisan electoral behavior.

Journalists who covered the vote-counting process left behind the most accurate estimate of straight- and split-ticket voting. After the polls closed, election officials often began their vote tabulating by first separating and counting the straight and split tickets.[59] Very occasionally, newspapers recorded the total number of each variety at this early stage in the vote-tallying process. The *Denver Republican* went to press around 1:00 A.M. on the day after the election of 1888. Up to that time, all that the judges and clerks in many voting places had managed to do was to enumerate the Republican, Democratic, and divided ballots. The paper detailed the vote breakdown for fourteen precincts from around the city (representing about one-third of the total vote cast in the county). Its findings appear in Table 4.1.[60] Ignoring the outlier value registered by the Twenty-sixth Precinct, the percentage of split tickets to the total cast ranged from 17.9% to 35.0%. The percentage of nonpartisan ballots cast across all fourteen precincts amounted to almost one-third (29.6%). The *Republican* found nothing remarkable or out of the ordinary in these numbers. Sixteen years later, another newspaper from a rural county in the southern portion of the state made a similar report. (See Table 4.2.) These thirteen precincts surveyed (representing nine towns and four precincts in the small city of Trinidad) furnished almost one-half (46.3%) of all votes cast in Las Animas County in 1904. There is a wider range in the percentage of split tickets, but no precinct recorded less than 19.3%. The percentage for all the precincts (37.4%) exceeded that reported earlier for Denver. Clearly, many voters in Denver and Las Animas, probably about one-third, had no reservations about going outside their chosen party in selecting their elected officials.[61] Even parties in seemingly "safe" districts had reason

58 *DT*, Nov. 3, 1880, p. 8.
59 California's election law mandated that the officials first separate and count the number of straight and split tickets. See *Statutes of California* (1891), No. 130, p. 176. This procedure would also apply to party-column ballots that allowed a voter to mark a "straight" party vote with a single check mark.
60 The 7,432 votes reported in Table 4.1 represent 37.4% of all votes cast for president in Arapahoe County that year. Since it was a presidential election and since neither party was troubled by internal division on the order of the 1882 or 1886 elections, the figures for 1888 plausibly represented a high point in party unity.
61 A handful of reports with similar results can be found from other places and times. See *DR*, Nov. 8, 1882, p. 4; Nov. 5, 1890, p. 2; *Silver Plume*, Nov. 12, 1892, p. 3; *Ontonagon Herald* (Mich.), Nov. 12, 1904, p. 1.

TABLE 4.1. *Straight and Split Tickets for Selected Colorado Precincts, Denver, 1888*

Ward	Precinct	Straight Tickets		Total Vote	Split Tickets	
		Rep.	Dem.		Total	Percentage (%)
1	2	130	136	324	58	17.9
2	8	120	133	389	136	35.0
2	10	151	118	393	124	31.6
2	11	280	156	561	125	22.3
3	12	317	160	618	141	22.8
4	18	256	169	552	127	23.0
6	33	176	187	477	114	23.9
8	22	253	184	587	150	25.6
8	23	268	175	620	177	28.5
8	24	261	195	654	198	30.3
8	25	263	140	473	70	14.8
8	26	106	103	710	501	70.6
9	30	166	190	482	126	26.1
9	31	230	210	592	152	25.7
TOTAL				7,432	2,199	29.6

Source: *Denver Republican*, Nov. 7, 1888, p. 3.

to worry about desertions in their ranks. Most of the "cutting" apparently was done at the bottom of the ticket. Candidates heading the ticket rarely emerged with the highest or the lowest vote totals in the precinct results. Instead, it was the candidates for sheriff or for state assembly who usually ran well ahead of or behind the slate. Party loyalty more easily attached itself to presidential or gubernatorial nominees. It did not automatically transfer to persons running for the state legislature or for county clerk. Ticket splitting was carried out in response to local political circumstances where factional discord was most intense. This may be one reason why the earliest experiments with the direct primary singled out local offices and only later applied the principle to posts elected statewide.

Frustration with an expensive and unreliable ballot-distribution system induced the major parties to embrace ballot reform. Around 1890 state governments began taking sole responsibility for the preparation of the ballots and their distribution at the polling places. Ballot reform helped the parties better contain partisan inconstancy within a bipartisan framework, though it could not prevent voters from straying to the main

TABLE 4.2. *Straight and Split Tickets for Selected Colorado Precincts, Las Animas County, 1904*

| Township | Straight Tickets | | | Split Tickets | |
	Rep.	Dem.	Total Vote	Total	Percentage (%)
Primero	98	9	471	364	77.3
Berwind	73	109	300	118	39.3
Starkville	88	102	243	53	21.8
El Moro	33	60	137	44	32.1
Segundo	138	89	306	79	25.8
Hohne	96	81	225	48	21.3
Sopris	286	84	506	136	26.9
Tercio	132	78	355	145	40.8
Hastings	347	80	529	102	19.3
Trinidad Ward 1	163	141	472	168	35.6
Trinidad Ward 2	66	117	311	128	41.2
Trinidad Ward 3	112	87	375	176	46.9
Trinidad Ward 5	109	81	334	144	43.1
TOTAL			4,564	1,705	37.4

Source: Chronicle News (Trinidad), Nov. 9, 1904, p. 7.

opposition party.[62] Third parties and fusion candidacies found it harder to get their candidates' names on the ballot in the first place. State administration of the ballot also protected the major parties from "treachery" from within. The opportunity for ticket peddlers or others to promote ticket splitting by passing out pasters or furnishing unsuspecting voters with bipartisan ballots was eliminated. The state now provided what was usually a single ballot to be marked up inside a voting booth. Another important provision in the laws designated that only one candidate's name could wear the party label for each office. This bestowed an "official" status on one candidate that branded all rivals as apostates. In the short term, there is some evidence that the new ballot laws promoted partisan voting primarily by denying mavericks or independent candidates and third parties access to the ballot. After a decade or so, however, ticket splitting reasserted itself, although it would now be more purely bipartisan

[62] John F. Reynolds and Richard L. McCormick, "Outlawing 'Treachery': Split Tickets and Ballot Laws in New York and New Jersey, 1880–1914," *Journal of American History* 72 (Mar. 1986): 835–58; Peter H. Argersinger, "'A Place on the Ballot': Fusion Politics and Anti-Fusion Laws," in *Structure, Process and Party: Essays in American Political History*, ed. Peter H. Argersinger (Armonk, N.Y., 1992), pp. 150–71.

in character; voters divided their choices largely between the Democratic and Republican nominees. Ballot reform did little to correct perceived abuses or shortcomings in the nomination process, but focused instead on inhibiting disgruntled elements from venting their frustration on election day.

Voters of the nineteenth century, and the ticket peddlers who assisted them, exhibited an independent streak that dismayed party stalwarts. Controversy surrounding how a nomination had been secured was often responsible for many of the split tickets cast on election day. Political parties cast about for mechanisms to check partisan inconstancy, which accounts for their support for ballot reform in the 1890s. The latter did succeed in curtailing independent and minor party candidacies, but it did not begin to address the grievances that could still express themselves in a vote for one or more candidates of the other major party. Ballot reform accomplished what it could, but party regularity eluded the partisan-minded reformers, prompting some to turn their attention to the nomination process. "If there is not an understanding, a full and entire agreement to abide by the nominations of a convention, of what service [is] a convention?" asked Colorado's *Trinidad Weekly News* in 1886. "We had as well go back to the old way of letting every man run for office on his own hook. The first thing the next state convention should do . . . is to devise a set of rules that shall make bolts and splits impossible."[63]

IV

For party leaders of the Gilded Age, achieving harmony was more a matter of outcomes than of process. They aimed chiefly to arrange for a proper division of the spoils of office among their party's major constituencies. This was the subject of the lengthy negotiations going on behind the scenes at the state and other conventions. California Democratic leader Stephen M. White offered words of encouragement to one close political associate working out a deal with the "Hon. O'Connor and his high toned associates." "It is hoped you will succeed, because that faction no doubt controls many votes – not enough to elect anybody but a sufficient number to do a good deal of 'knifing.'"[64] Efforts to placate all elements of the party gave rise to informal rules to guide the decisions. The application of term limits maximized the number of offices up for grabs at any party

[63] *Trinidad Weekly News*, Sept. 17, 1886, p. 1.
[64] White to W. D. English, July 31, 1886, Box 1, Letterbook for Mar. 4, 1885, to Aug. 26, 1886, White Papers.

conclave. The goal of a "balanced" ticket was to ensure that all the party's major players came away with something. Recognizing and rewarding the parties' numerous, locally organized power blocs was the preferred means of achieving party unity, but it was hardly a very reliable one.

The efforts of state and local conventions to parcel out offices among the parties' many factions induced delegates to take a dim view of any individual holding on to an elective office for very long. The same principle applied to appointive offices. In 1884, a Michigan Greenbacker articulated the democratic appeal of "rotation in office": "If office is a good thing, pass it around. If it isn't, don't impose it on one man all the time."[65] Rotation or "term limits" resonated with the political culture of the Gilded Age. Some prescribed the practice as an antidote to "an aristocracy of officialism."[66] Others emphasized the benefits that accrued to political parties in having a large number of offices to distribute on or after election day; it spurred partisans at all levels to vigorous efforts during the campaign season. (It also subjected the winners to an avalanche of requests for appointive positions that they could never hope to satisfy.) Rotation in office also accorded with the distributive mode of governance that historians identify as the hallmark of policy making in the party period.[67] Americans looked to government at all levels to dole out the nation's riches whether in the form of land, franchises, charters, or the like. Public office was one more asset in the government's possession that rightly should be passed around at the "Great Barbecue." But not least of the practical benefits associated with term limits was the abundant supply of elective offices made available to placate an insatiable party cadre.

Rotation in office brought an early end to many political careers. A congressman usually could not expect a third term or perhaps even a second on the basis of his experience, seniority, name recognition, or record.[68]

---

[65] *DFP*, Aug. 19, 1886, p. 3.

[66] Arthur Judson Pillsbury, "Plans for Effective County Organization of the Republican Party in California," p. 17, Bancroft Library.

[67] Richard L. McCormick, "The Party Period and Public Policy: An Exploratory Hypothesis," *Journal of American History* 66 (Sept. 1979): 279–98; Peter H. Argersinger, "The Transformation of American Politics: Political Institutions and Public Policy, 1865–1910," in *Contesting Democracy: Substance and Structure in American Political History, 1775–2000*, ed. Byron E. Shafer and Anthony J. Badger (Lawrence, Kans., 2001), pp. 126–31.

[68] *DFP*, July 30, 1880, p. 7; Aug. 8, 1888, p. 3; *NYT*, July 30, 1886, p. 1; Dallinger, *Nominations for Elective Office*, pp. 88–89. Samuel Kernell found the principle of rotation "a significant impediment to career development" of congressmen before 1890. See Kernell, "Toward Understanding Nineteenth Century Congressional Careers: Ambition, Competition, and Rotation," *American Journal of Political Science* 21 (Nov. 1977): 669–93.

The *Big Rapids Pioneer* asked a Michigan congressman contemplating a third term to "remember there are other pebbles on the beach – other tin cans in the alley – and other men in the district as well qualified as he for the office, and who desire as much as he to leave the heritage of an honored name on the pages of the Congressional Record to their posterity." A letter writer to a New Jersey newspaper urged Monmouth County's Democrats to observe a one-term rule for county offices. It claimed the county clerk's office earned the holder about twenty thousand dollars a year over a five-year term. "The Democratic idea of rotation in office should certainly be applied to such an office as this. One term of such a fat office ought to satisfy any man."[69]

Incumbents who ventured to overturn the rotation tradition usually came to grief. Michigan's Republicans honored a firm if unwritten rule that any state officeholder who had not proven himself incompetent was entitled to a second term – but no more. In 1882, a few state officeholders tried to hang on to their positions for a third term. Their efforts met with a storm of protest in the press and at Michigan's Republican State Convention. The secretary of state garnered just 9 percent on the vote on the first ballot, running last in a field of four. The state auditor also ran last in a three-man race; his candidacy met with "some rather pointed and very sarcastic remarks" in the nominating speeches of his rivals. This was enough to dissuade the other two-term officeholders from asking for similar consideration. In California, the bias against renominating candidates was not as intense, but there was no supposition that a single four-year term entitled the officeholder to another. California incumbents had to fight for their jobs like everyone else. In six state conventions between 1882 and 1890 a total of ten incumbents entered the race to succeed themselves: only one candidate met with no opposition, and four were turned down. Democrats even renominated their state controller to a third term in 1890 despite objections that "the people were opposed to third terms, which might cast disunion and ruin in the Democratic party."[70]

The partisan imperative underlying rotation in office also applied to fashioning balanced tickets. Given their role in securing victory, all factions expected some consideration from state and local conventions. In the 1880s, parties defined their political subdivisions by geography rather

[69] *Big Rapids Pioneer* (Mich.), Apr. 6, 1904, p. 2; *Red Bank Register* (N.J.), Oct. 8, 1888, p. 2.
[70] *DFP*, Aug. 8, 1882, p. 4; *DEN*, Aug. 30, 1882, p. 1; *SFE*, Aug. 23, 1890, p. 2.

than by political ideology or ethnicity. Although one finds appeals for veterans or farmers or even newspaper editors as a class of persons deserving of "recognition," their political clout was minimal. Ethnicity and occupation did not exert influence in a state convention in the same manner as counties or congressional districts did. Delegates from the same county met in caucus to agree to promote the interests of a particular candidate; delegates who shared an occupation, ethnicity, or other status did not. When politicians at a state convention spoke of a balanced ticket they usually meant one that included candidates from every region of the state. County conventions choosing minor officials worked out their own arrangements for townships and wards.[71]

A recurrent theme in the nominating speeches at conventions of all levels was to insist that one's county, township, or ward had been overlooked in the makeup of the ticket. Left unstated was the threat that a spurned constituency might not make the usual effort on the party's behalf come November. A speaker made his pitch for a northern California man for state treasurer in 1898 with the aid of a large map of the state. He drew a solid blue line across its northern portion and pointed out that the convention had yet to pick a candidate from the area. When a speaker's appeal drew heavily on the needs or rights of his home delegation, the candidate's qualifications might appear secondary. "I do not say of Judge [E. A.] Bridgford that the sun rises on his head before day and sets there as late as possible in the evening," a speaker acknowledged to a California Republican congressional nominating convention in 1894. Rather, the nomination properly belonged to Colusa County

by reason of her location; hers by right of the commanding talents of a man whose name I shall present; hers by the equity of rotation, and hers as a just reward for her unfaltering support of the party through all the years that are gone. . . . When other contingents have stood in the public trough with both feet and forehands filled until their teeth were afloat and squealing for more, the sentinels of the Colusa guard have filed past the tents of your captains and asked for commands. . . . Colusa has sent a very cranky delegation down here this year, and we will not be satisfied with a smile or a piece of soft soap.[72]

---

[71] *RMN*, Oct. 15, 1880, p. 4. Ethnic balance played a bigger role in municipal elections where immigrants represented a much larger share of the electorate. In Hudson County, New Jersey, the sheriff's office and the mayoralty of Jersey City were split between one man of Irish extraction and another of German. See George C. Rapport, *The Statesman and the Boss* (New York, 1961), p. 74.

[72] *San Francisco Chronicle*, Aug. 26, 1898, p. 1; *SFE*, Aug. 24, 1894, p. 2.

Colorado's women delegates provided one notable exception to the emphasis on geographically balanced tickets. As soon as they first appeared on the floor of state conventions in 1894, women in both major parties seized the state office of superintendent of public instruction for one of their own. Angenette J. Peavey organized a successful women's ticket in Denver's Republican primaries that year; the G.O.P. tendered her the nomination in deference to her political skills and those of women in general. Peavey's triumph was no small accomplishment given the obstacles women encountered in securing places in party organizations or in just getting themselves registered to vote. Mary C. C. Bradford performed a similar service for her sex among Denver's Democrats. She too would later be rewarded with the state education post. Men soon learned they had no business competing for the school superintendent's post in either party's state convention. After 1894, only women served as state superintendents of public instruction until the post was abolished some decades later. Unlike other groups, women delegates made their wishes known by caucusing together during the state conventions, even if they were not always able to unite as a voting bloc.[73]

The early success women enjoyed in winning some recognition on the ticket did not mean that they had influence in the convention that corresponded with their strength of numbers in the electorate or even in the convention. Indeed, Colorado's women politicians soon found themselves trapped in an educational ghetto. It was some years before female candidates were even considered for other statewide offices. Women could expect only a single seat in the state legislature and hardly any more on either party's state committee. "Not a woman spoke in the [Democratic State] Convention," wrote one exasperated female reporter in 1904, "and one wonders if a woman will ever be governor, or congressman, or mayor..., or even temporary chairman of a state convention. One wonders and wonders why there are women delegates at all. They seem to be a kind of superfluity; a kind of knob on the potato politic. They are

---

[73] DR, Sept. 7, 1894, p. 4; RMN, Sept. 14, 1894, p. 1; Aug. 21, 1894, p. 8; Aug. 30, 1894, p. 5; Katherine Kenehan, "The First 50 Years," unpublished manuscript in File Folder 1, the Colorado Federation of Jane Jefferson Clubs Collection, Colorado Historical Society, Denver; RMN, Sept. 12, 1900, p. 12; DP, Sept. 22, 1904, p. 1; Sept. 11, 1906, p. 4. State Board of Immigration, *Yearbook of the State of Colorado, 1918* (Denver, 1918), p. 200. In 1948 the state constitution was amended to replace the superintendent of public instruction with a commissioner of education appointed by a state board of education, a position that after 1951 was filled only by males. Colorado Department of Education, "A Brief History of the State Department of Education in Colorado" [http:www.cde.state.co.us/cdeedserv/historycde.htm] July 2005.

THE WOMAN AND THE HEELER.

FIGURE 4.3. The *Rocky Mountain News* welcomed women's suffrage in Colorado in 1894, taking note of the "hotbeds of iniquity and corruption which have grown into existence under masculine regime in politics, the worst of which are the primaries." (Aug. 20, 1894, p. 4.) Denver's Republican County Committee refused to admit women to their ranks, claiming they "should be at home minding the babies." (*RMN*, Sept. 6, 1894, p. 1.)

not on the inside, nor admitted to the 'holy of holies,' when officials are made and unmade before business ever reaches the conventions."[74] "It is easier for a rich man to go through the eye of the needle (or something like that) than for a mere woman to get the 'dope' at a Democratic Convention," grumbled a frustrated female reporter in 1908.[75] A resurgence in women's political activism manifested itself in the state conventions of 1908 and 1910. One woman mounted an unsuccessful drive to capture the Democratic nomination for secretary of state and another landed a Republican nomination for regent of the state university.[76] Even California's major parties took cognizance of women's growing political role by 1906. Democrats that year nominated a woman for superintendent of

[74] *DP*, Sept. 22, 1904, p. 5.
[75] *RMN*, Sept. 8, 1908, p. 4.
[76] *RMN*, Sept. 14, 1910, p. 1; Sept. 21, 1910, p. 3.

public instruction, and Republicans nearly did the same.[77] Racial minorities and interest groups such as organized labor did not yet have similar success in regularly securing a place in state government for one of their own. The convention system's ready response to its female base, however, suggests that it might have more readily accommodated other political constituencies once they became more organized.

Conventions where only one or a few offices were up for grabs, where there was no opportunity to divide up many offices, had their own formula for achieving balance. They rotated nominations over time. Congressional and legislative conventions agreed that each year a different county, township, or other political subunit would dictate the choice. In one legislative district the privilege of naming the nominee might be assigned to one county one year and to its neighbor the next.[78] Republicans in Berrien and Cass counties in Michigan shared the Seventh District state senatorial seat. In 1900, it was Cass's turn to come up with a candidate. The delegates from Berrien County attended the convention but cast blank ballots while the Cass delegation's votes deadlocked among three candidates. After eighteen fruitless ballots, the Berrien delegates elected one of their own to the spot, much to the chagrin of the Cass delegation.[79] Local understandings that combined the principles of term limits and balanced tickets reflected the outcome-oriented approach of the convention system.

Few partisans defended the principle of a balanced ticket for its own sake. Every convention affirmed that it had recruited the best-qualified men and women for each office. Editorials chastised conventions that appeared to lose sight of the credentials of the candidates in seeking to placate a cantankerous delegation. "Something is due to location and nationality," the *Rocky Mountain News* conceded in 1882, "but these are secondary considerations at most and must not be permitted to outweigh the more important qualification of eminent fitness." The parties rejected the premise that considerations of region necessarily compromised quality. A northern Michigan newspaper's equivocations in 1886 summarized this confusing argument: "No district should be considered, as a district, the merits of the men nominated being the only points to be considered. The Upper Peninsula can be relied upon to do its duty in the premises if the proper candidates are put in the field, without regard to section,

---

[77] *LAT*, Sept. 5, 1906, p. 1; Sept. 13, 1906, p. 1.
[78] O'Donnell to John Uglow, Sept. 17, 1906, Folder 30, T. J. O'Donnell Papers, Archives at the University of Colorado at Boulder Libraries.
[79] *DFP*, July 21, 1900, p. 3.

although we believe, by right, this district is entitled to a leading place on the [state] ticket."[80]

Putting the principles of balance and rotation into practice, however, sometimes proved problematic. Agreements and customs collapsed owing to a multitude of causes. Counties or townships laid claim to nominations based on "understandings" that might not be shared by the other political units in their district. There was also some question about whether "outsiders" should have a hand in deciding which candidate from the designated locality should take home the honors. Representatives from sparsely settled counties or townships had difficulty convincing their counterparts from more heavily populated areas that offices should be shared equally.[81] Legislative districts were often reorganized with the census, thereby terminating one set of arrangements and forcing politicos to negotiate another. Incumbents could be relied upon to point out some of the inequities and deficiencies of term limits and balanced tickets as they sought to cling to office.

The major political parties of the Gilded Age relied on unwritten "gentlemen's agreements" to produce a united front in the face of the enemy. These arrangements functioned rather like the cartels or "pools" organized in various industries of the time to check "ruinous competition." The cartels and political factions worked out a deal that promised each constituency a piece of the action and a stake in the outcome. Wrenching offices out of the hands of incumbents maximized the supply of available resources. A balanced ticket spread the spoils more evenly around. Incumbents chafed under the limitations, but they could exert little influence when decisions were made in conventions by persons after their job. As in the business sector, pooling agreements often proved ineffective and short-lived. Endemic ticket splitting and charges of treachery indicated that something more needed to be done.

V

As they approached the new century, party organizations exhibited new respect for rules and more formalized structure as bulwarks against factionalism and its consequences. The additional pressures brought to bear

[80] *RMN*, Sept. 21, 1882, p. 4; *Mining Gazette* (Houghton, Mich.), Aug. 19, 1886, p. 3.
[81] *Cape May County Gazette*, Sept. 9, 1892, p. 2; *Big Rapids Pioneer* (Mich.), July 21, 1898, p. 4; *DFP*, Aug. 20, 1882, p. 4; Frank Miller to Burns, Sept. 27, 1899, Box 2, Folder 3, Burns Papers; *Niles Daily Star*, May 20, 1904, p. 4.

on the convention system by aggressive vote getters prompted party officialdom to rationalize the nomination process. With more competition in the primaries, the utility of clear guidelines and detailed procedures became more apparent. Party unity remained the goal, but now it would be achieved with a rule book rather than through negotiation. "[Y]ou must have rules and organization, and you must enforce them, and if you don't you invite political destruction,"[82] U.S. senator Henry M. Teller advised Colorado's Democratic State Convention in 1908. For a variety of reasons, state and local party organizations proved inadequate at the task of bringing order to the nominating process. The parties' manifest failures at self-regulation opened the door to government intervention.

In the early 1880s, local party organizations enjoyed substantial autonomy in the nominating process, though their competence was often in question. Typically, the county committee confined its duties to announcing the date, place, and time of the county convention. The towns or wards of larger cities did the same for their caucuses and primaries. "This is the true and established Democratic usage," the *San Francisco Examiner* affirmed in 1880, "the right of the people of every political [*sic*], or community, locality to manage their own affairs in their own way." The laissez-faire approach came under mounting criticism for leaving the party vulnerable to manipulation or mismanagement. "Heretofore," the *Rocky Mountain News* complained in 1882,

these preliminary gatherings of the Democratic campaign . . . through the apathy of the average central committee, have been practically allowed to take care of themselves. The supervision of the authorized representatives of the party has been limited to naming the time and place for these meetings of the people. The rest has been trusted to luck, so that any industrious ward bummer, with a commission from an enemy or an ax to grind, could step in from the gutter, with a few followers on his trail, and run the primary to suit himself, or to meet the requirements of his bargain with our political opponents.

The *News* wanted Denver's Democratic County Committee to appoint the officials who would preside at the primaries. "Then, whatever the result may be, let it be honestly counted, openly declared, and thoroughly respected as the verdict of the party with no coddling for bolters."[83]

Impatience and frustration with the decentralized party management structure spurred urban county committees to usurp functions formerly handled by their political subdivisions. Their scrutiny of party functions in wards and townships intensified over time. The calls for caucuses and

---

[82] *RMN*, Sept. 9, 1908, p. 3.
[83] *SFE*, Apr. 21, 1880, p. 2; *RMN*, Sept. 11, 1882, p. 4.

primaries became more detailed, and the authority for administering these procedures shifted up the party hierarchy. The parties of the largest city in this study led the way. San Francisco's Democrats enacted a far-reaching restructuring of the delegate-selection process in 1882. Persistent factionalism and competition with the Workingmen's Party had left the city's Democratic Party with "scarce a grease spot . . . to mark its place," in the words of local leader Christopher Buckley. Appeals and threats from the Democratic State Committee induced the city's two major factions (Buckley's Yosemite Club and the more exclusive Manhattan Club) to form a "Committee of Fifty" to reorganize the party. The new plan called for replacing the two Democratic clubs with one for each of the city's forty-seven precincts. The county organization took responsibility for the initial formation of the clubs. It prescribed who could participate in the primaries, and how and when they would vote. Democrats credited the new system with securing their victory in the 1882 elections, the party's first clean sweep in fifteen years.[84] San Francisco's Republicans paid the plan the ultimate compliment by making similar changes in their own ranks, though not without provoking opposition. "What has the County Committee to do with this club?" demanded one irate Republican when the new regulations were put in place. "I regard this club as a body of independent, sovereign voters, and no power on earth, not even a county committee, can either control or lay down laws for it."[85]

A similar transition occurred in other large cities. The calls for the primaries issued by the county committees document the committees' expanding authority. Decisions about the time and place of the primaries were among the first responsibilities that moved from the local affiliates to the county organizations. Detroit's Democratic and Republican county committees of the early 1880s expected their ward committees to make the local arrangements and announce them in the press.[86] With three days to go before Wayne County's Democratic convention in 1882, the local party organ expressed alarm that no call had been issued for five of the city's thirteen wards. "The members of the ward committees evidently need a little punching up," the local Democratic organ editorialized. The five wards never did get their meetings advertised in the *Free Press*. Two years later, the call issued by the Democratic County Committee was

---

[84] William A. Bullough, *The Blind Boss and His City: Christopher Augustine Buckley and Nineteenth Century San Francisco* (Berkeley, Calif., 1979), p. 87; Committee of Fifty, "Address of the Committee of Fifty to the People [1882]," Bancroft Library.

[85] *SFE*, Feb. 28, 1882, p. 3; Aug. 12, 1882, p. 3.

[86] *DFP*, Aug. 5, 1880, p. 4; Aug. 13, 1882, p. 4; *Detroit Post and Tribune*, July 9, 1880, p. 2; Aug. 23, 1882, p. 2; Aug. 11, 1884, p. 6.

much more informative. Detroit's caucuses would be in session from 7:00 to 8:00 P.M. on the next Thursday evening, and those outside the city would be held from 3:00 to 5:00 P.M. Instead of one caucus for each ward the call stipulated one for each of the city's fifty-two election districts. The announcement further specified the use of ballots in the selection of delegates and listed the addresses of the meeting places, mostly private residences.[87]

As competition for delegates became more intense, urban county committees adjusted the proceedings to accommodate more voters. They expanded the hours for voting, an indication that the voice voting associated with the caucus was giving way to a primary using ballots. Detroit's Democrats lengthened the voting times from one to two hours in 1890 and upped this to six hours (2:00 to 8:00 P.M.) by 1894. Specifying the precinct rather than the ward as the unit of representation multiplied the number of voting places and made them more accessible. Denver's Democrats convened in 9 wards in 1890 and in 128 precincts in 1894. The city's Republicans followed suit two years later.[88] County organizations assumed responsibility for providing ballots and appointing officials to monitor the voting. In 1898, Republicans in Newark and its suburbs enrolled the voters' names on a party roster, arranged for the preparation of a designated ballot, and detailed how votes were to be counted.[89] The Executive Committee of the Los Angeles Republican Party that year set the dates, times, and places of the primaries, as well as of the caucuses that preceded them. The caucuses forwarded the names of prospective delegates to the secretary of the county committee. He prepared the ballots and turned them over to the district committee members. The latter were to bring the ballots to the primaries and "place the tickets in a conspicuous place, easily accessible to all Republican voters." A committee member objected to the plan and proposed retaining the old system whereby "the voters of each Assembly district should choose the delegates in such manner as they saw fit." His substitute motion received "scant consideration."[90]

---

[87] *DFP*, Aug. 18, 1882, p. 4; Aug. 6, 1884, p. 4; July 11, 1888, p. 4; Aug. 28, 1890, p. 4; June 15, 1894, p. 5. In later years, the call was not quite so meticulous, though the authority for choosing the time and place of the caucuses remained in the hands of the county committee.

[88] *RMN*, Sept. 20, 1890, p. 2; Sept. 5, 1894, p. 5.

[89] *NA*, Sept. 12, 1898, p. 5.

[90] *LAT*, Aug. 2, 1898, p. 14; Arthur Coffman Wolfe, "The Direct Primary in American Politics" (Ph.D. diss., University of Michigan, 1966), pp. 14–24.

As the major parties moved to assert control over their nominating procedures, they began taking steps leading to the dismantling of the convention system. The locally organized, informal caucus was dead in most large cities by 1900 or so. Few mourned its passing. Next to go was the county convention. In California and Michigan, urban voters began balloting on the names of the state delegates by 1904. New Jersey's Democrats and Republicans had been voting directly for their state delegates since at least 1880. The next logical step was to invest voters with the authority to select the nominees. Party-run direct nominations, the so-called Crawford County Plan, which dated back to the Jacksonian Era, began to spread rapidly in the 1890s.[91] About that time, the parties in New Jersey's heavily urban Hudson and Essex counties implemented a direct primary for county and legislative offices. At least one of the major parties in every county of rural South Jersey adopted a similar system by 1902. Republicans in Jackson County, Kansas, introduced a party-run direct primary as early as 1877. In an 1898 article, the local politico claiming responsibility for the innovation lauded its salutary effect on party unity. "There has been no bolting by defeated applicants; each having been satisfied that his friends did all they could for him, in turn cheered the winner.... The few fight it out in each precinct, and have it all over there without necessarily embroiling the whole party to its lasting damage."[92]

Past scholarship has linked the spread of the direct primary not to competition in the nomination process but to a lack of it in the general election. V. O. Key, Jr., and others argue that the appearance of the state-administered direct primary came in response to a decline in electoral competitiveness that followed the 1896 election. Lower competition acted as both a cause and an effect of changes in nomination procedures. Direct nominations tended to appear first in the less competitive states.[93] Once

---

[91] Alan Ware, *The American Direct Primary: Party Institutionalization and Transformation in the North* (Cambridge, U.K., 2002), pp. 97–100. Ware claims that the Crawford County system was mainly confined to rural areas in its early years. See also Ernest A. Hempstead, "The Crawford County or Direct Primary System," in *Proceedings of the Rochester Conference for Good City Government and the Seventh Annual Meeting of the National Municipal League [1901]*, ed. Clinton Rogers Woodruff (Philadelphia, 1901), pp. 197–217. Only Colorado cities (in the four state sample) preserved the two-step process of selecting county delegates who in turn appointed the state contingent.

[92] *NEN*, Jan. 4, 1903, p. 4; John S. Hopkins, "Direct Nomination of Candidates by the People," *Arena* 18 (June 1898): 735–36.

[93] V. O. Key, Jr., *Politics, Parties and Pressure Groups*, 5th ed. (New York, 1964), pp. 375–76. Wolfe, "Direct Primary," pp. 49–50. Key and Wolfe concede that the statistical evidence of a relationship is not very compelling.

in place, the direct primary bolstered one-party rule by Republicans in the North and Democrats in the South.[94] The majority party became the arena for resolving political issues, which rendered other forms of organized opposition – even the minority party – largely irrelevant. Key's hypothesis has not gone unchallenged. Alan Ware affirms that the decline in electoral competitiveness associated with the "System of 1896" is an illusion. He also fails to find an association between the appearance of direct primary laws and electoral competitiveness.[95]

The proper unit of analysis for understanding the appeal and adoption of direct nominations is the county rather than the state, and attention should focus on the actions of party officials rather than of state legislators. The practice of leaving the choice of nominees to the party faithful was introduced by political parties at the local level. Regrettably, records of the nominating practices of the Democratic and Republican organizations are hard to come by, especially at the local level. Fortunately, one pioneering political scientist did seek out such data. In 1902, James Judson Crossley mailed a survey to the Democratic and Republican county committees in all of Iowa's ninety-nine counties inquiring into their nominating practices. He found that Republican organizations in one-third of the state's counties employed the direct primary for selecting candidates for township, county, and legislative offices. The rest of the state continued to rely on conventions to make these nominations.[96] Republican county organizations were responsible for introducing the system of direct nominations, since state regulation of the nominating process was in its infancy.[97]

Just as Key would predict, what most clearly distinguished those Iowa counties replacing the indirect with the direct primary for local offices was the level of electoral competitiveness in the general election. Table 4.3 measures competition as the difference in the percentage of the total vote between the Democratic and Republican candidates for governor in 1901. The mean size of the Republican margin of victory was far larger in counties that employed the primary (42.5 percentage points) than those still

---

[94] Key, *Politics, Parties and Pressure Groups*, pp. 386–87; Pollock, *Direct Primary in Michigan*, pp. 30–31.

[95] Ware, *American Direct Primary*, pp. 162–95.

[96] James Judson Crossley, "The Regulation of Primary Elections by Law," *Iowa Journal of History and Politics* 1 (Apr. 1903): 165–92.

[97] Crossley was a member of the state assembly. In 1896 he and others introduced legislation authorizing or mandating direct nominations for local offices. Their bills failed to pass.

TABLE 4.3. *Electoral Competitiveness and the Party-Administered Direct Primary for Iowa Counties, 1902, Republican Party*

System of Nomination	N of Counties	Mean Differential in Percentage of Party Vote for Governor, 1901
Direct primary	34	42.5
Indirect primary	65	17.0

$Eta^2 = .45$; Sig. $= .000$

making do with conventions (17.0). The different nominating systems explained a prodigious 45 percent of the variance in electoral competitiveness.[98] As the minority party in the state, Democrats had less use for the primary system. They emerged with only 36.8% of the statewide vote in 1901 and employed the primary in only two counties: one was the banner Democratic county that year, and the other ranked fourth.[99] For a minority party, whose success relied largely on exploiting whatever divisions it detected within the ranks of the opposition, the selection of nominees might be better left with the professionals acting in a convention.[100] Local Republican organizations introduced and ran Iowa's earliest direct primaries in places where a G.O.P. nomination was tantamount to election (barring treachery and maverick candidates).

The association between direct primaries and one-party rule in Iowa and elsewhere may largely reflect a disparity of resources between entrenched majority parties and their feeble opposition. A primary made considerable demands on a party's campaign chest. A San Francisco Republican leader claimed that the G.O.P. spent fifty thousand to sixty

[98] Analysis of variance as used here inverts the cause-and-effect relationship. The assumption is not that the use of the primary accounted for the Republicans' wider victory margins, but that places that were less competitive to begin with opted for direct nominations over the indirect variety.

[99] Internal inconsistencies in Crossley's data do not make it clear if the two Democratic counties, Carroll and Davis, were joined by a third, Decatur.

[100] In the context of the 1901 gubernatorial election, "competitiveness" was really an indicator of how thoroughly Republican a county was. There were no counties where the Democrats enjoyed a substantial competitive edge; in the 1901 election, the banner Democratic county supplied the party with only 52.0% of the vote, and the party secured a very thin plurality of the vote in only seven other counties. A test for an association between degree of urbanization and the adoption of the primary found no association whatsoever and explained a mere one percent of variance whether one classifies urban areas as places of over 2,500 inhabitants or over 7,500.

thousand dollars on that city's primary contests in the 1890s.[101] Election officials needed to be paid, as did the proprietors of the polling places. In some localities, the parties equipped the polling places by providing voting booths, ballot boxes, and the ballots themselves. A majority party in a noncompetitive district could raise the needed revenue by making financial demands of its nominees that the minority party could not. One party was offering an opportunity to be carried triumphantly into public office; the other was tendering a ticket to political oblivion.[102] For a majority party the direct primary served as a sensible insurance policy. A party with overwhelming support among the electorate ran the risk of a competitive contest only if it produced a controversial nomination. A party in a competitive district, bracing itself for a hard-fought contest in the general election, might prefer to save its ammunition. A poor minority party might be priced out of the market entirely. A Newark, New Jersey, Republican leader outlined the cost-benefit analysis behind the party's switch to direct nominations for local offices in 1896. "When the present [nominating] system was adopted it was a question of expense, but it was decided to do it and save the cost in reducing the expenditures in meetings, parades and such demonstrations. We felt that if we satisfied the people that they had fair and honest primaries it would do more good than the parades.... It is a fact that we wouldn't go back to the old system if we wanted to."[103]

Rural areas and small towns generally did not feel it necessary to experiment with their nominating procedures. They probably could not afford a primary – direct or indirect – in any case. The county committees in the more remote counties of California continued to appoint their state delegates.[104] Rural county committees left townships with a free hand in determining when, where, and how their delegates would be chosen. Announcements about caucuses in the countryside continued to elude the press; locals presumably learned about them by word of mouth or perhaps

[101] *SFE*, June 13, 1894, p. 4. Chicago's primaries, according to one well-posted source, cost $28,000 in the mid-1890s. See National Conference on Practical Reform, *Proceedings*, pp. 74–81. The wide gap in costs between the two cities might reflect the fact that the polls in Chicago were open only a few hours whereas those in San Francisco operated all day.
[102] It also stands to reason that business interests that commonly donated to political parties (the utilities, saloons, contractors, and railroads) would be more generous to the party in power.
[103] *NEN*, Oct. 29, 1902, p. 1.
[104] *SFE*, Aug. 6, 1898, pp. 4, 29; *LAT*, Aug. 13, 1902, p. 1; *SFE*, Aug. 13, 1906, p. 6; Aug. 21, 1906, p. 4.

a poster. Small towns tended to schedule their caucuses for the evening whereas rural areas preferred the afternoon (night travel was hazardous). Voter participation remained minimal. The "office caucus," frequently held at a law firm, prevailed in communities where a party had as many as one hundred or more voters.[105] Reports from the hinterland indicate that the citizenry were only dimly aware of or concerned about state races. Candidates for statewide offices did not trouble themselves trying to elect friendly delegations in counties credited with but a handful of votes. In short, rural party officials were not under pressure to adjust their voting procedures to handle larger numbers of voters stirred up by the campaigns of gubernatorial or other candidates. The absence of competition in rural areas perhaps accounts for the reputation of their caucuses as less corrupt than primary elections in the cities.[106]

Party development of governing mechanisms and administrative capacity also lagged at the state level. County committees in many urban areas functioned with written bylaws by the 1880s,[107] but their state affiliates did not see the need for the same for some years to come. "I know nothing about the rules governing the organization of Democratic conventions," confessed Michigan Democratic leader (and U.S. postmaster) Donald M. Dickinson in 1891.[108] A national survey of state party organizations in the mid-1890s credited Democrats with formal rules in fifteen of forty-five states and Republicans in eighteen. Only half the states with guidelines had bothered to have them printed. Most of the states with published guidelines were located in the Northeast. In the copycat tradition of reform, one party's adoption of printed rules made it highly likely that state's other major party would do the same.[109] Bruising nomination struggles often

[105] *Ontonagon Herald* (Mich.), Aug. 27, 1898, p. 3; *Niles Republican* (Mich.), Apr. 16, 1900, p. 4; *Big Rapids Pioneer* (Mich.), Apr. 13, 1904, p. 2; *Aspen Democrat* (Colo.), Aug. 23, 1908, p. 2.

[106] National Conference on Practical Reform, *Proceedings*, p. 27; Charles B. Spahr, "Direct Primaries," in Woodruff, *Seventh Annual Meeting of the National Municipal League*, pp. 186–87; Dallinger, *Nominations for Elective Office*, p. 96. More recent scholarship questions whether rural areas were any less prone to corruption and "boss rule." See John D. Buenker, "The Politics of Resistance: The Rural-Based Yankee Republican Machines of Connecticut and Rhode Island," *New England Quarterly* 17 (June 1974): 212–37.

[107] *TTA*, Sept. 14, 1892, p. 3; *Burlington Gazette* (N.J.), Sept. 11, 1880, p. 2; Republican Party of San Francisco, "Rules and Regulations of the Republican Party of San Francisco, 1881," Bancroft Library.

[108] Sarasohn, "Regulation of Parties," p. 24.

[109] Daniel S. Remsen, *Primary Elections: A Study for Improving the Basis of Party Organization* (New York, 1895), pp. 38–39. Among those states where both parties operated with

provided the impetus for state bodies to take action. After the credentials committee of the Michigan Republican State Convention wrangled over a contested delegation in 1896, it appealed to the full convention to formulate regulations to avert future imbroglios. Two years later, the credentials committee at California's Republican State Convention made a like plea after a similar ordeal. Both state party conventions in Colorado went on record endorsing printed rules in 1902.[110]

The adoption of rules, printed or otherwise, hardly proved a panacea. Numerous factors undermined the efficacy of formal structures in bringing peace to party deliberations. Regulations often enjoyed but a short life span. State conventions viewed themselves as answerable to no one but the people. Rules adopted by one state or local convention might be amended, discarded, or ignored by the next. When Colorado's Republicans first enacted a set of rules at their state convention in 1902 it was alleged that the rules were designed to ensure that the Wolcott faction would remain permanently in power. Two years later, an opposing faction was in control of the state committee and they junked much of what was in place.[111] The seeming impertinence of a state committee's meddling with the regulations approved by a full convention was not unusual. A contemporary student of party governance noted how county or state committees routinely modified the rule books to better suit their present circumstances. Hence, "the servant is greater than the master. The committee is lord of the party." What parties needed, the author concluded, was a set of constitutional safeguards that were beyond the reach of a state committee or even a state convention,[112] but who could impose such a document?

State nominating conventions were imperfect instruments for establishing a framework of party governance in any case. The delegates interested themselves primarily in selecting candidates; they evidenced little patience for abstract issues of administrative structure. Rules and

printed rules were Connecticut, Indiana, Iowa, Kentucky, Massachusetts, Pennsylvania, and Virginia. Only in one state, North Carolina, did one major party (the Democrats) have printed rules and the other none.

110 *DFP*, Aug. 6, 1896, p. 1; *SFE*, Aug. 25, 1898, p. 4; *DT*, Aug. 7, 1902, p. 8; May 4, 1902, p. 2. Democratic Party of Colorado, "Plan of Organization and By-Laws of the Democratic Party of Colorado," Box 3, Costigan Papers. Colorado's parties were acting in response to the recently approved "Act Relating to Political Parties." See *Colorado Laws* (1901), Chap. 71.

111 *RMN*, Sept. 14, 1904, p. 1; *DP*, Sept. 14, 1904, p. 2.

112 Remsen, *Primary Elections*, p. 22; Merriam, Gosnell, and Overacker, *Primary Elections*, pp. 7–14.

regulations drawn up by a state committee were invariably approved by conventions without debate or opposition. State and local party organizations evolved rapidly from a condition of having no rules to one of having too many. Party committees and conventions further undermined whatever benefits clearer regulations had to offer by refusing to abide by them or even take cognizance of their existence. In 1906, Colorado's Republican State Convention engaged in a lengthy debate over a resolution granting women equal representation on the state committee. The body adopted the proposal "in the face of strong opposition," even though a supporter noted that the 1898 state convention had already mandated it.[113] Both parties' state conventions in California issued directives that demanded an end to the custom whereby county committees appointed delegates to state conventions. Nevertheless, a few county committees continued the practice without incurring the wrath or even the notice of the state committees or conventions. San Francisco's Democratic Committee selected the state delegates in 1894 and 1898; they were seated both times even though a contesting delegation from San Francisco – elected in primaries – appeared in the latter year.[114] However appealing the concept, haphazard implementation robbed rules of their viability.

Parties neglected to abide by their own directives partly owing to a lack of institutional memory. Party organizations existed for only a few months every two years, left few records, and experienced frequent turnover in leadership. Moreover, many county and local organizations believed that the state body had no business dictating how they did business. They too regarded themselves as autonomous entities, called into being by the people rather than by a state or national body. A county convention in Colorado in 1890 rejected a suggestion that it follow the rules of the party's national body on a matter involving a contested delegation. A delegate articulated the independent mindset at odds with the organizational imperative: "The Republican Party makes laws to purify itself, and it will make them whenever it is necessary, and in doing so it does not follow any statute but the wisdom of the majority."[115]

Whatever the rules might say, the final decision rested with the party's sovereign body, the nominating convention. The convention's verdict on cases of contested delegations offered an opening to shape the nominating process. Even without bylaws, some hoped that the state conventions

[113] *DP*, Sept. 15, 1906, p. 4.
[114] *SFE*, Sept. 3, 1886, p. 1; May 4, 1894, p. 2; *LAT*, July 26, 1898, p. 8.
[115] *RMN*, Sept. 17, 1890, p. 6.

might put in place a system of "case law" through their decisions on contested delegations. "I believe unless you do what is right and be controlled by rules and precedents that have been established, that you will suffer at the polls," a Republican delegate affirmed in 1890. Occasionally, debates over a credentials committee report raised concerns about setting precedents that might come back to haunt a subsequent convention. But credentials committees and full conventions evidenced little patience for abstract arguments over the legitimacy of one delegation vis-á-vis another. Delegates to county and state conventions grew impatient at the time lost "washing somebody else's dirty laundry." "These d ——— d Arapahoe [County] fellows get up these contests for the sole purpose of keeping the country delegates in Denver," a rural delegate growled.[116] In the interests of harmony and time, credentials committees and conventions frequently offered seats in the convention to both sets of contesting delegations.[117] In doing so, they passed on the opportunity to confer legitimacy on a delegation and thereby lay out rules governing the delegate selection process. Former governor Charles S. Thomas chided the 1908 Colorado Democratic State Convention as it prepared to recognize both sets of contesting Denver delegates: "[L]et me warn you, as long as you reward disobedience with compromise you will never have any harmony.... The only way to enforce harmony is to obey party law."[118]

The gubernatorial contest proved to be another important factor in undermining the convention's ability to implement guidelines over the nominating process. Delegates could not be trusted to judge a case by its merits or to abide by precedents if doing so worked against the interests of their gubernatorial favorite. They increasingly voted yea or nay on procedural issues primarily on the basis of whether the ruling would help or hurt their choice for governor. Before gubernatorial candidates came to dominate the convention proceedings the delegates could address the knotty issues associated with a contested delegation with open minds. Once delegates were elected on the strength of their association with a particular candidate their independence was compromised. Table 4.4 exposes this relationship by pairing a county delegation's vote on a contested delegation with its later vote on governor. It draws on the handful

[116] *RMN*, Sept. 19, 1890, p. 2; Sept. 18, 1890, p. 2.
[117] *RMN*, Sept. 22, 1882, p. 1; *DFP*, Aug. 19, 1886, p. 1; *TTA*, Sept. 15, 1892, p. 5; *SFE*, Sept. 1, 1886, p. 1; Sept. 4, 1902, p. 4; Aug. 23, 1894, p. 3; *RMN*, Sept. 11, 1900, p. 1; *DP*, Sept. 14, 1904, p. 5; *DFP*, June 27, 1902, p. 1. Under these arrangements, each delegate cast half a vote.
[118] *RMN*, Sept. 9, 1908, p. 3; *DP*, Sept. 1, 1906, p. 4.

TABLE 4.4. *First Ballot Roll Call Votes on Governor Correlated with Roll Call Votes on Credentials Reports*

	Yes Votes	No Votes
1884 Republican State Convention, Colorado		
Meyer	33	31
Eaton	45	10
Moynahan	10	1
Tabor	7	0
1886 Democratic State Convention, California		
Bartlett	5	9
Reddy	8	9
Berry	21	24
Torpey	18	7
Coleman	5	0
1890 Republican State Convention, Colorado		
Routt	22	228
Smith	24	18
Stanton	0	35
1896 Republican State Convention, Michigan		
Pingree	288	1
Bliss	9	155
Wheeler	1	42
O'Donnell	8	18
Aitken	2	19
Connar	13	1
1910 Democratic State Convention, Colorado		
Shaffroth	275	68
Jefferson	0	327

Pearson Corr. Credential Vote and Vote for Meyer $= -.34 \, r^2 = .11$; Pearson Corr. Credential Vote and Vote for Bartlett $= -.14 \, r^2 = .02$; Pearson Corr. Credential Vote and Vote for Routt $= -.45 \, r^2 = .21$; Pearson Corr. Credential Vote and Vote for Pingree $= .82 \, r^2 = .66$; Pearson Corr. Credential Vote and Vote for Shaffroth $= .60 \, r^2 = .35$;

of instances in the four sampled states where there is a record of a full convention's county-by-county vote on a credentials issue as well as on a competitive contest for governor.[119] The first such correlation was possible in Colorado's Republican State Convention of 1884. The table considers how supporters of the various gubernatorial candidates aligned themselves on a vote to decide which set of delegates to seat from Arapahoe

---

[119] A competitive contest is one wherein no candidate had more than 60% of the vote on the first roll call.

County (which then included Denver).[120] One portion of the table considers only counties that awarded all of their votes to a single candidate on the first ballot. Republican front-runner William H. Meyer, for example, secured all 64 votes allotted to eight counties. Meyer's delegates from these solid delegations narrowly voted (by 33 to 31) in favor of the majority report of the committee of credentials bearing on the Arapahoe contest. The delegates from counties unanimously supporting one of the three other gubernatorial aspirants (Benjamin H. Eaton, James A. Moynahan, and Horace A. W. Tabor) also voted for the majority report though by more lopsided margins. In 1884, the delegates settled the credentials issue without being much influenced by their preferences for governor; a majority of every gubernatorial candidate's delegates endorsed the credentials committee's action. The lack of relationship between the vote on governor and an earlier one on credentials was also apparent two years later in California's Democratic State Convention. It is presumed from this pair of conventions from the 1880s that the delegates' decisions rested on the merits of the case – or at least on factors external to their preference for governor.

As years passed, however, the votes on governor corresponded with those on procedural issues. The last two state conventions where linkages can be made between a vote on governor and another on credentials display patterns in stark contrast to those of the 1880s. This is most apparent in the Michigan Republican State Convention of 1896. All but one of Hazen S. Pingree's 289 delegates from solid delegations voted to seat a Pingree contingent from St. Clair County. Only 9 of the 164 delegates from counties uniformly backing his chief rival, Aaron T. Bliss, agreed with them. A dispute involving the Denver delegation at Colorado's Democratic State Convention in 1910 also clearly divided the supporters of Governor John F. Shafroth from those of his rival. If the analysis is broadened to consider the votes from all the counties, rather than the solid delegations alone, the trend over time remains visible. Pearson Correlation results, also appearing in Table 4.4, find little relationship between the vote on credentials and the vote on governor in 1884 ($r^2 = .11$) and 1886 ($r^2 = .02$).[121] The association was far closer by 1896 ($r^2 = .66$)

[120] In this case, the "Yes" and "No" votes pertain to a roll call wherein the full convention endorsed the majority report of the credentials committee by 191 to 98.
[121] Here the data utilizes the percentage of a county's vote going to the gubernatorial front-runner (i.e., the candidate who secured the most votes on the first ballot) and the percentage voting "yes" on the credentials roll call. The correlation brings with it the usual caveats of the ecological fallacy, but brings all counties into the analysis.

and 1910 ($r^2 = .35$). The struggle to land the top spot on the ticket was coming to dominate the credentials process just as it was other facets of the convention. Political commentators reported the roll call on a credentials fight as a reliable indicator of the voting strengths of the candidates. The reputation of delegates as honest brokers who could be trusted to judiciously resolve internal disputes suffered, and the opportunity to build a stable framework of party governance was lost along the way.

As the Progressive Era dawned around 1900, a nominating system that had pursued harmony through a judicious division of the spoils was giving way to one that sought the same end by relying on process. The change in approach was in part a response to the challenge posed by the hustling candidates. Focusing as it does on state conventions, this study has perhaps made it appear that gubernatorial candidates were the primal force for change, but in fact aggressive office seekers were putting pressure on the nominating process at all levels. The major parties' county and state organizations found it necessary to revamp their nominating procedures to better function in a more openly competitive environment. County committees adopted formal rules of procedures and supervised the actions of ward and township affiliates in the conduct of primaries and caucuses. The biggest changes occurred in the biggest cities, but even state organizations were taking steps to rationalize their operations. Majority parties in areas of one-party rule experimented with direct nominations; they had more resources and the most to lose when the nomination process went awry. But rules alone could accomplish only so much. Parties proved more adept at passing new rules than in enforcing existing ones. Greater attention to process served as one palliative to the problems posed by greater competition, but it fell well short of a remedy.

VI

There was no better indicator of the pressure on the major parties to reform than the mounting incidences of contested delegations showing up at state conventions. Here was conclusive evidence of an embarrassing breakdown in nominating procedures that posed a threat to party unity. In theory, closer supervision of the nomination process and greater clarity about procedures should have eliminated some of the confusion or abuses that left the legitimacy of a delegate's credentials in doubt. Party reform should have led to a reduction in the number of contests being filed,

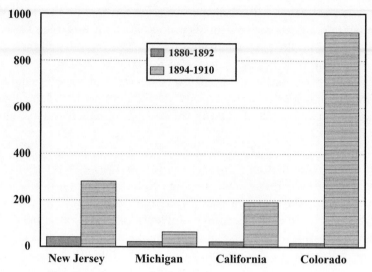

FIGURE 4.4. Number of contested delegates by state: Democratic Party.

but this is not what happened. Instead, heightened competition at the delegate selection stage led inexorably to an increase in the number of seats challenged in the state conventions of both parties.[122]

The increase in disputed delegations was most dramatic among the Democrats, as can be seen in Figure 4.4. The conventions are divided between the two political eras representing the Third and Fourth Party systems. The total number of disputed seats at state conventions in all four states between 1880 and 1892 amounted to 93. It skyrocketed to 1,459 during the decade and a half that followed. The number of counties sending contesting delegations to Democratic conventions leaped from eight to twenty-nine. Colorado accounted for most of the disputed delegates, but every state exhibited some increase in the number of convention seats challenged.[123] Republicans experienced a similar if less-striking trend in

---

[122] A contesting delegation is one that demands recognition from the credentials committee at the party's state convention. There were many more credential disputes that were settled at the county convention or that were never brought before the state credentials committee.

[123] In drawing comparisons between states it is important to remember that states that elected their state officers every two years (Colorado and Michigan) held twice as many conventions as California, where officials served a four-year term. In New Jersey, the governor's term was three years.

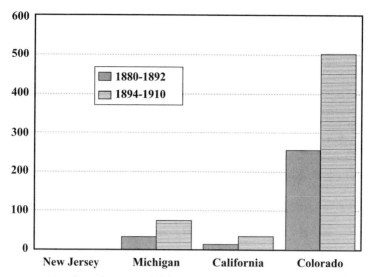

FIGURE 4.5. Number of contested delegates by state: Republican Party.

their own ranks, as seen in Figure 4.5. The number of counties involved in contests in the four states remained about the same over time (from 19 to 18); the number of seats contested, however, doubled (from 300 to 612). Only New Jersey's G.O.P. bucked the trend by avoiding contests in any of its eleven state conventions between 1880 and 1910. At the other extreme, Colorado Republicans displayed the most disharmony before and after 1894. The decline in competition in state conventions (as manifested in Figures 3.3 and 3.4) makes the increasing divisiveness over the makeup of delegations all the more remarkable. Despite their new rules and the greater likelihood of a predetermined outcome after 1892, the major parties found themselves arguing over the legitimacy of more and more delegates.

The growing problem that contested delegations posed for the major parties might call into question the efficacy of their efforts to better supervise the nomination process. Whatever the shortcomings in the parties' regulatory efforts, it would be wrong to dismiss these measures as ineffective. The disparity in the number of contested seats in Colorado versus those in New Jersey stands as testimony to the merits of reform. In the Garden State voters elected state delegates. There was no need for a county convention to complicate matters by issuing instructions or compelling a delegation to vote as a unit. Separate primaries for state

ARRIVAL OF THE SCHOOLMASTER.

FIGURE 4.6. Denver County's conventions frequently erupted into bitterly divisive struggles in both parties. Contesting delegations from Denver showed up at five of six Democratic and Republican state conventions between 1906 and 1910. Here the state Democratic organization hurries in to restore order in 1902 with the help of a rule book and switching sticks to produce harmony. (*RMN*, Sept. 9, 1902, p. 4.)

and local offices meant that the gubernatorial race was divorced from the factionalism that gripped county and municipal politics. By 1900 many New Jersey localities selected their nominees for local offices in party-run primaries. The state stepped in to supervise these proceedings in 1903, and it arranged for a direct primary for county and legislative positions in 1907.[124] By contrast, Colorado's indirect primary changed but little before 1910. Delegates selected in largely unregulated primaries met in

[124] *New Jersey Laws*, Chap. 248 (1903), pp. 603–29; *New Jersey Laws*, Chap. 278 (1907), pp. 697–700.

county conventions where much more was at stake. The full vote of the state delegation was often pledged to a single gubernatorial aspirant. The same conventions selected delegates for other legislative conventions and determined the ticket's composition on county and local races. Last but not least, state regulation of nominating practices in Colorado was minimal compared to what was in place elsewhere.[125] Colorado serves as a "control group" for the purposes of this study. Its political parties retained the same nominating procedures over time. The state's unhappy experience with contested delegations suggests that increased attention to rules and procedures offered the parties at least some protection from disruptive internal conflicts.

Yet for all their innovations, parties were unable to get ahead of the curve and bring their disaffected elements back into line. The hustling candidate bore chief responsibility for bringing more competition and dissension into the nomination process, especially at the grassroots level where the voters could express their preferences. The general thrust in party initiatives up to about 1900 was to replace the caucus with a more closely monitored primary. The party-run indirect primary was also giving way to the party-run direct primary. As parties adjusted their practices to accommodate competition, they invited more of it. Standardized procedures over how delegates would be selected made it easier for candidates to mount campaigns to capture them. Bringing more order to the primaries, caucuses, and conventions helped but was not enough to remove contention and controversy. The consequences could be fatal to the political ambitions of the winners. Like other organizations of their time, political parties discovered that internal reform offered only limited relief. As with other Progressive Era measures, state regulation would emerge as the logical alternative only after efforts at self-regulation had played themselves out.

---

[125] The state statutes in effect up to 1910 outlawed vote fraud. *Colorado Statutes*, "An Act to Prevent Frauds in the Nominating of Public Officers." Approved, Apr. 4, 1887.

5

"The Pivot of Reform"

Debating the Direct Primary

I

For two days in January 1898 some fifty or so notable citizens gathered at New York's Board of Trade and Transportation to discuss various mechanisms for improving the nominating processes of the major parties. Many of those attending would play important roles in overhauling the election systems of their states in the years to come. George L. Record had already drafted the nation's first direct primary bill four years before, only to see it voted down in the New Jersey legislature. He and others viewed the first (and apparently last) "National Conference on Practical Reform of Primary Elections" as a watershed event. "As all of you know," Record reminded the assembly, there had been "very little interest in primary reform, and it has been practically impossible to get anybody to pay any attention to it." Yet, a change in the political climate seemed palpable. Four years of investigation and agitation on a variety of municipal issues had convinced the Chicago Civic Federation that "if any permanent reform were to be secured, it must be through the purification and utilization of the party primaries." "The primary is the pivot of reform," another delegate affirmed, and so it seemed for some years to come. Despite the obscurity that soon awaited it, the primary reform conference's claim to historical significance is not without merit. The conclave demarcated that point in time when an overhauling of the convention system became a cause célèbre for scholars, journalists, and partisan-minded legislators. The presentations and discussions offered a preview to the debates that would soon appear prominently in magazines, party functions, and state houses around the nation. The conference proceedings laid out the diverse rationales for the direct primary that would account for its wide appeal inside and outside the major party organizations.[1]

The disparate backgrounds of the conference participants and sponsors constituted one of its most noteworthy features. The conference call, issued by the Chicago Civic Federation, expressed the popular prejudice that a corrupt and dysfunctional nominating system was largely an urban phenomenon. Almost all the participants were city dwellers, a majority from the Northeastern states and another third from the Midwest.[2] The New York conference brought together two groups that would come to constitute the yin and yang of the direct primary movement. The call appealed for input from "the practical and political reform workers from many large cities." Those whom the conference report would label "municipal reformers" comprised a constellation of intellectuals associated with the era's many political crusades. The names of Carl Schurz, E. L. Godkin, and Richard H. Dana adorned the conference call, along with those of college faculty (Nicholas Murray Butler from Columbia University and John R. Commons, then at Syracuse University) and presidents (William R. Harper of the University of Chicago). Representatives of many local "good government" associations swelled the ranks of the municipal reformers. Arrayed on the other side were those identified as "political workers." Albany's Republican "boss," William Barnes, Jr., signed the call, as did the mayors of New York, Milwaukee, New Orleans, San Francisco, Providence, Toledo, Chattanooga, Boston, Buffalo, Des Moines, and Atlanta. Among the state legislators attending the sessions was a California senator who had recently authored the state's revised primary law. The major political parties sent members of their state committees, the Allied Political Clubs of New York, and the Republican League. Former congressman Robert M. La Follette signed the announcement; so did Edward Scofield, the man who had defeated La Follette for the gubernatorial nomination in the previous Wisconsin

---

[1] National Conference on Practical Reform of Primary Elections, *Proceedings of the National Conference on Practical Reform of Primary Elections, January 20 and 21, 1898* (Chicago, 1898), p. 86; *NYT*, Jan. 21, 1898, p. 2. For more on the conference, see Alan Ware, *The American Direct Primary: Party Institutionalization and Transformation in the North* (Cambridge, U.K., 2002), pp. 81–84.

[2] The handful of representatives from Southern states were mostly mayors of large cities, and the conference paid little heed to the electoral changes then underway in the states of the former Confederacy. Mississippi's Democratic Party, for example, would introduce the direct primary in 1902. See Charles Edward Merriam, Harold F. Gosnell, and Louise Overacker, *Primary Elections* (Chicago, 1928), pp. 40–59; Frederick W. Dallinger, *Nominations for Elective Office in the United States* (New York, 1903), p. 127.

Republican State Convention.[3] A scattering of merchant associations and labor unions also endorsed the document, though their representatives did not play a significant role in the proceedings. The conference organizers had brought together an unlikely coalition of independent political thinkers and partisan-minded practitioners that would soon bring an end to the convention system.

The reformers and the politicians shared a common goal, even if they prioritized their concerns differently. The reform element appealed for greater participation in the nominating process, particularly by those commonly referred to as "the respectable element." They condemned the influence of those they branded "the worst class of citizens" at the caucuses and primaries. The ignorance and venal behavior ascribed to these mostly poor and immigrant voters reduced the primaries to a fraud and a farce in the eyes of these self-described "better citizens." It was conceded that the best citizens often evinced a deplorable indifference to the candidate selection process, but their disgust and alienation was understandable under the circumstances. "We may protest against the lack of interest manifested by that portion of our population representing the majority of property and intelligence," averred one participant, "but so long as this class knows that present methods will obtain, so long will they decline to participate in primaries." Theodore Roosevelt articulated the concerns of the municipal reformers in a telegram sent from the Department of the Navy: "The problem before this people is very largely how to stir reputable citizens up to their duties, and to make those duties easy to perform, while at the same time depriving the less reputable portion of the community both of the chance to commit frauds in politics and the opportunity to be rewarded for committing them."[4]

If reformers valued increased participation by the "respectable element" as a prerequisite to good government, party leaders endorsed greater participation as indispensable to party unity. John E. Milholland,

---

[3] In February 1897, La Follette made a speech at the University of Chicago where he first took up the issue of reforming the nomination process. See Allen Fraser Lovejoy, *Robert M. La Follette and the Establishment of the Direct Primary in Wisconsin, 1890–1904* (New Haven, Conn., 1941), p. 45; and Arthur Coffman Wolfe, "The Direct Primary in American Politics" (Ph.D. diss., University of Michigan, 1966), p. 27. The Chicago Federation issued the conference call only some months after La Follette's speech. Yet the future Wisconsin governor apparently did not attend the conference and his thoughts on the subject do not appear in its report. La Follette's appearance later in Michigan also helped convince the influential "Michigan Club" to endorse the initiative. *DEN*, Aug. 2, 1904, p. 2.

[4] National Conference on Practical Reform, *Primary Elections*, pp. 14, 30.

the chair of the committee on arrangements, expressed the views of the party stalwarts. "Party harmony, about which we have heard so much sighing, will also be one of the inevitable results of this reform," he predicted in his opening remarks. "Where every voter has an opportunity to express his preference in a nominating convention little fault can be found with the result of any honest minority." Milholland assured the reform types that "the overwhelming majority of all public men are with us."

Does this statement surprise you? Well, it should not, for I make the assertion without fear of successful contradiction, that the Civil Service Reform and the Australian Ballot law owe more to the efforts of the practical politicians than has ever yet been acknowledged. The best politicians are in favor of genuine Civil Service Reform, because it is their only salvation from the clamor of unsatiable constituents. They favored the Australian Ballot law because it meant a tremendous saving of their money on Election Day. They are in favor of this reform, too, when it is properly and fairly represented, because they have become as tired of the fraudulent practices connected with the primaries in great cities as the rest of the people.

A member of the Republican League from Buffalo, New York, later outlined a direct nomination system recently endorsed by the party's city and county conventions. He too reassured his audience that Republicans embraced the new nominating procedures out of an enlightened self-interest. "That a partisan committee has gone so far, may strike you as somewhat strange; but I trust you will give thoughtful party men the credit of recognizing it as axiomistic that the larger the party, the more successful will it be, and the fairer its primaries and conventions, the fewer its bolters." The Buffalo delegate hinted that the direct primary was essential to the very survival of the major parties. "We of Buffalo have been impressed with the fact that factional discord has been on the increase, not only in New York, but all over the country.... We have been made aware that during the past four or five years, owing to the concentration of party power in the hands of a few – a concentration which is an outgrowth of the Australian ballot system – a disintegration of parties seems almost at hand." The recent chair of the Republican County Committee for New York echoed this sentiment: "I say, as a party man, that it is the true interest of each party to make honest, straight primaries the possibility, and to render it impossible ... to accomplish any result by fraud. The cleaner the primary the stronger the organization."[5]

5 National Conference on Practical Reform, *Primary Elections*, pp. 12, 131, 109.

Partisans and reformers concurred that a restructuring of the nominating process was in the best interests of both major parties. The remarks of Oscar L. Straus, the newly installed president of the National Primary Election League formed at the conference's close, evoked wide applause: "I understand that the object of this conference is not to break down parties, but to strengthen parties, and to make them representative of the people instead of mere cliques. We recognize the necessity of parties in a free government, and we want to make them what they were intended to be – the preservers of the rights and liberties of the people, instead of being the barrier between their rights and liberties." Straus and others also insisted that their movement posed no threat to those outside the bipartisan framework. The conference's agenda, he insisted, "is not antagonistic to the independent party . . . but is devoted to securing laws which will enable the honest element in any and all parties to register its will at the nominating caucus or primary." But if not hostile to third parties and independent candidacies, the ultimate goal of the National Primary Election League was to render them irrelevant. "If party organizations secure good government," Straus and others predicted, "independent parties will naturally disappear."[6]

Many attending the conference had already concluded that state governments had a key role to play in advancing their cause. While party organizations grew frustrated with rules that often went unenforced, calls for state regulation arose from various quarters. Government intervention in party affairs had been underway since the 1880s, when most northern states began defining and outlawing various forms of vote fraud in caucuses, primaries, and conventions. The party-run direct primary – or Crawford County Plan – was one of many experiments discussed at the New York conference, though many no longer regarded it as practical. Most attendees seemed interested in limited state supervision of the nominating process, proposing legislation leading up to the adoption of the direct primary. Following the conference, reformers and partisans pressed their demands on separate fronts. In the end, both groups enjoyed at least partial success. Voter participation in the primaries increased while the most blatant forms of fraud decreased. The major parties did gain more control over the nominating process to better defend themselves from the depredations of bolters, third parties, and independent movements. But the task of instituting government supervision over the nominating process was the responsibility of state legislators, and it was their interests

---

[6] National Conference on Practical Reform, *Primary Elections*, p. 132.

and those of other elective officeholders that would be most fully realized by reform.

II

The legislative lineage of the direct primary dates back to the first laws defining and outlawing vote fraud or bribery at partisan functions. Such bills generally failed to arouse much opposition or controversy in New Jersey, Michigan, Colorado, or California. Yet, they marked an important first step in the political parties' new status as organizations with a public purpose that warranted intervention by the state. Statutes regulating how parties conducted their primaries, caucuses, and conventions followed. Here, too, bills that gradually integrated the convention system into the general election process rarely met with opposition. When state laws bearing on the nomination process were contested in the courts, the judiciary usually affirmed their constitutionality based on the special character of political parties in furnishing candidates for the general election.[7] By the time agitation for the direct primary appeared, around 1903, state regulation of the parties was an accomplished fact in most states.

Over a span of thirty-four years following California's Porter Law of 1866, the four states under review enacted a total of eleven laws cracking down on bribery and vote fraud in the nomination process. In New Jersey, Colorado, and California, all but two of twelve bills aimed at eradicating vote buying or ballot box stuffing became law. Most of the time senators and assemblymen in these three states passed the legislation either unanimously or by an overwhelming margin. Because the statutes were mostly outlawing practices already illegal in a general election, it is easy to understand why they encountered so little opposition. Only in Michigan did bills aimed at vote fraud face serious opposition. The Michigan House devoted the better part of a full day debating the proposition in 1877. Legislators puzzled over House Bill 114's purposes and effects. Newspapers lampooned representatives "straining at imaginary gnats" who offered "innumerable objections and amendments."[8] Democrats consistently mobilized behind legislation promising to clean up the primaries while Republicans united to weaken or defeat such measures. "The opposers of the bill are generally republicans of the most ignorant

---

[7] Leon D. Epstein, *Political Parties in the American Mold* (Madison, Wis., 1986), pp. 155–99.
[8] *DEN*, Mar. 22, 1877, p. 2.

and bigoted order," one Democratic newspaper noted, "who fancy that because a democrat introduced the bill it is a deep, dark, democratic trick to swindle them out of office."[9] In 1887 Michigan became the last of the four states to outlaw vote fraud in primaries, caucuses, and conventions, after having killed three bills to this purpose in 1877, 1879, and 1885. Significantly, no one argued that actions taken in a private men's club, which was all political parties were in the eyes of the law up to this time, were outside the purview of the state.

It was one thing to enact laws attacking flagrant fraud by candidates, voters, and officials; enforcing the statutes was an entirely different matter. If the laws enacted in the 1880s and 1890s purified the primaries no one seemed to notice. It was rare indeed to find even a few isolated arrests at the voting places, and usually the charges were dropped right after the polls closed.[10] Prosecution was virtually unheard of. "It is a source of wonder to the uninitiated why evidence is not gathered and proceedings commenced against the offender," Michigan governor Hazen S. Pingree noted dourly. "It has become a matter of common knowledge... that these practices are indulged in by candidates for all public offices, including prosecuting attorneys and circuit judges. Since the men who are charged with the duty of prosecuting criminals are themselves guilty of infractions of the law, it is quite apparent that they will not and cannot prosecute others who have offended the law in the same manner." In 1894 an Oakland, California, police judge declared the state statutes aimed at scotching fraud in the pending primary null and void; the *Examiner* could summon neither surprise nor indignation: "These views are uniformly supported by the courts, and if anybody has been convicted for frauds at primaries in the last dozen years the circumstance has escaped our memory.... Primaries are called for the purpose of stuffing ballot boxes and committing other frauds, and police judges and other magistrates are expected to carry out the intentions of the politicians and free any of their adherents who happen to get arrested."[11]

---

[9] *DFP*, Mar. 24, 1877, p. 2.
[10] *NEN*, Sept. 10, 1892, p. 1.
[11] Stephen B. Sarasohn, "The Regulation of Parties and Nominations in Michigan: The Politics of Election Reform" (Ph.D. diss., Columbia University, 1953), p. 30; *SFE*, June 16, 1894, p. 6; *DR*, Aug. 29, 1888, p. 6. The *Rocky Mountain News* heaped praise on a Denver judge who called upon the grand jury to investigate the city's 1884 Republican primaries but soon had to report that the body had lost interest in the matter. "It is rumored that certain members of the present grand jury bought votes in the recent Republican primary election." Sept. 3, 1884, p. 4; Sept. 5, 1884, p. 4.

The official recognition accorded parties by laws aimed at fraud and bribery in their nominating procedures was enhanced when state-prepared ballots replaced party-printed tickets in the general election. The adoption of an official ballot spurred governments to get more involved in party affairs and was another big step on the path to the direct primary.[12] Most states overhauled their election machinery between 1888 and 1892 primarily to counter intimidation, vote buying, and vote fraud in the general election; all were practices said to be facilitated by the use of party tickets on election day.[13] A state-printed ballot available only inside the polls would be harder to "stuff." Greater privacy at the polling place promised to reduce intimidation and bribery. Booths and barriers around the polls made voting a more impersonal experience that especially appealed to middle- and upper-class voters. All of these features of the so-called Australian ballot commended it to third parties and reformers wishing to promote a brand of nonpartisan or at least bipartisan politics.

But many early supporters of ballot reform eventually came around to denounce the resulting legislation as a Trojan Horse that only further entrenched bossism. The laws specified that those state officials charged with preparing the ballots were to assign only one candidate with a given party label. When this matter was in dispute, the public officials or the courts followed the dictates of whomever they recognized as the "regular" party organization. This undermined the maverick candidates who chose to run without the blessing of the official party organizations. Third parties also found it harder to get their names on the ballot or to fuse with some one of the major parties. A letter writer to the *New York Times* in 1898 deplored the impact of ballot reform on independent political action.

The bosses have been steadily amending the election laws so as to throttle opposition . . . until now they have us tied hand and foot and gagged. . . . [T]here was better opportunity to defeat unfit nominations under the old regime, when no

---

[12] Ware, *American Direct Primary*, pp. 31–56; William H. Hotchkiss, "The Movement for Better Primaries," *Review of Reviews* 17 (May 1898): 583–89; Merriam, Gosnell, and Overacker, *Primary Elections*, p. 23.

[13] L. E. Fredman, *The Australian Ballot: The Story of an American Reform* (East Lansing, Mich., 1968); Eric Falk Petersen, "The Struggle for the Australian Ballot in California," *California Historical Quarterly* 51 (Fall 1972): 227–43; John F. Reynolds and Richard L. McCormick, "Outlawing 'Treachery': Split Tickets and Ballot Laws in New York and New Jersey, 1880–1914," *Journal of American History* 72 (Mar. 1986): 835–58. The relevant statutes in the other states under review include *Statutes of California* (1891), No. 130, pp. 165–78; Colorado Statutes, "Elections" (1891), pp. 143–66; *Michigan Public Acts* (1891), No. 190, pp. 256–71.

troublesome formula had to be followed in order to set up independent candidates than there is now, with the mongrel thing called the "party column ballot" and the hedges which have been placed to hinder anything but machine-made tickets from being voted. There may be, possibly, less corruption at the polls now than then, but the boss attains his ends just as well, for he keeps competition out of the field.[14]

Over many past campaigns, as Mark Summers has pointed out, the major parties had resorted to all manner of extralegal means to crush or marginalize outside elements in the form of third parties and independent candidates. "Behind the gaudy show that the two major parties...put on, the system was rigged to give the professional politicians every unfair advantage."[15] The official ballot opened a new chapter in allowing the major parties to call upon the state to achieve the same end.

By certifying certain candidates as "regular" or official nominees, the new ballot removed any illusion that the Democratic and Republican parties were strictly private entities beyond the proper reach of the law. This paved the way for the greater public regulation of parties to follow. "[P]rimaries to select nominees to public office are public matters, not organization matters; public elections, not private elections," one proponent of the direct nominations would later insist. "It would seem self-evident... that when the state permits upon the official ballot... the name of but one person as representative of a given political policy, it would be the name of the man who... has proved by the actual votes cast in his favor in an open and fair contest that he has a larger popular following than any competitor."[16] There remained those, like Charles Frederick Adams of Manhattan, who regarded the recognition afforded parties as too high a price to pay for any purification of the political process. "What we must 'abolish' (if democracy is to live) is the prevailing folly of giving by law to the results ground out by the 'machines' the fatal weight which they now get by being recognized and treated as the final, authentic

---

[14] *NYT*, Feb. 6, 1898, p. 9; see also *The Nation*, Dec. 2, 1897, pp. 431–32.

[15] Mark Wahlgren Summers, *Party Games: Getting, Keeping, and Using Power in Gilded Age Politics* (Chapel Hill, N.C., 2004), p. 280. See also Peter H. Argersinger, "'A Place on the Ballot': Fusion Politics and Anti-Fusion Laws," in *Structure, Process and Party: Essays in American Political History*, ed. Peter H. Argersinger (Armonk, N.Y., 1992), pp. 150–71.

[16] Horace E. Deming, "Some Dangers of the Control of Permanent Political Organizations of the Methods of Nomination to Elective Municipal Office," in *Proceedings of the New York Conference for Good City Government and the Eleventh Annual Meeting of the National Municipal League [1905]* ed. Clinton Rogers Woodruff (Philadelphia, 1905), p. 361.

'nominations' of the 'parties.'"[17] Most party leaders thought otherwise, and gladly endured government regulation as the price they paid for their semiofficial status.

In the wake of the official ballot, state regulation of party primaries expanded significantly, especially in California and Michigan. Partisan-minded legislators in the 1890s also acted in response to the calls from Republican and Democratic organizations for government assistance in bringing more order to their deliberations. Given the implications these laws had for their own political careers, legislators acted with caution. They applied the statutes only to a few urban areas, or perhaps made them optional. The earliest legislation bearing on the nomination process itself was conservative in purpose. It aimed to preserve the convention system by standardizing practices and removing features that brought it into disrepute. "Once let the caucus be officially regulated, perfectly fair and largely attended," one reformer predicted in 1898, "the agitation for the abolition of the convention and for direct nominations by the people will disappear."[18]

Government regulation of the indirect primary in California came as politicians lost patience with the convention system. No less an authority than Daniel M. Burns, kingmaker in Republican state conventions between 1882 and 1898, found the conduct of San Francisco's 1894 primaries "highly displeasing." "Some illegal voting is going to occur," he conceded, "but the percentage of such voting is much smaller at regular elections than it is at primaries. So I have thought that perhaps it would be well to put the primaries under the control of regularly elected officials of the different counties."[19] County conventions and major newspapers that year added their voices to the call for greater regulation over the nomination process.[20] "Every friend of honest politics should favor the placing of the primary under the laws which guard regular elections," the *San Francisco Examiner* affirmed. That same year, the *Los Angeles Times* interviewed 128 of that city's local businessmen and professionals from both parties. They concurred that the nominating system was broken, even if they did not agree on how to fix it. "I do not see how we could possibly have anything worse than the present system," one

[17] *NYT*, Jan. 28, 1898, p. 6.
[18] Hotchkiss, "Better Primaries," p. 587.
[19] *SFE*, June 4, 1894, p. 10. Martin Kelly, another San Francisco G.O.P. leader, concurred. *SFE*, June 12, 1894, p. 9.
[20] *Tulare County Times*, May 17, 1894, p. 4; *LAT*, June 10, 1894, p. 9; June 19, 1894, p. 1.

banker grumbled.[21] Distrust of existing practices prompted San Francisco's Democratic County Committee to dispense with primaries entirely in 1894 and 1898, and appoint the state delegation itself, an action that angered many.[22]

Party officials in San Francisco and Los Angeles seriously considered a "postal primary" in 1894. The procedure allowed the rank and file to mail in their ballots instead of attending a caucus or primary. Advocates of the plan emphasized that it would induce more citizens to participate by sparing them the turmoil, confrontations, and even bodily harm that might await them at an urban polling place. For party officials the main appeal of the plan was not in accommodating their busy and timid voters. Rather, by leaving the postal service with the responsibility for collecting and delivering the ballots, the program relied on the federal government to help party leaders canvass the returns. With the ballots in the hands of the postal authorities "there is no possible chance to tamper with them in any way," one advocate affirmed with stupefying naiveté. Efforts to persuade the Democratic State Convention of 1894 to endorse the plan failed; many delegates feared entrusting so important a partisan function to postal employees, who were hardly nonpartisan. The convention's resolution committee countered with a platform plank vaguely calling for further state regulation of the primary. The compromise evoked only "mild applause" when it was read before the full convention, an indication that the issue had yet to generate much attention around the state.[23]

When next the California legislature met, outgoing Republican governor Henry H. Markham also urged it to broaden government supervision over the nomination process. "The danger to our government lies in the loose and very profligate manner in which these [primary] elections are conducted. . . . This is an evil growing by which it feeds on, threatening the liberties of the people by debarring them from the free and untrammeled

[21] *SFE*, July 16, 1894, p. 4; *LAT*, May 17, 1894, p. 4; May 19, 1894, p. 4.

[22] *SFE*, July 27, 1894, p. 10. The committee defended its action by claiming that former "boss" Christopher Buckley would have returned to power through corrupt primaries had they been allowed to go forward. "There never has been an honest primary held in San Francisco, neither on the Republican nor the Democratic side," one committee member insisted. The committee repeated the action in 1898, this time prompting the filing of a contesting delegation. *SFE*, Aug. 3, 1898, p. 14.

[23] *LAT*, May 20, 1894, p. 8; June 2, 1894, p. 5; *SFE*, June 10, 1894, p. 12; Aug. 24, 1894, p. 2. Democrats introduced a postal primary plan to the 1909 California Senate (SB No. 24) that would have required all voting be done by mailed ballots. The measure was voted down (26 to 7) in the face of formidable Republican opposition. See Franklin Hichborn, *Story of the Session of the California Legislature of 1909* (San Francisco, 1909), pp. 27–30.

exercise of personal choice."[24] The legislature responded with a statute setting the date and hours for primaries in San Francisco and Los Angeles, and mandating the use of the same ballot box as in November.[25] Subsequent legislatures assigned responsibility for furnishing ballots with local government authorities and set guidelines on the apportionment of delegates. A later statute put election officials serving at primary elections on the public payroll and mandated that the polling places resemble what voters encountered at a general election.[26] This 1901 law was mandatory in the dozen cities with populations over seventy-five hundred and was optional elsewhere. Most of the preceding statutes passed both houses of the California legislature by overwhelming margins, as noted in Table 5.1. Only an 1899 bill that would have arranged for the election of party officials in the primaries met with significant opposition. California's major parties and their representatives in the legislature welcomed government support and oversight of their nominating processes.

New Jersey's legislators did not move as swiftly to intercede in the party nomination process (see Table 5.2). The state's laissez-faire attitude changed abruptly, however, in the aftermath of the highly contentious and controversial Essex County Democratic primary of 1901. The 1902 legislature unanimously approved a commission to draw up the necessary legislation. The committee recommended that primary elections follow a routine similar to that of the general election.[27] New Jersey leaped ahead of other states with a law that was statewide in its application and introduced a direct primary for local offices. Laws setting the apportionment at state conventions and arranging for the election of party officials in the

[24] H. H. Markham, "Second Biennial Message," *Appendix to the Senate and Assembly of the Thirty-First Session of the Legislature of the State of California*, 2 vols. (Sacramento, Calif., 1895), vol. 1, p. 20.

[25] *California Statutes* (1895), No. 181, pp. 207–18. The law was slightly revised two years later with the so-called Stratton Law. *California Statutes*, (1897), No. 106, pp. 115–34. That same year the courts found the Stratton Law unconstitutional. *SFE*, Aug. 9, 1898, p. 3. The next legislature rushed through a constitutional amendment to authorize the legislature to regulate the nominating process, which won overwhelming approval by the voters. Senate Constitutional Amendment (1899), No. 4.

[26] *California Statutes* (1899), No. 46, pp. 47–56; *California Statutes* (1901), No. 197, pp. 606–19. Strictly speaking, the 1901 law was optional for the parties, but it was the only means by which their nominees could have their names automatically enrolled on the ballot. Choosing not to abide by the statute would require that a party's candidates qualify for a place on the ballot with petitions.

[27] George L. Record, "The First Primary Law," *Trenton Evening Times*, Oct. 8, 1924, p. 3; *NEN*, Jan. 5, 1903, p. 1. The bill introduced a direct primary for nominees for ward and township offices. Hence, part of the legislative maneuvering behind Senate Bill 87 is put off for discussion in conjunction with Table 6.2.

TABLE 5.1. *Landmark Legislation Introducing State Administration of the Indirect Primary, California*

Year	Bill	Law	Description	Lower House				Senate			
				Vote "Yea"-"Nay"	Party Index of Like.	Eta² for Urban	Eta² for Comp.	Vote "Yea"-"Nay"	Party Index of Like.	Eta² for Urban	Eta² for Comp.
1895	A751	181	Sets date, officials, ballot boxes, polling place for cities	49-3				31-1			
1897	S140	106	County administration of indirect primary	58-0				26-1			
1899	A911		Election of party committees at primaries	45-0				8-18	97.0	.05	.06
1899	S30	46	State provides blanket ballot, sets apportionment	53-1				32-2			
1899		SCA	Constitutional amendment to regulate political parties	U				29-1			
1901	A793	187	Selection and functions of state committees defined	63-0				30-0			
1901	A109	197	State-run indirect primary for cities over 7,500	53-2				24-0			

Year	Bill	Description		X						
1905	A748	Voters declare party identification when register	26-35		.09	.09				
1905	A916 179	Voters declare party intend to support at primary	52-0				22-0			
1907	A934 352	Voters declare party identification at registration; closed primary	38-31	41.3	.07	.08	23-4			
1907	S829 340	Parties can establish own test for party identification	42-18	66.7	.22	.15	25-0			
1907	A794	To regulate the nomination of candidates in conventions	31-37	69.1	.04	.21	10-22	30.3	.17	.01

Abbreviations: U = Unanimous approval; X = Minority party constitutes fewer than 5 voting members.

TABLE 5.2. *Landmark Legislation Introducing State Administration of the Indirect Primary, New Jersey*

Year	Bill	Law	Description	Lower House				Senate			
				Vote "Yea"-"Nay"	Party Index of Like.	Eta² for Urban	Eta² for Comp.	Vote "Yea"-"Nay"	Party Index of Like.	Eta² for Urban	Eta² for Comp.
1902	S173	150	Establish commission to consider regulation of primaries	U				U			
1903	S87	248	State furnishes ballot box and officials, sets date and hours	58-0				17-1			
1904	S232	241	Sets apportionment for state conventions	57-0				12-0			
1905	S100	117	Party committees to be elected at primaries	56-0				11-0			
1906	S294	235	Sets same date for indirect primaries for both parties	55-0				11-7	X	.23	.00

Abbreviations: U = Unanimous approval; X = Minority party constitutes fewer than 5 voting members.

primaries met with similar unanimous approval. The only instance when legislative unanimity broke down came when senators from rural districts objected in vain to a proposal in 1906 that arranged for Democratic and Republican primaries on the same day. Regulation advanced rapidly in the Garden State because the government was only taking ownership of procedures already put in place by party organizations in many parts of the state.

Michigan's legislature also moved rapidly to regulate party nominating practices in the aftermath of the official ballot. Here too the laws addressed conditions in the cities, not in the countryside. The first such bill set hours for voting and required use of a ballot in cities of twenty thousand or more; it passed the state senate in 1885 before getting tabled in the house (see Table 5.3).[28] When similar legislation appeared in 1893 it met with hardly any opposition.[29] The next legislature unanimously mandated that Detroit administer the primaries much as it did the general election. In the interests of a more peaceful and orderly process, the law stipulated that voters mark their ballots in private, present them to the officials, and promptly leave the polling place. Another law passed that session authorized smaller localities – if they so chose – to offer the same services if one of the major parties so requested.[30] Regulation expanded to other urban areas in an 1899 statute that set hours for polling from 2:00 to 8:00 P.M. in places with populations over thirty thousand and 4:00 to 8:00 P.M. in smaller cities.[31] The last four bills enjoyed unanimous or near-unanimous support. Heated gubernatorial races directed attention to the shortcomings in the nomination process, as did the occasional, more localized, internal party fracas. The reflexive and piecemeal measures taken by Michigan's legislators did not follow any larger blueprint of reform. "The acts previous to 1900," concludes one careful student of the legislation, "do not seem to have resulted from any conscious attempt to alter the party system through extensive regulation, . . . but were rather the result of efforts to prevent the repetition of certain specific abuses which had aroused public comment from time to time."[32]

---

[28] "Senate Bill No. 250" [File #224], Michigan State Library, Lansing.

[29] *Michigan Public Acts*, 1893, No. 175, p. 274–75. This bill also required proper notice of primaries with announcements in newspapers and public places. It applied to cities in excess of 25,000 population.

[30] *Michigan Public Acts*, 1895, No. 411, pp. 348–54; 135, pp. 264–69.

[31] *Michigan Public Acts*, 1899, No. 22, p. 31.

[32] Sarasohn, "Regulation of Parties . . . in Michigan," p. 29. For evidence of the public condemnation of Detroit's primaries, see *DFP*, Nov. 16, 1894, pp. 3–4.

TABLE 5.3. *Landmark Legislation Introducing State Administration of the Indirect Primary, Michigan*

Year	Bill	Law	Description	Lower House				Senate			
				Vote "Yea"-"Nay"	Party Index of Like.	Eta² for Urban	Eta² for Comp.	Vote "Yea"-"Nay"	Party Index of Like.	Eta² for Urban	Eta² for Comp.
1885	S250		Sets times and arranges for election officers	T				19-8	75.0	.01	.19
1893	A646	175	Sets polling places, hours, vote by ballot for cities over 25,000	71-2				18-0			
1895	A239	135	Cities over 50,000 can provide voting booths and ballot boxes	58-4				25-0			
1895		411L	Detroit primaries regulated for hours, day, administration	U				U			
1899	A203	22	Sets voting hours in cities (other than Detroit)	70-1				U			

Abbreviations: T = Tabled (no vote); U = Unanimous approval; L = Local acts.

174

Of the states under review, Colorado proved the most reluctant to revise its nomination procedures, perhaps because of an unhappy early experiment with government regulation. A bill allowing for state-supervised primaries passed both houses in 1883 with but a single dissenting vote (see Table 5.4).[33] Optional in its implementation, the statute put the Centennial State in the vanguard of the primary reform movement before there was any such movement. Political parties that opted to abide by its guidelines would select delegates using the same balloting procedures as in the general election. The law kept the polls open for designated hours that varied by the size of the electorate. (To hold down expenses, the officials presiding over the voting at the primaries were paid by the parties rather than out of the public coffer.) Both major parties availed themselves of the law in 1884, but, if anything, government intervention in the Republican primary only exacerbated a bitter factional feud. The law's champion, Denver newspaper editor Nathaniel P. Hill, made full use of its provisions to nominate a set of state legislators in Denver agreeable to returning him to the U.S. Senate. According to the local Democratic newspaper, Hill gained control of the Republican County Committee "by dark and devious means." The committee scheduled Denver's primaries twenty days in advance of the state convention – when the normal time span was less than a week. The law authorized Hill's friends on the county committee to appoint all the officials who staffed the polling places – the men who counted and (as it turned out) recounted the votes until Hill's slate emerged victorious.[34] Hill's *Denver Republican* cast the election as a "contest of the respectable element in politics as against the bummers, and the respectable element won."[35] Republicans elsewhere in the state apparently did not agree; the contesting delegation from Denver won recognition at the state convention.

Hill's triumph in the primaries proved short-lived, as did his election law. The 1885 legislature opted not to return him to the Senate. It also rescinded the primary law – "that unique and monumental statutory blunder" – by the same overwhelming margin that had put it on the statute books two years before.[36] Bills to restore some form of regulation met

---

[33] *Colorado General Laws*, "An Act to Regulate Primary Elections." Approved Feb. 28, 1883, pp. 182–91.

[34] *RMN*, Aug. 19, 1884, p. 4; Aug. 23, 1884, p. 4. The *News* was vexed when local Democrats elected to run their primaries under the same statute. *RMN*, Sept. 9, 1884, p. 4.

[35] *DR*, Aug. 22, 1884, p. 1.

[36] *Colorado General Laws*, "An Act to Repeal an Act Regulating Primaries." Approved Apr. 6, 1885.

TABLE 5.4. *Landmark Legislation Introducing State Administration of the Indirect Primary, Colorado*

Year	Bill	Law	Description	Lower House				Senate			
				Vote "Yea"-"Nay"	Party Index of Like.	Eta² for Urban	Eta² for Comp.	Vote "Yea"-"Nay"	Party Index of Like.	Eta² for Urban	Eta² for Comp.
1883	S4	3/28	Sets hours, voter qualifications, outlaws fraud (optional)	34-1				22-0			
1885	H320	4/6	Repeals law of Mar. 28, 1883	31-0				20-1			
1891	H182		To regulate the holding of primary elections	37-4				T			
1895	S225		Regulating the primary	RF							
1897	H173		In relation to primary	20-37	68.1	.18	.13	24-6	62.5	.16	.00
1901	S17	71	Party state committees decide regularity of nominations	??				26-0			
1907	H100		Outlawing fusion candidates	38-20	5.0	.10	.05				
			Make special order for Mar. 27					18-14	14.3	.44	.13
			Amend to allow fusion of Dem. and Rep. nominees					16-17	19.0	.28	.18
1909	H282		Concerning nominations and regulation of political parties								
			Motion to strike out enacting clause	25-27	X	.04	.01				
			Motion to refer bill back to committee	39-11	X	.07	.07				
1909	S14		Regulation of political parties								
			Making special order for Feb. 10	22-10				22-10	82.5	.03	.00

Abbreviations: RF = Reported Favorably by Committee; T = Tabled (no vote); X = Minority party constitutes fewer than 5 voting members; ?? = The bill number cannot be found in the index.

with grief in the Republican legislatures of 1891 and 1895. Another bill failed in 1897 with Populists lined up in favor and Democrats averse. The only legislation of any note, passed in 1901, invested final authority in passing on the regularity of any nomination with the respective state committees.[37] Thereafter, county and state conventions joined governors in demanding a primary election law, but nothing substantive materialized in the legislature until the first direct primary law made its debut in 1910.[38]

When a bill occasionally produced a divisive vote – defined here as one with 15 percent or more of the legislators voting in the minority – statistical analysis endeavored to distinguish its supporters from its opponents. Partisanship sometimes played a role in dividing the legislators, but rarely were party lines drawn very tight. The "Index of Likeness" value appearing in Tables 5.1–5.4 provides a simple indicator of the level of bipartisan support each bill enjoyed. The Index measures the gap between the percentage of Democratic legislators voting "yea" on a bill or motion and the like percentage for Republicans. The value of the Index ranges from 0.0 to 100.0. The higher number registered when Democratic and Republican legislators backed a bill by nearly identical percentages. An Index value of 0.0 would result from a roll call wherein all Democrats supported a bill and all Republicans opposed it (or vice versa). An Index value ranging above 75 will be treated as evidence of negligible partisan differences, and results falling below 25 can be viewed as highly partisan. The Index is not computed if either party had fewer than five legislators voting on a particular roll call. This was usually the case in Michigan, where Democrats occupied but a handful of seats – if any – in legislatures after 1900; Michigan was something close to a one-party state where partisanship could not take hold. The lone divisive vote in New Jersey also fails to register an Index owing to the small size of the state senate (21 seats).

Partisan squabbling over regulating the parties was more apparent in the western states. Only one of California's half dozen contested roll calls qualified as truly bipartisan. In each case, Democratic assemblymen and senators were more supportive of stronger regulatory measures than were their Republican colleagues. Colorado Democrats viewed House Bill 100 in the 1907 session as hostile to their interests. The measure outlawed the fusion candidacies that Democrats had been arranging with Silver Republicans. Democrats voted squarely against the measure in the house

[37] *Colorado Statutes* (1901), No. 71, pp. 169–73.
[38] *RMN*, Sept. 9, 1902, p. 9; Sept. 13, 1902, p. 2; *DP*, Sept. 13, 1906, p. 6; *Senate Journal*, Jan. 10, 1903, p. 84.

and senate, producing three indices that ranged from 5.0 to 19.0. In three other roll calls, covering as many different bills, the partisan divide was less evident (values ranging from 62.5 to 82.5). In Colorado, it was the Republicans who were more eager to pass legislation imposing regulation on political parties.[39] In brief, partisanship occasionally emerged as a key variable separating advocates and opponents of the earliest legislation governing the nomination process – but party did not; California Democrats embraced regulation while those in Colorado dug in their heels.

Urban and rural delegates likewise did not tend to disagree on the need to regulate the convention system. Testing for the influence of urbanization on a legislator's voting record in Tables 5.1–5.4 called for use of analysis of variance. The statistic produces an Eta^2 value recording the amount of variance in the urbanization index "explained" by a vote of "yea" or "nay" on any given roll call.[40] (See Appendix B for how "urbanization" was operationalized in the current context.) A high Eta^2 value – one that approaches 1.00 – would indicate a pattern of urban legislators voting one way and their rural counterparts voting the other. Only Eta^2 numbers of .05 or higher merit discussion, and a total of twelve votes across all four states met this cut off. About half of these roll calls raised broad issues of regulation; the other half more narrowly focused on closed primaries and fusion. But there is little consistency from vote to vote. Legislators from more urban areas backed regulatory efforts four times and opposed such efforts on two other roll calls: hardly much of a difference especially given the many other votes when no association manifests itself. It bears noting that the early bills on the indirect primary in California and Michigan applied only to the larger cities. Legislators from the localities affected always introduced the bills. It probably did not matter much to a rural legislator how the citizens of Grand Rapids or Sacramento selected their party's candidates. The six other votes dealing with the scope of participation also failed to uncover an enduring urban/rural division within the upper or lower chambers. Legislators from California's cities supported

---

[39] Only in 1891 did Colorado's Democratic legislators back a bill regulating primaries by a larger margin than their rivals.

[40] This use of Eta inverts the relationship between the dependent and independent variables (urbanization influences how a legislator votes; a legislator's vote is not thought to influence how urban his home constituency is). But the concept of "percentage of variance explained" is more helpful for comparative purposes, which is all that is of concern here. The procedure is explained more fully in R. Darcy and Richard C. Rohrs, *A Guide to Quantitative History* (Westport, Conn., 1995), pp. 145–48.

an open primary (on 3 roll calls), while Colorado's urban representatives endorsed the closed variety (on the other 3 roll calls).

Analysis of variance can also test for the influence of two-party competition on a legislator's disposition on party regulation. Party competition proved to be a powerful predictor for which Iowa counties would adopt a system of party-run direct primaries (see Table 4.3). Competition did not prove to be nearly so helpful in explaining a legislator's attitude toward state regulation of the indirect primary. Of the sixteen divisive roll calls appearing in Tables 5.1–5.4, the amount of variance in the competition index explained by the legislators' votes met or exceeded 5% in eleven instances. Most of these votes dealt with measures bearing on the participation of voters and candidates in the primaries. Legislators from noncompetitive districts in California and Colorado evidenced firmer support on five of six measures that would close the primary to all but voters and candidates of the given party.[41] The temptation for voters and candidates associated with the minority party (Democrats mostly) to cross party lines when a nomination was in play was perhaps greatest in areas of one-party rule; officeholders already affiliated with the majority party in safe districts had no use for the interlopers.[42] In the five remaining bills touching on the more mundane mechanics of regulation no pattern emerged separating legislators from competitive and noncompetitive districts.[43] In short, the one-party rule associated with "the system of 1896" was not responsible for introducing the state-administered indirect primary, but legislators from noncompetitive districts did prefer a closed primary.

The regulation of political parties was a process well advanced in the states under review (and elsewhere) well before the appearance of the first direct primary law.[44] The chronology of reform called first for laws defining and punishing various forms of bribery and fraud in the nomination process. These were followed by statutes that became more detailed in specifying the times and procedures for voting, often dedicating state equipment, staff, and facilities for this purpose. State laws followed closely behind the less than satisfactory efforts of the major parties to organize

[41] The relationship between competition and support for closed primaries is given more definitive support by the binary logistic regression analysis appearing in Tables B.1 and B.4 in Appendix B.

[42] See also Argersinger, "'A Place on the Ballot."

[43] Senators and representatives from noncompetitive districts supported regulatory legislation in three roll calls, and they opposed it in two.

[44] On trends elsewhere at this time, see Ware, *American Direct Primary*, pp. 57–94.

and administer the increasingly contentious primaries, especially in the major cities. Legislators often acted at the behest of party leaders and platforms, and in the aftermath of an especially ugly nomination fracas. Politicians smoothed the transition by making the initial legislation either optional or applicable only to the cities. The sheer novelty of some of the earliest bills aroused partisan suspicions that drove Democrats and Republicans apart (California in 1866; Michigan in 1877, and New Jersey in 1894), but over time, they enacted much of the legislation in a spirit of bipartisanship. When opposition to further government encroachments on party activities did appear, it lined up along neither an urban/rural axis nor a competitive/noncompetitive one. By 1903, state-administered indirect primaries operated across New Jersey and in the major cities of Michigan and California. The distance yet to be traveled from the indirect to the direct primary proved not very far.

III

Not long after the 1898 New York conference on the reform of the nominating system the direct primary emerged as the logical alternative to the convention system. Robert M. La Follette would get much of the credit for popularizing the idea in speeches he delivered at the Universities of Chicago and Michigan in 1897 and 1898, respectively. "Waste no more time on vain sermons of the duty of attending the caucus," he admonished. "It is too late for that." As governor of Wisconsin, La Follette helped enact the first fully realized, statewide direct primary law in 1903.[45] The National Municipal League later took up the cause,[46] and books and popular magazine articles extolling the direct primary proliferated. Like electoral reforms past and those to come, the direct primary was prescribed as a tonic to relieve some of the nation's most serious political ills. Voter turnout would rise, money's influence would wane, and a better character of public officials would come to the fore. The bossism and corruption that thrived in a complicated and often secretive decision-making process could not survive in the simple and open format of a primary election. There were those who could be labeled "party stalwarts" who remained unconvinced. They generally expressed less confidence in the

[45] Lovejoy, *La Follette*, p. 79.
[46] Clinton Rogers Woodruff, ed., *Proceedings of the Chicago Conference for Good City Government and the Tenth Annual Meeting of the National Municipal League [1904]* (Philadelphia, 1904); Woodruff, *Eleventh Annual Meeting of the National Municipal League*.

electorate's willingness or ability to assume the duties of "the best representative men." What further divided proponents and opponents of direct nominations was how parties could best maintain unity in an increasingly candidate-dominated political environment. Amid all the ink spilt debating direct nominations, it is important to note that almost everyone concurred that parties were vital to the democratic process and needed to be strengthened.

Research on the Progressive movement in recent decades has hamstrung any attempt to link it to either a core constituency or a coherent agenda.[47] Today, historians are most likely to speak of "a complex and many faceted phenomenon" that reflected an explosion of interest groups at the turn of the century.[48] The direct primary could also be classified as one more reform framed to satisfy a well-connected pair of interest groups: the Democratic and Republican parties. As simple and satisfying as such an interpretation might be, it overlooks the work accomplished by reformers inside and outside the major parties in making the case for change. The direct primary was the special concern of a body of reforming professionals found in the newly nonpartisan (more accurately "bipartisan") urban press, in independent political organizations (like the National Municipal League), and in the academic community.[49] A key motif of those who identified themselves as "progressives" was an appeal to the public interest. Their rhetoric was replete with references to "efficiency,"

---

[47] David W. Noble, "Progressivism," in *Encyclopedia of American Political History*, ed. Jack P. Greene (New York, 1984), vol. 4, pp. 992–1004; Peter G. Filene, "An Obituary for the Progressive Movement," *American Quarterly* 22 (Spring 1970): 20–34; Daniel T. Rodgers, "In Search of Progressivism," *Reviews in American History* 10 (Dec. 1982): 113–32.

[48] Thomas R. Pegram, *Partisans and Progressives: Private Interest and Public Policy in Illinois, 1870–1922* (Urbana, Ill., 1992), p. ix; Arthur S. Link and Richard L. McCormick, *Progressivism* (Arlington Hts., Ill., 1983), pp. 47–58; James J. Connolly, *The Triumph of Ethnic Progressivism: Urban Political Culture in Boston, 1900–1925* (Cambridge, Mass., 1998) pp. 39–76; Philip J. Ethington, *The Public City: The Political Construction of Urban Life in San Francisco, 1850–1900* (Cambridge, U.K., 1994), p. 288.

[49] For other works that situate professionals at the center of various political reforms during the Progressive Era, see Kenneth Finegold, *Experts and Politicians: Reform Challenges to Machine Politics in New York, Cleveland and Chicago* (Princeton, N.J., 1995); Philip J. Ethington, "The Metropolis and Multicultural Ethics: Direct Democracy Versus Deliberative Democracy in the Progressive Era," in *Progressivism and the New Democracy*, ed. Sidney M. Milkis and Jerome M. Mileur (Amherst, Mass., 1999), pp. 195–96; Steven J. Diner, *A Very Different Age: Americans of the Progressive Era* (New York, 1998), pp. 200–232; John D. Buenker, "Sovereign Individuals and Organic Networks: Political Cultures in Conflict During the Progressive Era," *American Quarterly* 40 (June 1988): 187–204.

"morality," "good government," and "the best men" who served the interests of all. They confronted political "bosses" who they claimed served only "selfish" interests. Businesses seeking political favors – in the form of franchises, lower taxes, or a protective tariff – subsidized the bosses' political organizations. The machines delivered "the goods" to railroads, public utilities, banks, insurance companies, and others.[50] Their control over the nomination procedures allowed the machines to ride roughshod over public opinion. The boss and his minions packed the caucuses, staffed the voting places, counted the votes, and constituted the party organization. The direct primary was one of many measures that promised to break the monopoly the machines allegedly exercised over the political process. Let the voice of the citizenry be heard, progressives averred, and the public interest would again be served.

Opposition to political machines at the turn of the century ought not to be misconstrued as opposition to political parties. Reformers drew a distinction between "parties" and "machines." The former represented a body of citizens united on a broad public agenda, the latter a cabal of greedy politicians using government to suit their own private interests. As one reformer expressed it, "[O]ne may be a strong Party man without necessarily being a strong Organization man." It was the bosses who were fundamentally nonpartisan, charged the reformers. Party lines meant nothing to Republican and Democratic leaders who regularly cooperated with one another to please the same clients or masters, who might be the Southern Pacific Railroad in California, the Public Service Corporation in New Jersey, or the mine owners in Michigan's Upper Peninsula. The *Chatauquan* attributed the defeat of many progressive candidates in 1908 to just such collusion between Democratic and Republican machines in various states.[51] "[T]he words 'Republican' and 'Democrat' have no more significance for the 'practical' politicians who trade and dicker in offices and votes than they had in the days of Mr. Tweed," another progressive organ insisted. Many advocates of direct nominations insisted that they

[50] Finegold, *Experts and Politicians*; Richard L. McCormick, "The Discovery that Business Corrupts Politics: A Reappraisal of the Origins of Progressivism," in *The Party Period in Public Policy: American Politics from the Age of Jackson to the Progressive Era*, ed. Richard L. McCormick (New York, 1986), pp. 311–56; Connolly, *Ethnic Progressivism*, pp. 39–76.

[51] Horace E. Deming, "The Functions and Opportunities of Political Organizations under the Municipal Nominating Law," in Woodruff, *Tenth Annual Meeting of the National Municipal League*, p. 377; *Chautauquan* 52 (Nov. 1908): 325; National Conference on Practical Reform, *Primary Elections*, p. 139; SFE, Aug. 20, 1898, p. 6.

AN UNEQUAL MATCH.

FIGURE 5.1. A common complaint among the reform press concerned the complicated, multitiered convention system that posed a barrier to all but the professional
politicians. The simplicity of the direct primary would allow even political ama-
teurs to offer the political machines serious competition. (*LAT*, Sept. 9, 1906,
p. 4.)

were the true partisans, determined to protect their party's principles and
return the party to its rightful owners. Progressive reformers concurred
with partisan leaders of years past that putting the voters in charge would
reinvigorate the political parties by removing a chronic source of friction. Thus could La Follette promote his plan as one that would destroy
machines but strengthen parties "by eliminating most of the causes for
bolting the party."[52]

Bossism in American politics, many concluded, was the inevitable outcome of a complicated nominating process. The arcane rules and multiple layers of the convention system – the caucus, and the county and
state conventions – offered protection to the boss and the special interests he served. For George L. Record, much of the appeal of the direct

[52] George Walton Green, "Facts About the Caucus and the Primary," *North American
Review* 137 (Sept. 1983): 260; Lovejoy, *La Follette*, p. 45.

primary lay in the prospect of circumventing the tiresome business of recruiting delegates: "To fight the machine you must build up an organization and get men to run as delegates to conventions. Because we find it hard, in most cases impossible, to get men to stand as delegates [or to get them elected, he might have added], we have fought for the abolition of conventions and the establishment of the direct primary."[53] "At present the professionals are the only ones who understand the complex delegate system and how to operate it," lamented Charles B. Spahr to the National Municipal League in 1900. "So long as nominations are made through conventions the machine is enthroned." A leader of California's Independent League came to a similar conclusion in 1906: "There is no way to dispose of the boss and machine except to abolish the present system of nominations." Abolish the convention, La Follette promised, and "no longer...will there stand between the voter and the [elected] official a political machine with a complicated system of caucuses and conventions, by the easy manipulation of which it thwarts the will of the voter."[54]

Foremost among the benefits reformers associated with the direct primary was the prospect that it would bring out more voters. Middle- and upper-class citizens in particular, who had abandoned the convention system in disgust, were expected to flock to the primaries once they were cleaned up. "The most serious indictment of our primary system is that so few voters attend, and usually those only of the obedient kind," one proponent of primary reform complained. It had long been charged that political machines deliberately suppressed voter participation among the "better element" by situating polling places in dangerous or undesirable locations. They staffed or surrounded the polls with "toughs" and disreputable types whose very presence at the polls drove decent voters away. "Our Republican ring," complained a "gentleman from Buffalo" as early as 1883, "tries to keep away respectable voters from the caucuses by appointing inconvenient times and places, giving short notice, and sometimes getting up rows, or so 'fixing' the organization before hand...that respectable people will not go to them." Another "gentleman" from Cincinnati, "whose name is well known in that city," agreed:

[53] *Jersey Journal*, Mar. 1, 1911, p. 12.

[54] Amos Parker Wilder, "Primary Election Laws," *Proceedings of the New York Conference for Good City Government and the Sixth Annual Meeting of the National Municipal League* [1900], ed. Clinton Rogers Woodruff (Philadelphia, 1900), p. 220; *SFE*, Sept. 9, 1906, p. 27; Austin Ranney, *Curing the Mischiefs of Faction: Party Reform in America* (Berkeley, Calif., 1975), p. 125.

"The game is to make the caucuses and primaries so disorderly and nasty that well behaved people are glad to remain away."[55] Much of the regulatory legislation over the indirect primary endeavored to make voting less intimidating: putting election officials instead of party heelers in charge, evicting all but voters and officials from the polling place, and providing a secret ballot. A state-regulated indirect primary eliminated some of the worst abuses, but it had not induced large numbers of citizens to turn out.

Proponents of direct nominations conceded that the record of voter participation had been disappointing, but they laid the blame on the system, not on the electorate. Some attributed stubbornly low voter participation under the convention system to the largely meaningless process of voting on delegates. "There is no interest in a primary because you do not do anything at a primary," Record assured the New York conference on reforming the nomination process.

As long as you elect a delegate at a primary you perform no function whatsoever.... Ask [the voters] their choice for delegates and they would stare at you in blank amazement; they have no interest in it; it does not appeal to them. But ask them who is their choice for governor of New York State on the Republican ticket next fall and every man in this state who is a member of that party would have an opinion on it;... he would be rejoiced down to the bottom of his heart for the privilege of casting one vote at the primary for the candidate of his party for governor.

La Follette shared Record's confidence in the electorate. "If we provide the same safeguards, the same certainty, the same facility for expressing the will of the people at the primaries as now prevail at the elections, we shall have the same general interest, the same general participation in the one as in the other." "Our citizens are not indifferent as to better municipal government – they are helpless," a proponent of direct primaries insisted in 1900. "There is a distinction. Push a man under water and if he does not seek to come to the surface he is indifferent as to his life. But hold him under water, and he is helpless. Don't add to his plight by styling him indifferent."[56]

55 Hotchkiss, "Better Primaries," p. 587; Issac M. Brickner, "Direct Primaries Versus Boss Rule," *Arena* 41 (Aug. 1909): 550–56; *The Nation,* July 19, 1906, p. 48; Charles Baldwin Cheney and David F. Simpson, "Political Organization and Primary Legislation in Minnesota," in Woodruff, *Eleventh Annual Meeting of the National Municipal League,* pp. 344–45; Green, "Facts About the Caucus."
56 Lovejoy, *La Follette,* p. 36; National Conference on Practical Reform, *Primary Elections,* p. 88; Wilder, "Primary Election Laws," p. 221.

On no point were the proponents and opponents of the direct primary further apart than on the electorate's willingness or ability to take
responsibility for selecting their parties' candidates. Stalwarts questioned
whether most voters had the capacity, patience, or desire to choose judiciously among scores of candidates for numerous offices. A delegate at
the 1898 conference challenged Record's claim that voters would thrill
to the prospect of voting directly on their gubernatorial nominees. Ralph
M. Easley of the Chicago Civic Federation pointed out that his city's voters in the last presidential election had been handed a ballot containing
the names of three hundred and seventy candidates. "The average voter
didn't know a sole [*sic*] on the ticket and didn't care to. He was either
for the nominee for the republican or democratic party as he favored the
'single' or 'double standard.' I apprehend that, if Mr. Record will inter-
view one hundred 'average' citizens in Jersey City, he will discover the
same general principle is true there." A New Jersey Democratic politician later echoed this sentiment: "The masses of voters are not in close
enough touch with public affairs and are so without acquaintance with
public men that unless they have the benefit of suggestions of those who
are in the swim and know what the requirements of an office are and
where to look for the man fitted to fill it, they are at sea." "The trouble
with the average American citizen is that he is politically lazy," a rural
New Jersey newspaper boldly asserted in 1911. Political "fads," like the
direct primary bill then before the legislature, "cannot permanently cure
a condition that has its origin in the indifference of the individual to the
welfare of the community."[57] Statements opposing direct nominations
on principled grounds opened critics to charges that they believed "the
people are not fit to govern themselves at all, and representative government is a failure."[58] Perhaps this is why so many defenders of the status
quo remained anonymous and why the argument rarely surfaced inside
legislative chambers.

---

[57] National Conference on Practical Reform, *Primary Elections*, p. 93; *NYT*, Oct. 16, 1911,
p. 7; *Hunterdon Republican*, Mar. 15, 1911, p. 2. Opponents of La Follette's direct
primary bill expressed similar reservations. "The voters would be required to select candidates from a list of names of men of whom, in many cases, they would have but slight
knowledge, and some of whom they would not know even by reputation, and upon whose
qualifications and fitness for office they could not, in the nature of things, pass intelligent
judgment." Emanuel L. Philipp, *Political Reform in Wisconsin* (Madison, Wis., 1973),
p. 56. For like commentary, see *LAT*, May 20, 1894, p. 8; *NYT*, Feb. 6, 1898, p. 9; *DEN*,
Mar. 25, 1903, p. 3.
[58] Brickner, "Direct Primaries," p. 553; *DEN*, Apr. 9, 1903, p. 2.

Advocates for abolishing conventions expected to see a qualitative improvement in American politics as well as a quantitative one in voter turnout. Transferring authority for making nominations over to the people would better educate the citizenry on government affairs. Moreover, successful candidates would have to address broad public concerns rather than the narrow interests of the party's convention goers. The direct primary, one averred, "places responsibility upon the people, and makes politics consist not in courting and buttonholing and bribing individuals, but in persuading and educating the whole people. . . . The system that puts responsibility for men and measures directly upon the conscience of the whole people is the only system through which the whole people can be stirred to think and feel and act for the public welfare." "Under this system all representatives must apply for a nomination, and would be compelled to state and define their position on all public questions before receiving the vote of the people," predicted another. The direct primary would become "the great common school of American politics" leading to public meetings and debates, and ultimately to "a better class of public men in office."[59] Progressives expected direct nominations to bring into better focus the broader public interest so often lost sight of in the convention system where politicians wrangled over how to divvy up the spoils.

Direct nominations were also expected to bring an end to the deal making and trading on offices that reformers charged had sidetracked many highly qualified candidates in the past and opened the door to corruption.[60] "Heretofore, in the making of nominations particular attention has always been given to the matter of location and racial extraction," the *Detroit Free Press* complained in 1904. "To secure the support of the Germans a German has almost invariably been given a place on the ticket. . . . These rules have been well defined and adhered to with precision." This would not be possible under a direct primary, the paper noted approvingly. Voters would give little heed to racial or ethnic considerations – or to a balanced ticket for the sake of a balanced ticket. "No longer will the prime qualification for a local office be that the nominee for it

---

59 Charles B. Spahr, "Direct Primaries," in *Proceedings of the Rochester Conference for Good City Government and the Seventh Annual Meeting of the National Municipal League [1901]*, ed. Clinton Rogers Woodruff (Philadelphia, 1901), pp. 195–96; Brickner, "Direct Primaries," p. 551.

60 Eric Falk Petersen, "The Adoption of the Direct Primary in California," *Southern California Quarterly* 54 (Winter 1972): 368; *LAT*, June 19, 1894, p. 1; *RMN*, Sept. 9, 1908, p. 1; *Outlook*, May 20, 1899, pp. 150–51.

is a 'well known east side German' or a 'representative of the colored citizens,' but that he is well equipped to discharge the duties that success may impose on him." Another supporter likened the direct primary to civil service reform, ensuring promotion only on the basis of merit. In this respect, the direct primary resembled another popular progressive measure, at-large elections whereby a single, aggregate vote overrode local power networks through which minorities secured representation.[61] The direct primary, in the eyes of reformers, would allow the "best men" and an overarching "public interest" to trump a fractured set of ethnic identities and private interests.

Whether party unity was better served with or without the carefully crafted tickets made possible by the convention system was a major point of contention. Many politicians defended the negotiations and compromises that went into preparing a full slate of candidates as vital to party unity. A properly balanced party ticket ensured that all the major elements of the party had a stake in the outcome and would stand by the party. Voters could not be expected to be quite so politic and evenhanded in making their selections in the primary. A Michigan legislator denounced a 1903 direct primary bill because it "renders it impossible to consider locality and nationality in the make up of the ticket." "I assert without fear of successful contradiction: There is not a county in the state of Michigan so overwhelmingly republican that the party dares to nominate a ticket regardless of locality and nationality. To do so is to court inevitable defeat for part or all of a ticket."[62] Stalwarts viewed their parties as disparate and unstable coalitions that had to be placated with a demonstrably "fair" division of the offices. Proponents of direct nominations countered that trades and deal making had brought the parties into disrepute and sowed discord on election day. They argued that the best means of unifying the party was by nominating the person with most support among the rank and file. La Follette allowed that efforts at a balanced ticket would suffer some at the polls under a system of direct nominations, but he insisted that the party would still come out ahead. Primary winners would be "so strong as to out-weigh all considerations of geography or nationality."[63]

[61] Samuel P. Hays, "Political Parties and the Community – Society Continuum," in *The American Party Systems: Stages of Political Development*, ed. William Nisbet Chambers and Walter Dean Burnham (New York, 1967), pp. 33–55.

[62] *DEN*, Mar. 25, 1903, p. 3; Clarence J. Hein, "The Adoption of Minnesota's Direct Primary Law," *Minnesota History* 35 (Dec. 1957): 345; *DEN*, Mar. 26, 1903, p. 1.

[63] *DFP*, Aug. 6, 1904, p. 4; Deming, "Municipal Nominating Law"; Lovejoy, *La Follette*, p. 45.

The corrupt and demoralizing impact of money in elections was another affliction of the body politic that was supposed to be remedied by the direct primary. A long-standing complaint lodged against the convention system was that it was rigged against men of moderate means. The bias against the relatively poor candidate came about when party insiders took stock of his financial assets. Politicians salivated at the prospect of nominating a rich man for office who could liberally fund the fall campaign. The *Detroit Free Press* complained in 1882: "If a candidate for Governor is to be selected – in either party – the first question is 'Can he afford to run?' If he has no money to spend or no moneyed friends to spend it for him, and thereby establish a lien on him, he is set aside, no matter what his qualifications may be or even what his availability in a partisan sense may be.... It is the same thing on a smaller scale if the office in question is that of Alderman." Candidate assessments and the additional demands of voracious politicians (ward heelers, newspaper editors, and even other candidates) were converting politics into an exclusively rich man's sport. "It has come to pass in most of the states that none but millionaires can be governors and senators," the *Detroit Evening News* complained in 1884. "[T]he days of men like Hamilton and Jefferson and Douglas and Lincoln and Webster, who remained in office and in comparative poverty all their lives, is rapidly passing away."[64] Mounting concern over expensive electioneering prompted futile legislative efforts to rein in runaway costs. Corrupt practices acts, appearing as early as the 1870s, sought to demarcate a clear line of separation between legitimate campaign expenditures and those that bordered on bribery.[65] The "Australian" or official ballot was supposed to hold down campaign expenses by relieving candidates of the costs of paying for the production and distribution of the ballots.[66] More ambitious laws would follow demanding an accounting of funds raised and spent, and even putting a cap on total campaign expenditures.[67]

---

[64] *DFP*, Aug. 11, 1882, p. 4; *DEN*, Aug. 13, 1884, p. 2. See also, *NEN*, Sept. 12, 1889, p. 1; *Courier* (Georgetown, Colo.), Sept. 23, 1886, p. 2.

[65] *New Jersey Laws* (1878), Chap. 204, pp. 318–19; *New Jersey Laws* (1883), Chap. 134, pp. 171–74; *California Statutes* (1895), Chap. 185, pp. 227–28; *Colorado Statues* (1887), "Act of April 4," pp. 347–50; *Michigan Public Acts* (1877), No. 180, pp. 193–207; *Michigan Public Acts* (1895), No. 135, pp. 264–69. Payments to print or to distribute tickets or for renting halls for campaign events passed muster; money or goods or services going to voters or delegates did not.

[66] Fredman, *Australian Ballot*; Reynolds and McCormick, "Outlawing 'Treachery.'"

[67] *New Jersey Laws* (1911), Chap. 183, pp. 284–324; *California Statutes* (1897), Chap. 106, pp. 115–34; *California Statutes* (1907), Chap. 350, pp. 671–78; *California Statues* (1909), Chap. 405, pp. 691–711; *Colorado Statutes* (1910), Chap. 4, pp. 15–44.

AFTER THE "BATTLE OF THE BARRELS."

THE VICTOR: "SHAKE HANDS, BOYS, AND LET'S ALL BE THANKFUL THAT NO RANK OUTSIDER TOOK THE PRIZE."

FIGURE 5.2. Michigan's 1900 Republican gubernatorial race featured three millionaires (Aaron T. Bliss, Dexter M. Ferry, and Justus S. Stearns) whose lavish campaign expenditures reflected the more aggressive campaigns mounted by hustling candidates. The [money] barrel campaign aroused enough indignation in Democratic and Republican ranks as to induce newspapers and county conventions to demand the direct primary. (*DEN*, June 29, 1900, p. 1.)

Prior to about 1900, concern over the corrupting influence of money in electoral politics was confined mainly to the general election. As the hustling candidates appeared to contest the primaries, however, the problem of the so-called barrel campaign now became associated with the nomination process. The scramble by three millionaires in 1900 to secure Michigan's Republican gubernatorial nomination resulted in an exorbitant amount of electioneering expenditures that shocked members of both parties. It was not merely that dispensing cash before the nomination had upped the ante for prospective candidates. The use of money to elect or to secure the support of delegates amounted to bribery in the eyes of many. The Republicans of Barry County, Michigan, denounced "the use of money to pack caucuses or control conventions in the interest of any candidate for office." They branded such practices as "unjust, unfair, un-Republican, accomplishing the debauchery of citizenship and the degradation of our public life." Like county conventions elsewhere, Barry County's Republicans concluded in 1902 that the solution was the direct primary.[68]

In retrospect, it is passing strange that supporters of the direct primary could not see that requiring candidates to win two elections instead of one would make far more demands of a candidate's bank account. Certainly the opponents of the direct primary understood that it represented an expensive proposition for the candidates. "It will take money to make a campaign of the state," a Michigan state senator warned. "The lieutenant governor receives $3 a day and the privilege of presiding over this Senate. A rich man can afford to make a campaign of the state, but a poor man can't."[69] Proponents of the direct primary shrugged off such prognostications because they focused on the savings that candidates would realize by not having to dicker with the delegates. An article extolling the virtues of the Crawford County Plan of party-run direct primaries insisted that the plan placed a rich man and a comparatively poor man on a level playing field. "It is only when candidates get to spending money freely with leading party workers that the cost grows, and this is not a necessary expense nor is it a fault peculiar to the system." This, indeed, was where most of the money went during the 1890s, when candidates relied on their surrogates to carry the day. A Republican insider in Michigan estimated the total costs of winning a gubernatorial nomination in 1896 at $40,000. Almost half of this money went to the candidate's staff and intermediaries: $5,000 for the campaign manager, $10,000 for agents in the field, $2,000 for local workers.[70] Most striking to the modern eye is the mere $5,000 set aside for advertising. Candidates for statewide offices at the turn of the century made but limited use of newspapers or other forms of mass media to get their names before the public.

There was mounting evidence, for those who dared to look, that the direct primary placed a new set of burdensome levies on candidates.

---

[68] *DFP*, July 15, 1900, p. 3; June 10, 1902, p. 2; *RMN*, Oct. 4, 1898, p. 4; *SFE*, Aug. 13, 1902, p. 2.

[69] *DEN*, May 25, 1905, p. 3. See also *RMN*, Sept. 26, 1910, p. 1.

[70] Ernest A. Hempstead, "The Crawford County or Direct Primary System," in Woodruff, *Seventh Annual Meeting of the National Municipal League*, p. 206; Arthur C. Millspaugh, "The Operation of the Direct Primary in Michigan," *American Political Science Review* 10 (Nov. 1916): 714.

Advertising costs would far outpace whatever savings office seekers might realize by cutting out the middlemen. The pattern was apparent early on in Cleveland, which had longer experience with direct nominations than most cities. A local lawyer expressed reservations about the city's experience with the Crawford County Plan at the 1898 conference for reforming the nomination process. None of his listeners could have appreciated the prescience of his remarks. "Candidates seem to proceed upon the theory that the people are only waiting to vote for any person for any position, without regard to fitness or ability, and that ready success lies in a vigorous advertising campaign." "It is said the best advertisers get the most votes," another close observer of party-run direct primaries concluded two years later.[71] "Knowing none of the candidates, the citizen, obeying an impulse of human nature, votes for the fellow whose picture he has most often seen in the newspaper."[72] A full appreciation of the extra costs entailed by the direct primary awaited its implementation. Not long after the direct primary appeared, some states passed laws to curb various forms of political advertising.[73] Advocates of direct nominations held the electorate in too high esteem to suppose that a candidate could curry public favor with the same strategy employed for touting patent medicines or soap.[74]

The supporters of direct nominations were aware that the system was not without its drawbacks. One particularly vexing problem concerned the nominee's winning margin. In a multicandidate race it was likely that no one would emerge with a majority of the vote. Could such nominees really claim to be the choice of the rank and file? The convention system averted this scenario by requiring multiple ballots until a majority of delegates agreed on a nominee; this was an important safeguard for

---

[71] National Conference on Practical Reform, *Primary Elections*, pp. 100–101. The speaker believed that "these criticisms do not apply" to rural areas, where "people vote for [a candidate] with some knowledge of his fitness to fill the place he is seeking."

[72] Wilder, "Primary Election Laws," p. 219. See also Emily Newell Blair, "Every Man His Own Campaign Manager," *Outlook*, Feb. 25, 1911, pp. 426–33.

[73] *Michigan Public Acts* (1909), Chap. 281, p. 539. The law made it illegal for candidates to advertise in any "magazine, program, bill of fare, ticket for any ball or other entertainment." It stipulated that newspaper ads were to use pictures of 1.5 in. by 2 in., and that large type was to constitute no more than 10 percent of all text. It even outlawed the posting of campaign materials outdoors and of handbills any larger than 2.5 in. by 4 in. For laws elsewhere, see Leon E. Aylsworth, "Primary Elections – Legislation of 1909–1910," *American Political Science Review* 6 (Feb. 1912): 60–74.

[74] Some attributed newspaper support for the direct primary to the added revenue the papers anticipated from advertising. National Conference on Practical Reform, *Primary Elections*, p. 102.

ensuring party unison in the eyes of party stalwarts.[75] Many advocates of the direct primary saw merit in majority rule and debated whether a mere plurality of the vote should be enough to label a contender as the party's choice. The runoff primary, between the two highest vote getters, did not generate much support outside the South. Some proposed that the choice go to a convention when a leader's percentage of the vote fell below a given threshold – such as 40%. The most fervid supporters of the direct primary put their faith in a system of preferential voting. Under this procedure voters ranked all the candidates rather than voting for just one; the votes would then be tabulated to see which candidate first emerged with a majority by combining first, second, and other choices.[76] This complicated voting process reflected the confidence progressives harbored for the electorate's patience and attention to matters political. None of these solutions proved very satisfactory. The prospect of candidates taking a party nomination with only a minority of the vote tarnished the direct primary's appeal as a party unifier and an instrument of democracy.

Another troubling issue concerned the standards for determining who was and was not a member of any given political party. "[J]ust about every conflict over making the parties more representative or more democratic or more responsive or more effective," notes Austin Ranney from his survey of party reform in the United States, "turns on the basic question of who should be treated as party members." The problem arose whether the indirect or direct system of nomination was in place, but became a matter of contention when state regulation became more extensive. The early legislation regulating the primaries (by outlawing fraud or mandating specific voting procedures) left the major parties with the discretion of setting voter qualifications. Complaints of "ringers" helping a candidate or faction to carry a primary or caucus became more

---

[75] National Conference on Practical Reform, *Primary Elections*, p. 96; William B. Shaw, "The Direct Primary on Trial," *Outlook*, Oct. 24, 1908, pp. 383–89; Hempstead, "Crawford County System," pp. 205–8; Winston Allen Flint, *The Progressive Movement in Vermont* (Washington, D.C., 1941), p. 68. Although delegates to conventions were selected by pluralities, the convention system worked on the principle that nominees secure the support of more than half the delegates. Nationally, the Democratic Party required a two-thirds vote to land a presidential or vice presidential nomination, but this standard was not adopted by the four state affiliates under review.

[76] Daniel S. Remsen, *Primary Elections: A Study for Improving the Basis of Party Organization* (New York, 1895), pp. 79–87; *NEN*, Oct. 11, 1907, p. 5; Charles Edward Merriam, "Some Disputed Points in Primary Election Legislation," *Proceedings of the American Political Science Association* 4 (1907): 185–88.

vociferous and eventually induced legislators to lay down some guide-lines. The problem faced by partisans and reformers was how rigidly to define Republican or Democratic membership. The participants at the 1898 New York conference agreed that only bona fide party members should vote in party councils, but their standards for determining affiliation varied widely. Some were satisfied with a statement from prospective voters promising that they would support the party's nominees in the coming election. For others, nothing less than an affirmation that the voter had cast a straight party ticket in the last election would suffice.[77]

Experience convinced most early devotees of direct nominations of the value of the "closed primary." Certainly there were some proponents of the direct primary who wanted to leave the door to the primary wide open in the interest of nonpartisanship. The National Municipal League pressed for an open primary system for city elections.[78] Michigan's outgoing governor Hazen S. Pingree issued a characteristically brusque endorsement of the open primary in 1901: "[P]rimary election laws should be so framed as to encourage independence in voting, whether it destroys parties or not."[79] Most advocates of direct nominations did not share Pingree's indifference to the fate of political parties under the new system. Reformers generally viewed the direct primary as a mechanism of party governance and believed in safeguards to keep out intruders.[80] Minneapolis's unhappy experiment with the open primary in 1900 would be cited again and again. Large numbers of Democrats participated in the city's G.O.P. primaries and put former Democrat Albert A. Ames in the mayoral chair. When the Ames administration came under attack for corruption and bossism, many reformers held the meddling Democrats

[77] Ranney, *Mischiefs of Faction*, p. 145; National Conference on Practical Reform, *Primary Elections*, pp. 107, 109, 123.

[78] Clinton Rogers Woodruff, "The Unsatisfactory Character of Present Methods of Nominating to Municipal Elective Office," in Woodruff, *Tenth Annual Meeting of the National Municipal League*, pp. 366–75.

[79] Hazen S. Pingree, "Governor's Message," *Journal of the Michigan House of Representatives Session of 1901*, 3 vols. (Lansing, Mich., 1901), vol. 1, pp. 29–35. La Follette's first proposal for a direct primary in 1897 stipulated that it be closed to all but party members, but he reverted to an open primary in the bill he sent to the Wisconsin legislature three years later, Ranney, *Mischiefs of Faction*, pp. 148–49.

[80] Dallinger, *Nominations for Elective Office*, pp. 141–53; Edward Insley, "How to Reform the Primary Election System," *Arena* 17 (June 1897): 1019; Edward P. Costigan, "Remarks of Edward P. Costigan ... at Austin Texas, Feb. 9, 1923," Box 38, "General Personal" file, Edward P. Costigan Papers, Archives at the University of Colorado at Boulder Libraries.

responsible.[81] Progressive organs labeled the open primary "a most igno-
minious failure." Proponents of direct nominations everywhere faced a
similar conundrum, noted the political scientist Charles Edward Merriam
in 1907: how to open the process to "the honest, independent voter without admitting at the same time, the dishonest and venal."[82]

Reformers enjoyed only partial success in mobilizing the public behind
the direct primary. It was an article of faith among progressives that the
measure enjoyed broad popular support. Independent newspapers lined
up solidly behind the proposition, as did many partisan ones. "[T]here
is not an intelligent man in the state of Michigan who does not know
that eight out of ten voters in the commonwealth are heartily in favor
of the direct nomination of all candidates for public office," the *Detroit
Evening News* affirmed in 1903.[83] When voters were called upon to issue
an opinion on the matter, the direct primary won handily. La Follette's
direct primary proposal won the approbation of 62 percent of Wisconsin's
voters in a referendum.[84] California's voters backed an amendment to the
constitution authorizing the legislature to enact a direct primary law by
a 3 to 1 margin in 1908. In Michigan, a referendum on the state's 1905
primary election law passed with the assent of over 80 percent of the
electorate. Michigan authorized counties to adopt the direct primary for
local offices if first approved in a referendum. Voters endorsed the switch
to direct nominations in fifty-three of fifty-six counties polled between
1905 and 1909.[85]

[81] *Outlook*, May 20, 1899, pp. 150–51; Oct. 6, 1900, pp. 288–89; Sept. 27, 1902,
pp. 189–90.
[82] Edward Insley, "Needed Political Reforms," *Arena* 29 (Jan. 1903): 71–75; *Outlook*,
Aug. 15, 1908, pp. 823–24; Merriam, "Some Disputed Points," p. 183. In truth, the
distinction between closed and open primaries was largely a matter of degree. In the
purely open primary, such as that briefly in force in Minnesota, the elector was handed
a ballot for each of the parties and then allowed to select his choice in the privacy of the
voting booth. More common were procedures calling for the voter to ask for a party's
ballot, whereupon his or her affiliation could be challenged – though not easily refuted.
Party affiliation was often tied to how the individual voted in the past, and with the secret
ballot in place it was difficult to dispute anything a voter might say under oath. Only
when states began keeping lists of voters organized by party, with procedures making it
difficult to switch from Democratic to Republican or vice versa, was a primary effectively
closed. See Ranney, *Mischiefs of Faction*, pp. 148–49.
[83] *DEN*, May 13, 1903, p. 1; May 7, 1903, p, 2; *TTA*, Feb. 24, 1911, p. 1.
[84] Lovejoy, *La Follette*, p. 91. In 1914 a plurality of Vermont voters (45%) backed a direct
primary over the existing caucus system (30%) or a preferential primary that was non-
binding (25%). Flint, *Progressive Reform in Vermont*, p. 64.
[85] Petersen, "Direct Primary in California," p. 368; County Canvassers' Statements, "Referendum of June 12, 1906," Michigan State Archives, Lansing. The reports do not include

Yet, if direct nominations enjoyed wide support, it does not appear to have been very deep. The states' third parties (the Populists, Prohibitionists, and Socialists) did not trouble themselves much about regulating the major parties.[86] Some correctly saw the laws as a threat to their well-being. California's "Nonpartisan Party" challenged the constitutionality of the state's 1897 law claiming that "the inevitable tendency of the operation of the act will be to overwhelm and destroy all small political parties."[87] A Socialist speaker in Detroit was contemptuous of the direct primary's potential for reforming capitalist political parties: "The republicans and democrats have just found out that they are all rascals, and now the rascals want us to pass a primary law which will help precent [sic] themselves from being rascals."[88] A cursory inspection of the papers of various emerging professional, trade, and special interest organizations fails to uncover much attention to – much less agitation about – the subject. The Michigan Grange formally endorsed the direct primary, but there was little to show for it. In 1903, a direct primary bill hung in the balance in the Michigan legislature. A Detroit newspaper called upon members of the Grange, the National Municipal League, and other groups to form a "petition in boots" to descend on Lansing "and urge the senators to give the people the sort of general primary election law

data from Wayne County, though it was reported that the proposal met with "unanimous support" in Detroit. *DFP*, June 13, 1906, p. 2; Sarasohn, "Regulating Parties . . . in Michigan," p. 161.

[86] Colorado's Populist governor loaded up the plate of the 1894 legislators with thirty-two issues he wished to see it address, none of which touched on a direct primary. See R. G. Dill, *The Political Campaigns of Colorado with Complete Tabulated Statements of the Official Vote* (Denver, 1895), pp. 230–32. The three major third parties did warmly embrace the direct election of U.S. senators; the Australian ballot; and the initiative, referendum, and recall; but their state and county platforms had virtually nothing to say about reforming the nominating process. The platforms of California's minor parties can be found in Winfield J. Davis, *History of Political Conventions in California, 1849–1892* (Sacramento, Calif., 1893). For Colorado's Socialist Party, see Box 3, Folders 18 and 19, the William Penn Collins Collection, Archives at the University of Colorado at Boulder Libraries. For the Prohibitionists, see *SFE*, Aug. 28, 1902, p. 12; *RMN*, Sept. 10, 1908, p. 6. Concerning the Populists, see James Edward Wright, *The Politics of Populism: Dissent in Colorado* (New Haven, Conn., 1974), p. 117; *RMN*, Sept. 10, 1902, p. 9; Carl H. Chrislock, "Sidney M. Owen: An Editor in Politics," *Minnesota History* 36 (Dec. 1958): 109–26.

[87] "Charles A. Spier vs. Robert Baker et al." (1898), 120 Cal 370, p. 372.

[88] *DEN*, July 6, 1902, p. 5. Socialists in Colorado and Indiana nonetheless did mail ballots to their memberships allowing them to choose among candidates nominated in conventions. See Lewis E. Floaten, "Memo from State Headquarters," June 7, 1908, Box 7, Folder 15, Collins Collection; Ora Ellen Cox, "The Socialist Party in Indiana Since 1896," *Indiana Magazine of History* 12 (June 1916): 107.

they are clamoring for." A week later, one senator pointed out "that while newspapers were declaring that the people were clamoring for the passage of a sweeping primary election bill, no delegation had appeared here to urge the legislature to take favorable action on any bill."[89] In New Jersey, the People's Lobby spearheaded the drive for the direct primary and other measures to make government more transparent and responsive. With a statewide membership of five-hundred, however, the group hardly constituted a mass movement to intimidate any legislator; most politicians regarded the organization as a curiosity. A Republican state senator from Denver contended in 1909 that the newspapers were the only ones interested in promoting the direct primary. "The people don't want it. I have never received a single communication from a constituent telling me to do anything in relation to the primary bill." One authority on Michigan's early primary laws concluded that "the people of Michigan were perfectly willing to endorse the direct primary when somebody went to the trouble of asking their opinion, but there was no great popular uprising on its behalf."[90] In brief, Republican and Democratic legislators backed the direct primary because it suited their purposes, not because public opinion or powerful interests dictated that they do so.

Although politicians and, later, scholars would claim that the direct primary undermined political parties, this was clearly not the intent of most of its early proponents. Supporters and opponents of direct nominations differed over how best to secure harmony within party ranks. The latter envisioned the parties as factional groupings that had to be kept together through careful deliberations that insured that all elements had a vested interest in carrying the election. The former believed that the dissension that wracked the parties was a product of public disgust with a corrupt and undemocratic candidate selection process. Direct nominations would strengthen the Democratic and Republican parties by restoring public

[89] *DEN*, May 7, 1903, p. 1; May 13, 1903, p. 3. The *News* countered that the legislative committee of the state Grange had twice visited the legislature that session and that the Grange had endorsed the direct primary. But the Grange was also concerned about many other bills that more directly impacted on the Michigan farmer's welfare. In 1909, when a full-scale direct primary bill was under consideration, the Grange ignored the issue entirely. It devoted its efforts to blocking a pay raise for the superintendent of public instruction, endorsing local option in the regulation of the liquor trade, and making the telephone companies common carriers. See the *Lansing Journal*, Feb. 23, 1909, p. 1. The State League of Republican Clubs was far more vocal in its support for the direct primary but does not qualify as a nonpartisan special interest group. *DFP*, June 22, 1902, p. 3.
[90] *NEN*, Mar. 7, 1907, p. 5; *RMN*, Mar. 26, 1909, p. 2; Sarasohn, "Regulating Parties . . . in Michigan," p. 161.

confidence in their internal workings. The support the closed primary enjoyed among reformers should dispel any doubts about their fidelity to the major parties. It certainly was true that reformers expected direct nominations to produce a different variety of nominees: men – and in some cases, women – whose appeal rested on their qualifications rather than on any additional votes they could bring to the ticket. Reformers expected and desired that political parties would remain a fixture of American politics, even if they expected them to do business differently in the future.

IV

The sudden appeal of the direct primary after 1900 was mainly a consequence of changes wrought in the nominating process over the preceding decade. Two broad developments had rendered conventions superfluous, if not downright antidemocratic. Government regulation of the primaries and even of conventions had been substantially accomplished. Anticorruption statutes in the 1880s laid the groundwork for official recognition of party candidates that came with the official or Australian ballot late in the decade. This was followed by ever-widening state controls over the nominating process bearing on voter eligibility; the dates, times, and format for voting; and the proceedings of the nominating bodies themselves. It was no longer possible to argue that party nominating practices were a matter of concern only to Democrats or Republicans. The major parties had clearly been stamped as quasi-public agencies. Here was the first hint that the trajectory of party development in the United States would follow a different path than that of other Western democracies where formal regulation of parties by the state was never an option. In the debate over the direct primary it was rarely suggested that the government had no business involving itself in party management. Political parties in the United States generally welcomed state supervision over their sometimes chaotic affairs. Government regulation appeared only after the party organizations themselves had notably failed to regulate themselves. The nation's highly decentralized political parties lacked much of an organizational framework save for the few weeks preceding the general election. They could neither effectively supervise their internal affairs nor resist state encroachment on their prerogatives, even if they wanted to.

The logical next step in the evolution from the indirect to the direct primary would not have won such ready acceptance had the hustling candidate not already made his presence felt. Implicit in the logic of the direct primary was the proposition that when voters went to the polling places there were candidates to be voted on. This had generally not been the case during the 1880s, but it was becoming more and more the norm thereafter. At one time, prospective candidates were entreated to remain aloof from the delegate selection process and the actions of nominating bodies at all levels. The best representative men, selected for who they were rather than for whom they supported, had a freer hand in deciding on the parties' standard-bearers. Little by little, however, would-be state legislators, congressmen, and governors intruded on the process. They circulated at conventions, lined up slates of friendly delegates, made publicized visits to their friends around the state, and injected more competition and pressure on the nominating process than it was designed to handle. The phenomenon appeared across all layers of government but was more advanced when it came to local offices. Matters sometimes got out of hand, leading to contested delegations and charges of bossism and corruption that imperiled the entire ticket. Local party organizations turned to some version of direct nominations – the Crawford County Plan – but found that their administration of the proceedings could be another source of contention. Faced with ever more dissension in the nominating process, legislators and party officials came to view the state not as an unwelcome interloper but as a serviceable referee.

There were still those who praised the convention as an "opportunity for deliberation, for conference, for weighing the merits and availability of candidates."[91] But as more and more delegates went to conventions pledged to specific candidates, the image of the convention as a deliberative body lost credibility. At one time, the reputation of the convention rested securely on the reputations of the people who attended it. Now, men of standing found their way to the convention blocked if they were not ready to endorse a local favorite for governor, or they might be beaten in the balloting by a mere clerk or political functionary. The persons of more modest standing who replaced them could expect less deference in the press or in party councils. Elected on behalf of some candidate, delegates were expected to "take programme" rather than exercise their own discretion. In this context, neither committed or uncommitted delegates commended themselves to New York's governor Charles Evans Hughes: "If they are absolutely pledged they are simply registering devices and an unnecessary and cumbersome addition to the party machinery. If they are not pledged absolutely the party voter has not proper assurance either of their allegiance or of their deliberation. They lend themselves easily to

[91] Brickner, "Boss Rule," p. 553.

secret control by party managers and furnish the means not for true representation, but for nonrepresentation, or misrepresentation of the party."
"The very best the convention can do is to express the judgment of the
voters of its party," the *Rocky Mountain News* concluded in 1908. "Why
not let those voters express their own judgment?"[92]

---

[92] Charles A. Beard, "The Direct Primary Movement in New York," *Proceedings of the
American Political Science Association* 7 (1910): 196; *RMN*, Sept. 9, 1908, p. 14.

6

The Direct Primary in the Reform Tradition

I

Michigan's voters had never witnessed anything resembling Chase S. Osborn's barnstorming for the Republican gubernatorial nomination in 1910. Touring the lower peninsula in an automobile caravan over several weeks that summer, Osborn's entourage logged in twelve thousand miles – sometimes tooling along at an alarming thirty miles per hour. The "cow path campaigning" stopped "wherever we found a crossroads, a blacksmith shop and a bird's nest." His savvy handlers sent an organizer to towns ahead to ensure that Osborn was greeted by a band and an enthusiastic crowd. Osborn was a "natural campaigner," writes his biographer, "energetic, colorful, highly egotistical, a complete extrovert" and a good public speaker. Primary day left him hoarse from seven hundred mostly extemporaneous speeches. Osborn gloried in the glad-handing techniques perfected by candidates for lesser offices, but he did not overlook the tactics that had nominated governors past. He wrote numerous letters, hired a retinue of local campaign promoters, and even sought to enlist the census takers in his cause. It proved to be an expensive undertaking. Much of the thirty-five thousand dollars Osborn spent came out of his own bank account after his fellow mine owners proved less than generous. Some of the payments violated the state's new limitations on campaign expenditures, but it was easy enough to find loopholes in the statute. A longtime supporter of direct nominations, Osborn's ready adaptation to its demanding regimen accounted for his victory that fall. "Where, O where, would we be in this

WHAT KEMBLE SAW AT THE DEMOCRATIC STATE CONVENTION OF
NEW JERSEY

FIGURE 6.1. Shortly after being nominated for governor in 1910, Woodrow
Wilson broke with New Jersey Democratic Party tradition by speaking before
the convention. The candidate-centered campaign appears here in this candidate-
centered sketch of the proceedings. The less than flattering portraits of most of
the delegates was in keeping with their negative image during the Progressive Era.
(*Harper's Weekly*, Sept. 24, 1910, p. 7.)

fight," pondered his campaign manager, "if it wasn't for the direct primary."[1]

II

As it did in most states, legislation introducing a mandatory direct primary for state officials appeared around 1910 in California, New Jersey, Michigan, and Colorado. The bills, debates, and roll calls in all four states reveal similarities in the issues and coalitions surrounding the legislation. Urban areas turned against the convention system, and the Democratic Party proved more willing to invest voters with responsibility for selecting the parties' nominees. Opposition came from those elements in the parties that most benefited by the bargain and trade enshrined in the convention system. The ranks of the stalwarts who defended the status quo were thin, and nowhere were they in a position to block the reform entirely. Nonetheless, the path to the direct primary through the legislatures was not smooth. Agreement on the principle of direct nominations left unresolved many vital questions bearing on its administration. Extraneous issues concerning the conduct of the general election or the direct election of U.S. senators further complicated matters. The built-in inefficiencies of senates and assemblies convinced some that the political machines were seeking to kill the legislation.[2] Yet the direct primary emerged victorious everywhere with remarkable speed and little rancor. It did so primarily because it addressed the major parties' long-standing efforts to promote harmony and to disarm dissident elements.

Although both of California's major party state conventions endorsed the principle of direct nominations in 1906, constitutional roadblocks delayed legislative action until 1909.[3] Republicans held a better than 3 to 1

[1] Robert Mark Warner, "Chase S. Osborn and the Progressive Movement" (Ph.D. diss., University of Michigan, 1957), pp. 119–27. It is instructive to contrast Osborn's 1910 effort with his previous campaign for the nomination in 1900. His diary covering his activities the weeks before the state convention that year makes hardly any mention of his gubernatorial ambitions. He divided his time between his home in Sault Ste. Marie and the state capital where he served as state railroad commissioner. See Osborn's "Diary" for 1900, Box 111, Chase S. Osborn Papers, Bentley Historical Library, University of Michigan, Ann Arbor.

[2] A revealing description of the many complications that attended legislating in this era appears in *NEN*, Oct. 11, 1907, p. 17. "Lack of system," a veteran legislative reporter complained, was "a more serious hindrance to intelligent lawmaking than anything else this side of corporate influence."

[3] *LAT*, Sept. 8, 1906, p. 3; Sept.13, 1906, p. 4. The 1907 legislature had to submit a referendum to the voters authorizing it to enact a direct primary. The public gave its approval in 1908, paving the way for the 1909 legislature to act. See Eric Falk Petersen,

edge over the Democrats in both houses of the legislature that year. Prior to the opening of the session, the Direct Primary League mailed all legislators a draft of what would become known as the "Wright-Stanton" bill. The league's cover letter assured legislators that "instead of disrupting . . . parties [the bill] will result in strengthening and building up parties by popularizing party organization."[4] The bill mandated a direct primary for almost all elected offices as well as for the U.S. Senate,[5] and it applied to any political party that amassed 3% or more of the vote in the previous election. Anticipated opposition to the bill from the so-called Herrin machine (associated with the Southern Pacific Railroad) failed to materialize.[6] According to the *Examiner*, Republican regulars concluded that the direct primary "may not turn out to be such a bad thing after all. It is openly designed to preserve party organization, and the machine leaders are hoping that here their district organization may stand them in good stead."[7] One section that surely pleased partisan-minded legislators prohibited candidates defeated in the primaries from running for the same office in the general election.[8] As the legislation neared passage, a reporter circulating among the state senators noted that "the general comment today was that a law of this kind would work to the serious disadvantage of good government leagues and other political side shows not classed among the regular parties."[9]

All but a handful of California senators and assemblymen in 1909 endorsed the concept of a statewide direct primary. Only two issues divided the state's upper house when the bill first came up for

"The Adoption of the Direct Primary in California," *Southern California Quarterly* 54 (Winter 1972): pp. 368–69.

[4] Petersen, "Direct Primary in California," p. 369.

[5] School elections in rural areas were exempted under the statute. *California Statutes* (1909), Chap 405, p. 691. State legislatures at this time still had formal authority in appointing U.S. senators. The Wright-Stanton bill included a provision allowing legislative candidates to pledge that they would support the candidate who won the U.S. Senate primary. For detailed coverage of the passage of the law, see Franklin Hichborn, *Story of the Session of the California Legislature of 1909* (San Francisco, 1909), pp. 68–120.

[6] Among the members of the state assembly long associated with the Republican organization, only Grove L. Johnson openly opposed the measure: "I don't like this bill and I'm going to fight it. . . . I've come to the conclusion it is a covert blow at the Republican Party in California. It will help the rich and work against the poor." *SFE*, Feb. 26, 1909, p. 1. A year later Johnson's son Hiram, who testified before the legislature on behalf of the Wright-Stanton bill, would become the state's first governor elected under its provisions.

[7] *SFE*, Feb. 27, 1909, p. 13.

[8] Chap 405, pp. 695–96.

[9] *SFE*, Feb. 12, 1909, p. 1. The quote referred to a separate bill, but its provisions found their way into what became the state's first direct primary law.

consideration. One amendment would have tightened registration requirements to keep outsiders from participating in the primaries.[10] Legislators from less competitive districts generally supported efforts to keep their primaries closed to outsiders.[11] Another amendment stipulated nominations by convention when primary winners took less than 40% of the vote for a state office or less than 25% in local races. Legislators voted down both propositions by margins of more than 2 to 1. (The disposition of these and other roll calls appears in Table 6.1.) Urbanization proved to be a notable factor dividing the legislature on the amendments, especially when it came to retaining the convention when pluralities fell below a given threshold ($Eta^2 = .24$). Senators from urban areas, most notably San Francisco, wished to retain the nominating convention when no runaway winner had emerged. When the bill got to the state assembly, language was added making the primary vote on the U.S. Senate seat strictly advisory. This amendment passed despite the opposition of Democrats and legislators representing rural areas. Democrats also objected to a proviso that required all candidates to endorse state and national platforms, possibly a ploy to tie Democrats to their more controversial national issues.[12] The senate was closely divided on whether to accept the assembly's changes.[13] The two houses squabbled mainly over the implications of the primary for the U.S. Senate seat. The assembly's "advisory" language eventually made its way into the final bill, despite the opposition of senators from the more urbanized counties. California's success in enacting a full-scale direct primary law on its first try was perhaps unusual. The state's long experience in regulating political parties possibly facilitated the transition to direct nominations.

New Jersey took up the direct primary earlier and went through a more protracted and contentious process as it gradually implemented the

---

[10] Although the senate voted down an amendment for a closed primary, the final bill allowed participation only by voters who had registered with the party at least twenty days prior to the primary.

[11] See in particular the binary logistic regression results in Table B.1 of Appendix B.

[12] These provisions never made it into the final bill, which required only that the candidate aver that "he affiliated with said party at the last preceding general election." Chap. 405, p. 694.

[13] There are numerous hints in the press that the division over the senate issue reflected the interests of specific candidates thought more likely to benefit by one set of rules or another. See *SFE*, Mar. 4, 1909, p. 13; Mar. 10, 1909, p. 1; Mar. 12, 1909, p. 22. The rules of the state senate required twenty-one votes to approve the bill as modified by the assembly. Hence, senate ratification fell short by one vote even though the bill enjoyed a bare majority among those voting.

TABLE 6.1. *Landmark Legislation Introducing the Direct Primary, California*

Year	Bill	Law	Description	Lower House				Senate			
				Vote "Yea"- "Nay"	Party Index of Like.	Eta² for Urban	Eta² for Comp.	Vote "Yea"- "Nay"	Party Index of Like.	Eta² for Urban	Eta² for Comp.
1909	S3	405	Primary for state offices and Senate	58-0				27-0			
			Require conv. if winner has less than 40% vote					13-27	83.3	.24	.00
			Amend to mandate a closed primary					9-29	87.4	.11	.11
			Amend to add U.S. Senate to offices voted on	38-36	71.5	.20	.00				
			Require candidate support state and nat'l platform	26-42	74.5	.14	.00				
			Require candidate support past platforms	37-31	55.8	.18	.00				
			Accept assembly changes to bill					20-19	61.4	.20	.00
			To add U.S. Senate to offices to be voted on					20-18	60.2	.17	.02
			Accepting senate amendments	29-42	41.9	.08	.00				
			Accepting conf. comm. report	65-0				37-1			

primary across a series of offices. Democratic governor George T. Werts urged the legislature to enact George L. Record's direct primary proposal in 1894, apparently the first such bill in the nation.[14] The Republican-dominated assembly nixed the idea on a very nearly straight party vote. (See Table 6.2.)[15] The 1902 legislature gave unanimous consent to the creation of a commission to investigate nominating practices and propose legislation. The legislators acted at the behest of Governor Franklin Murphy, a man never to be associated with the Republican Party's budding "progressive" or "New Idea" wing. Murphy mainly desired to make primaries less disorderly after the chaos of Essex County's Democratic primary a few months earlier and a more recent uproar among Republicans in Camden.[16] The independent *Newark Evening News* expected – even welcomed – opposition from the party hierarchy. "If the report of the Primary Reform Commission does not meet with the opposition of political bosses and ward heelers it will not be the kind of a document that will receive the approval of the people."[17]

The commission's draft bill, modeled on Minnesota's statute, met Murphy's objectives by introducing state regulation over the delegate selection process. Commission member Record later took credit for an additional provision requiring direct nominations of candidates for township and ward offices. The governor was "very highly pleased" with the commission's recommendations, which also enjoyed "the practically unanimous endorsement of the state press." "Machine dictation," the *News* predicted, "will receive a blow from which recovery will be impossible."[18] The bill did meet with some short-lived opposition from a few party

[14] The governor assigned such importance to the proposed bill that he had it reprinted in *Minutes of Votes and Proceedings of the One Hundred and Eighteenth General Assembly of the State of New Jersey* (Trenton, 1894), pp. 24–42. The draft indicated that a primary winner would be required to garner some unspecified percentage of the total vote. Other language sought to preserve at least the appearance of candidates responding to a call from the people, by proposing that citizens submit petitions to put individuals on the ballot, after which the candidate would be officially asked if he would consent to run. Only persons who voted for the party's gubernatorial nominee at the last election could sign the nominating papers or vote. Parties retained the option of continuing to nominate in conventions if they so chose.

[15] The roll call is analyzed more thoroughly in Table B.2 in Appendix B.

[16] *NEN*, Apr. 1, 1903, p. 5. According to one insider, "direct nominations never appealed to [Murphy], but he did feel that the election of convention delegates should be conducted in a decent, orderly fashion." Ransom E. Noble, *New Jersey Progressivism Before Wilson* (Princeton, N.J., 1946), p. 132.

[17] *NEN*, Jan. 5, 1903, p. 6.

[18] George L. Record, "The First Primary Law," *Trenton Evening Times*, Oct. 8, 1924, p. 3; *NEN*, Feb. 24, 1903, p. 6; Jan. 4, 1903, p. 4.

TABLE 6.2. *Landmark Legislation Introducing the Direct Primary, New Jersey*

				Lower House				Senate			
Year	Bill	Law	Description	Vote "Yea" - "Nay"	Party Index of Like.	Eta² for Urban	Eta² for Comp.	Vote "Yea" - "Nay"	Party Index of Like.	Eta² for Urban	Eta² for Comp.
1894	S79		Record's direct primary bill	23-31	8.8	.05	.14	11-8	48.9	.02	.35
1903	S87	248	Direct primary for ward and township offices	58-0				17-1			
1906	S301		Direct nominations without conventions	14-25	62.2	.31	.03	12-1			
1907	A535	278	Direct primary for all offices but governor and Congress	26-12	7.7	.31	.00	16-0			
1909	A40		Direct primary for Congress	26-32	27.3	.09	.01				
1909	A41		Direct primary for governor	23-35	20.5	.07	.01				
1910	A5,6		Direct Primary for Congress and governor	19-36	10.0	.01	.00				
1911	A175	183	Direct Primary for Congress and governor	34-25	41.1	.02	.04	17-0			
			Substitute for bill w/o blanket ballot or registration	11-47	81.5						
			Require approval in a referendum	27-32	37.9	.03	.04				

organization men. The chair of the Essex County Republican Party, Carl Lentz, testified against the bill along with four other county committee chairmen. Lentz had helped introduce a Republican-run direct primary in his county in 1896. He balked at the prospect of turning authority over the administration of the primary to an elected official (the city clerk) who sometimes might be aligned with the opposition party. Legislators mollified Lentz and other party officials with revisions that expanded the party organization's authority in the management of their primaries.[19]

Administrative responsibility for the voting process proved not to be the most controversial feature of the 1903 legislation. Provisions that compelled voters to officially register their affiliation with a political party before they could take part in its primaries drew bipartisan fire. The Republican-aligned *Jersey Journal* and the Democratic *Trenton True American* condemned this and other provisos that threatened "the independent voter in the secrecy and independence of the ballot."[20] Record defended the provision, reminding legislators that the bill "was not drawn in the interest of the independent voter but to create and maintain party harmony."[21] Ironically, the state's major independent newspaper endorsed Record's position. "Ours is government by party," the *Newark Evening News* explained. "Only Republicans are expected to participate in Republican primaries." The *Trenton True American* was not persuaded. "The bill as it stands today is entirely acceptable to the bosses, and, in fact, in some respects makes it easier for them to control primaries."[22] Despite the opposition of a few independent-minded partisan newspapers, the bill sailed through the senate with a single dissenting vote and received unanimous approval in the assembly.[23] Record credited Governor Murphy and Murphy's successor, Senator E. C. Stokes, another party regular who served on the commission, for bringing the legislators around.[24]

[19] *TTA*, Mar. 31, 1903, p. 1; *NEN*, Apr. 1, 1903, p. 5.

[20] *TTA*, Mar. 20, 1903, p. 4; *NEN*, Jan. 28, 1903, p. 6.

[21] *TTA*, Mar. 31, 1903, p. 1. Record later defended the law when it was challenged before the state supreme court on the grounds that it violated a voter's constitutional right to secrecy. The court decided that there was no such constitutional right and that a voter's electoral preferences were not wholly compromised: the law specified only that the voter had chosen a majority of a party's candidates in the previous election. See "Andrew Hopper vs. Maurice Stack, County Clerk of Hudson County," *New Jersey Law Reports*, 69, pp. 562–71.

[22] *TTA*, Mar. 31, 1903, p. 1; *NEN*, Jan. 28, 1903, p. 6; Jan. 6, 1903, p. 6; *TTA*, Mar. 28, 1903, p. 4.

[23] Earlier, the Republican caucus voted to make the bill a party measure on a vote of 22 to 13. *NEN*, Apr. 1, 1903, p. 5.

[24] Record, "First Primary Law."

Efforts to expand the number of offices covered by the direct primary encountered greater resistance. In 1907 senators and assemblymen approved a statute subjecting themselves and other county officials to the direct primary. The bill met with some opposition in the assembly. Here, Democrats enacted the measure on another largely straight party vote.[25] Democrats decided, mostly in the interests of economy, not to apply the law to gubernatorial and congressional offices.[26] In years when the G.O.P. controlled both legislative chambers (1906, 1909, and 1910), its members dug in their heels at bills, adding congressional and gubernatorial offices to the list of positions to be voted on. In 1909 and 1910, Democratic assemblymen unanimously supported such bills, while most Republicans voted them down.[27] Division within Republican ranks was mainly along an urban/rural axis. This pattern is revealed by isolating four roll calls listed in Table 6.2 calling for direct nominations for Congress or governor or both in 1906, 1909, and 1910. Only a small minority of the total of number of votes cast by G.O.P. assemblymen in all four roll calls favored enlarging the range of offices subject to direct nomination (40 out of 178, or 22.5%). Republicans supporting a gubernatorial or congressional direct primary represented counties that were more urban (75.3%) than were those opposed to the proposition (53.8%).[28] Rural intransigence sprang from mundane political considerations. Opponents complained that candidates from densely populated cities would have a big advantage over candidates from the hinterland. Rural legislators did not object to the direct primary when applied only within their counties. When it was adopted across a congressional district or statewide, however, they feared it would diminish their political clout.[29]

Given their steady support for direct nominations, the Democrats' sweeping electoral victory of 1910 presumably doomed the state and

---

[25] The legislature voted on several direct primary bills that year, Assembly Bill 535 was the only one that survived a session that dragged on into October.

[26] A gubernatorial primary would cost the state fifty thousand dollars and would undermine the Democrats' promise to lower government expenditures after years of campaigning against Republican "extravagance." *NEN*, Oct. 11, 1907, p. 5.

[27] Democrats endorsed the direct primary for gubernatorial and congressional candidates in their 1907 state platform, while Republicans demurred. *NEN*, Sept. 17, 1907, p. 4; Sept. 19, 1907, p. 3.

[28] See also the binary logistic regression results in Table B.2 of Appendix B on these same votes.

[29] *NEN*, Oct. 11, 1907, p. 5; Feb. 24, 1909, p. 5. Table 2.1 documents how the apportionment law of 1904 benefited the state's rural counties.

congressional nominating convention.[30] Democrats controlled both branches of the New Jersey legislature, yet it was no easy matter getting the so-called Geran Act passed in 1911. The mostly rural Republicans remaining in the assembly continued to oppose the proposition. In 1911, however, they were joined by a number of Democrats, pushing the Index of Likeness in the direction of bipartisanship.[31] It was not that Democrats had experienced a change of heart on the principle of direct nominations. The 1911 law was a broad piece of legislation that had more important implications for the general election than for the primaries. Newly installed Governor Woodrow Wilson had irked his fellow Democrats by turning to Record to draft the legislation.[32] Opposition to the bill among Democrats (from Jersey City and Newark) focused not on the direct primary provisions, but on a complicated voter registration and ballot system that they feared would disfranchise their largely immigrant voting base. A substitute measure drawn up by the disaffected Democrats retained the provision for a direct primary for all elected officials but omitted the new voter registration and ballot features.[33] The motion to replace the Geran Bill with its substitute won the endorsement of only eleven dissident Democrats. A provision that would have required the Geran Bill to be approved in a popular referendum fared better owing to Republican support but still failed of passage (27 to 32). The direct primary was a controversial issue among Garden State Republicans – but not among Democrats. The division and wrangling that accompanied the 1911 law was due to extraneous issues related to its provisions for the general election.

Like New Jersey, Michigan implemented the direct primary on a piecemeal basis. The idea met more determined resistance in Michigan, as is

---

[30] Over the objections of Hudson County Democrats, the Democratic state platform of 1910 deleted the endorsement of the direct primary that had appeared in the 1907 document. The 1910 version committed the party to attempt nothing more than the simplification of the nomination process. Woodrow Wilson's political mentor, Col. George B. Harvey, rewrote this portion of the document. "The platform is in accord with the views of Dr. Wilson," he assured the press. "His views might be called 'conservatively radical.'" *NEN*, Sept. 15, 1910, p. 1.

[31] Fifteen of eighteen Republican assemblymen voted against the bill's final passage, as did ten of forty-one Democrats.

[32] Record was a Democrat when he authored his first direct primary bill in 1894 but later affiliated with the G.O.P. Noble, *New Jersey Progressivism*, p. 15.

[33] For fuller coverage of the debate over the bill, see *NEN*, Mar. 21, 1911, p. 1; John F. Reynolds, *Testing Democracy: Electoral Behavior and Progressive Reform in New Jersey, 1880–1920* (Chapel Hill, N.C., 1988), pp. 140–45. For a summary of the law, see Arthur Ludington, "Election Laws: The New Geran Law in New Jersey," *American Political Science Review* 5 (Nov. 1911): 579–85.

apparent by the sheer number of roll calls recorded in Table 6.3. Governor Hazen S. Pingree urged the adoption of the system in his first message to the legislature in 1897 and again in 1899.[34] The state press did not exude much enthusiasm for the idea. Most editors had little to say on the subject as very loosely sketched out by the incoming governor. One "machine" organ, aligned with U.S. senator James McMillan, conceded that the system might be appropriate "in large cities, if it can be reduced to practice, which is the important factor to be demonstrated." Still, the paper remained skeptical of its effectiveness in mobilizing support behind the nominees. "There is no likelihood that the fellow that gets thrown down will feel any better satisfied with the result."[35] Pingree never made direct nominations a top priority during his four years in office, and he never prevailed upon his party to endorse the idea. It was the "carnival of crime and corruption" surrounding the fight to succeed Pingree at the 1900 Republican State Convention that finally provoked the legislature into taking action.[36]

As elsewhere, urban areas played a pioneering role in bringing the direct primary to Michigan. "In Detroit, Grand Rapids and other cities there is strong demand for the direct nomination of candidates," the *Detroit Free Press* concluded in 1902. "In the rural district the voters are satisfied with the existing system, and are strongly opposed to any change."[37] In 1899, Wayne County Republicans appealed to the legislature to inaugurate the system in Detroit and its suburbs, but the senate narrowly shelved the plan. It was alleged that Senator McMillan blocked any legislation that would tamper with the Republican organization in his political base in Detroit.[38] The next legislature decided that the state's second largest city, Grand Rapids, was a more suitable locale for the

---

[34] *Journal of the Michigan House of Representatives, Session of 1897*, 2 vols. (Lansing, Mich., 1897), vol. 1, p. 64; *Journal of the Michigan House of Representatives, Session of 1899*, 2 vols. (Lansing, Mich., 1899), vol. 1, p. 60.

[35] *State Republican* (Lansing), Jan. 7, 1897, p. 1; *Evening Press* (Grand Rapids), Jan. 7, 1897, p. 1; *Adrian Daily*, Jan. 7, 1897; *Evening News* (Benton Harbor), Jan. 8, 1897. "The most charitable inference" that the Democratic *Detroit Free Press* could draw from the governor's proposal was that "having found in his own experience to what improper uses the caucus and convention can be put," he intended to make it "impracticable" for anybody else to follow his example. *DFP*, Jan. 8, 1897, p. 4.

[36] *DFP*, July 31, 1902, p. 2; *DEN*, May 25, 1905, p. 3.

[37] *DFP*, June 27, 1902, p. 2.

[38] A careful study of the Michigan scene maintains that many of the early supporters of the direct primary were hostile to the McMillan organization. See Stephen B. Sarasohn, "The Regulation of Parties and Nominations in Michigan" (Ph.D. diss., Columbia University, 1953), p. 83.

TABLE 6.3. *Landmark Legislation Introducing the Direct Primary, Michigan*

Year	Bill	Law	Description	Lower House				Senate			
				Vote "Yea"-"Nay"	Party Index of Like.	Eta² for Urban	Eta² for Comp.	Vote "Yea"-"Nay"	Party Index of Like.	Eta² for Urban	Eta² for Comp.
1899	H114		Direct primary for Wayne County local and legislative offices	52-28	97.2	.07	.01				
			To indefinitely postpone					13-12	X	.15	.13
1901	H46	292	Direct primary for Grand Rapids – city provides ballots	79-0				17-9	X	.01	.16
1901	H87		Direct primary for state offices – but with convention	64-14	92.3	.00	.07	BIC			
1901	H376		Direct primary for Wayne and Washtenaw counties	71-7				BIC			
			Motion to discharge from committee of whole	20-47	66.1	.01	.03				
1903	H1		Statewide direct primary	79-14	83.1	.02	.06				
			Making bill special order for next week	48-49	56.0	.02	.03				
			Amend bill to provide for an open primary	29-62	34.7	.01	.00				
			To substitute with a senate-drafted bill					21-9	X	.20	.09
			Passage of substitute bill					27-5	X	.04	.02

(continued)

TABLE 6.3 *(continued)*

				Lower House				Senate			
Year	Bill	Law	Description	Vote "Yea"-"Nay"	Party Index of Like.	Eta² for Urban	Eta² for Comp.	Vote "Yea"-"Nay"	Party Index of Like.	Eta² for Urban	Eta² for Comp.
1905	H184		To provide for a direct primary								
			Referring back to committee	52-41	X	.01	.00				
1905	H553		Direct primary for gov., lt. gov., and legislators	92-1							
			Adoption of substitute prepared by comm. of whole	53-42	X	.00	.00				
			Substituting senate bill								
			Motion to take bill out of special order	16-14	X	.07	.04	25-6	X	.04	.01
1905	S292	181	Direct primary for gov. and lt. gov., if they get 40% of vote	89-8	X	.01	.01	30-2			
			Amend to require 40% of vote instead of majority					24-8	X	.08	.25
			Amend to eliminate 40% requirement	27-68	X	.02	.00				
1905	S243		To provide for holding direct primary					25-6	X	.04	.01

Year	Bill	Description								
1907	H173	To regulate and protect primaries	74-7	X			16-16	X	.02	.09
		Amend to remove 40% requirement	48-37	X	.00	.01				
		Amend to require winner have 20% of votes	34-50	X	.00	.00				
		Amend to apply to all state officials	46-38	X	.03	.02				
		Amend to prohibit all but small photographs	38-40	X	.01	.00				
1909	S34 281	Direct primary for gov. and lt. gov. – no 40% requirement					21-5	X	.06	.00
		Amend to include U.S. Senate	79-12	X	.01	.03	17-9	X	.02	.05
		Amend to apply to all state elected officials					10-16	X	.04	.02
		Apply law to all local offices if voters so choose	37-45	X	.03	.02				
		Apply law to circuit judges if voters so choose	61-22	X	.00	.09				
		Amend to apply to all state elected officials	51-40	X	.00	.07				
		Passage of bill prepared by conf. comm.	72-4				27-4			

Abbreviations: BIC = Buried in Committee; X = Minority party constitutes fewer than 5 voting members.

experiment.[39] The *Grand Rapids Evening Press* welcomed the opportunity to apply direct nominations to local offices under a bill introduced by one of the city's state representatives. "Popular sentiment emphatically demands a reform in the primary elections," the *Press* allowed, "but the proposed abolition of conventions is so radical a departure from long established methods that conservative actions are advisable."[40] House Bill 46 required the city clerk to administer the party primaries by preparing the ballots, paying the election officials, and preparing the voting places. The arrangement of the voting places (with booths, railings, and ballot boxes) followed the format of the general election. Grand Rapids and surrounding Kent County recovered part of the costs by imposing a fifteen dollar filing fee on candidates. Registered voters were free to participate in any party's elections, a more "open" format than what state election laws mandated for indirect primaries elsewhere.[41] Without much ado, subsequent legislatures added three other heavily urban counties to the list: Wayne and Muskegon in 1903, and Alpena in 1905.[42]

The policy of introducing the primary for local offices on a county-by-county basis became official Republican doctrine in 1904. The Republican State Convention that year voted down a direct primary plank by 774 to 304. Delegates from the state's most urban counties (Wayne and Kent) strongly backed the proposal, while "the country delegates were almost a unit against reform." The party's platform finessed the issue by preaching the virtues of local autonomy: "We favor a general primary election law that will enable every municipal and political district in the state to decide for itself the method by which it shall nominate its candidates for public office and delegates to state conventions."[43] The 1905 legislature translated this sentiment into statute form.[44] It empowered counties to hold referendums to determine if a party's nominees for county, legislative, and

---

[39] Disappointed Wayne County Republicans went ahead with their own party-run direct primary for selecting local candidates, following a set of rules framed by a former Pingree lieutenant and labeled the "McLeod Plan." *DEN,* July 1, 1902, p. 2; Sarasohn, "Regulation of Parties . . . in Michigan," p. 101. Candidates running in the primary were assessed a fee representing 1 percent of the annual salary of the office sought.

[40] *Grand Rapids Evening Press,* Jan. 13, 1901, p. 4.

[41] The voter requested "the ballot of the political party with which he then and there states he is affiliated." *Michigan Local Acts,* 1901, No. 292, p. 52.

[42] These bills were passed without opposition in either chamber. *Michigan Local Acts,* 1903, Nos. 292 and 502, and 1905, No. 476, respectively. The four counties functioning with a direct primary for local offices by 1905 were among the state's seven most urban counties according to the 1900 census.

[43] *Niles Daily Star,* July 1, 1904, p. 2; *DFP,* May 18, 1904, p. 3; July 1, 1904, p. 2.

[44] *Michigan Public Acts,* 1905, No. 181, pp. 247–66.

even congressional offices should thereafter be selected in a primary. The greater appeal that direct nominations carried for the dominant party is evident in the decisions of local party organizations to avail themselves of the statute. By 1909, Republicans in fifty-eight of the state's eighty-three counties had adopted the system; Democrats employed the direct primary in only seventeen counties.[45] In short, the route the direct primary took in Michigan was through local initiatives touching on county or local rather than on statewide offices.

The appearance of the direct primary for statewide offices in Michigan owed largely to the success of the house of representatives in gradually wearing down opposition in the state senate. The League of Republican Clubs also played a role in popularizing the idea in party circles by citing the salutary effects of direct nominations on party unity.[46] It was partly through the league's efforts that two-thirds of the Republican county conventions endorsed the principle by 1903.[47] That year, a direct primary bill for all state offices passed overwhelmingly in the lower house but was killed in the upper chamber; the bill met its strongest opposition from senators representing rural constituencies.[48] By 1905, the senate had become reconciled to the expediency of a direct primary for governor and lieutenant governor. Senate Bill 292 was amended to require nomination by convention if winners in the statewide canvass garnered less than 40% of the vote. The house's attempt to eliminate the condition fell far short (27 to 68), and proponents of the direct nominations had to be satisfied with a partial victory.[49] When the House again took up the issue in 1907 (House Bill 173), it succeeded in lifting the 40% requirement and placed all statewide elected officials on the primary ballot. This bill failed in the senate on a tie vote. Two years later the senate retreated from the 40% proviso, but limited the law's applicability to the state's two principal executive officers and its U.S. senators. The house deferred

---

[45] *Journal of the Michigan House of Representatives, Session of 1909*, 2 vols. (Lansing, Mich., 1909), vol. 1, pp. 42–43. Minor political parties made even less use of the provision.

[46] *DFP*, June 22, 1902, p. 3.

[47] *DEN*, Jan. 10, 1903, p. 2.

[48] Senators voted in favor of substituting the house-passed bill with one addressing only certain abuses in the nominating system but retaining the convention. Those senators who opposed switching the bills came from counties that were 55.0 percent urban, while those who backed the motion came from counties that registered only 22.1 percent, hence the Eta^2 value of .20.

[49] The 40 percent minimum did not prevent the incumbent governor, Fred M. Warner, from winning renomination in 1906 and an unprecedented third term in 1908.

to the senate's wishes in the conference committee, and the choice of the state's two chief executives was finally taken entirely out of the hands of the state convention.[50]

Primary reform in Michigan was an almost exclusively Republican affair. The state's Democratic Party teetered on the edge of extinction after 1900. Much of the time Democrats occupied fewer than five of the one hundred seats in the lower house; in the senate the number of Democrats dropped from one in 1901 and 1903 to zero thereafter. During the time that Democrats had at least a minimal presence in the house (1899–1903), their voting records resembled those of their Republican colleagues.[51] The most partisan division in the legislature manifested itself in a failed effort by house Democrats to amend the 1903 bill to allow for an open primary. Democrats fought for their right to participate in Republican primaries, while the G.O.P. endeavored to keep them out. If, as some scholars have suggested, the direct primary undermined minority parties by making the primary of the majority party the decisive arena for political decision making, Michigan's Democrats were complicit in effecting their own demise.

During the first five legislative sessions to take up the direct primary in Michigan (1899–1907), the bills met the stiffest resistance from representatives from the Upper Peninsula. Here too opposition was based on very tangible political considerations. Beginning in 1896, the custom of Republican state conventions had been to award the lieutenant governorship to an Upper Peninsula man. Legislators from those parts worried that leaving the choice of lieutenant governor to the voters would bring an end to the practice. During the debate over the 1905 direct primary bill, a legislator tried to induce his colleagues to see the matter their way. "It is an advantage for us in the Upper Peninsula to have the office of lieutenant governor, since we can't have anything else.... We brought down 28% of the republican majority in the last election of republicans, and you in the lower peninsula have 90% of the population. For these reasons we demand some consideration."[52] Table 6.4 reveals the frosty reception the direct primary met once it crossed the Straits of Mackinac. The table

[50] *Michigan Public Acts*, 1909, No. 281, pp. 514–42.

[51] The 1902 state Democratic platform rated the need for a direct primary law as "imperative." *DFP*, Aug. 1, 1902, p. 10.

[52] *DEN*, May 25, 1905, p. 3. It was alleged that mining interests in the Upper Peninsula were especially eager to hold on to the office because the lieutenant governor served on the State Board of Equalization responsible for the very favorable taxation rates established for the industry. *DFP*, July 18, 1900, p. 5.

TABLE 6.4 *Roll Call Votes on Direct Primary Bills by Region, Michigan House and Senate, 1899–1909*

	Total Votes in Favor of Direct Primary	Total Votes Opposed to Direct Primary	Percentage Favorable
1899–1907			
House			
Upper Peninsula	19	45	29.7
Detroit/Grand Rapids	101	30	77.1
Lower Peninsula*	295	206	58.9
Senate			
Upper Peninsula	1	12	7.7
Detroit/Grand Rapids	24	4	85.7
Lower Peninsula*	53	51	51.0
1909			
House			
Upper Peninsula	21	11	65.6
Detroit/Grand Rapids	36	12	75.0
Lower Peninsula*	110	74	59.8
Senate			
Upper Peninsula	3	3	50.0
Detroit/Grand Rapids	12	3	80.0
Lower Peninsula*	33	24	57.9

*Not including Detroit or Grand Rapids.

aggregates a total of eleven roll calls in the house and eight in the senate and classifies the "yeas" and "nays" on various motions as indicative of either support for or opposition to a system of direct nominations.[53] The votes of legislators from the Upper Peninsula are contrasted with those of their peers from the state's two largest cities and those of the rest of the lower peninsula. Prior to 1909, less than one-third (29.7%) of the votes cast by Upper Peninsula house members supported some one of several direct primary bills. Senators from the region displayed even greater cohesion in voting down the proposition. Just as they feared, once the party's voters made the selections under the 1905 law, the Upper Peninsula's grip on the lieutenant governorship was broken; the post went to a candidate from Lansing in 1906 and again in 1908. Once deprived of this political

[53] All roll calls in Table 6.3 are included here except the final vote on passage of the senate substitute for House Bill 1 in 1903, since that was not a direct primary law. The previous motion adopting the substitute (which had the effect of killing the direct primary bill that originated in the house) is included.

plum, legislators from the Upper Peninsula had no vested interest in the convention system, and they came out in support of direct nominations during the 1909 session.

As in New Jersey, the principle of direct nominations was championed in the Great Lakes State by urban legislators. Table 6.4 displays the voting patterns of senators and representatives from the state's two largest cities. Legislators from Detroit and Grand Rapids endorsed the direct primary by a ratio of 3 to 1 or better across the time periods.[54] Rural legislators contended that their urban counterparts championed the direct primary for reasons other than a devotion to democratic process. "Should this bill become a law," one representative from the Upper Peninsula predicted, "Detroit, Grand Rapids and one or two other cities in the lower peninsula could and would dominate state politics." One rural representative depicted the contest as a blatant power play: "When one class of voters resides within a few minutes walk of the polls while the other must come by team from one to ten miles, the conditions are too unequal for anyone to contend that farmers, miners and lumbermen can protect themselves, or that candidates for state offices in rural areas could have a possible show of success.... Will a farmer or group of farmers stop a threshing machine in order to drive ten miles to participate in a primary election? The promoters know that they will not. Hence their activity in its advocacy."[55] Table 6.4 neatly demarcates the battle lines over the direct primary in Michigan. Senators and representatives from the Upper Peninsula stood on one side, and those representing the state's largest cities occupied the other. Or, to put the matter more simply, the table reveals the division between those who expected to forfeit power under a system of direct nominations and those who planned to gain.

Like California, Colorado only belatedly interested itself in the direct primary, but the Centennial State enacted the reform almost as swiftly. As early as 1903, Democratic governor James B. Orman urged the legislature to produce "a primary law which shall put the nominating power solely in the hands of the people."[56] While Republicans evaded the issue of

---

[54] The Eta² values in Table 6.3 and the binary logistic regression results in Table B.3 in the Appendix concur that the urbanization index was not very helpful in separating the direct primary's supporters from its opponents. The suggestion is that while legislators from Detroit and Grand Rapids embraced the reform, those from the state's smaller cities often did not.

[55] *DEN*, Mar. 26, 1903, p. 1.

[56] *Colorado Senate Journal*, 1903, p. 84. Orman favored a law modeled on Minnesota's statutes. The outgoing governor had been denied renomination to a second term.

direct nominations, the Democrats endorsed the principle in their state platforms beginning in 1906.[57] The 1908 elections left Democrats with preponderant influence in the house, a safe majority in the senate, and the governorship.[58] Legislators who arrived in Denver in 1909 were prepared to invest voters with final authority for selecting their parties' nominees. Identical bills, drafted by future U.S. senator Edward P. Costigan of the Direct Primary League, appeared in the house (Bill 2) and the senate (Bill 14).[59] The league's draft mandated a closed primary.[60]

The issue that would give rise to much legislative bickering in the months to come involved a provision allowing party conventions to vote on candidates prior to the direct primary. New York governor Charles Evans Hughes had recently proposed institutionalizing pre-primary conventions in his draft of a direct primary law; this may have been the inspiration for their appearance in House Bill 282.[61] Officially, the so-called assemblies were to endorse no one. The single roll call taken on the candidates vying for a specific office would determine whose names would automatically appear on the primary ballot and in what order. There were those, like the *Rocky Mountain News*, who insisted that "A primary law so framed that a convention comes between the voters and the candidates is no primary law at all."[62] House Democrats concurred in this sentiment and House Bill 282 was exiled back to committee (see Table 6.5). When House Bill 2 reached the senate, however, it was amended to put the assemblies back in.[63] The house refused to accept the senate's amendments on a close vote (29 to 34). This key house vote exposed

---

[57] *DP*, Sept. 13, 1906, p. 6; *RMN* Sept. 9, 1908, p. 4. The closest the Republican state platform came to expressing an opinion on the matter was in 1908: "We favor the enactment of a primary elections law." *RMN*, Sept. 13, 1908, p. 3.

[58] Labor strife combined with a disputed gubernatorial election in 1904 represented a major political distraction in mid-decade. They probably explain why the first direct primary bill to get serious consideration did not appear until 1909. For historical background, see Carl Abbott, *Colorado: A History of the Centennial State* (Boulder, Colo., 1976), pp. 132–35, 202.

[59] *RMN*, Jan. 28, 1909, p. 14. After House Bill 2 appeared in the upper house, Senate Bill 14 was dropped at the request of its sponsor.

[60] *RMN*, Mar. 1, 1909, p. 1. The league denounced bills that were less rigorous in this respect – such as House Bill 282.

[61] Charles A. Beard, "The Direct Primary Movement in New York," *Proceedings of the American Political Science Association* 7 (1910): 192.

[62] *RMN*, Feb. 26, 1909, p. 12; Feb. 28, 1909, p. 14. The *News* also put it more graphically: "[T]he convention system is an excrescence on the direct primary." Feb. 19, 1909, p. 14.

[63] The amendment was made during the deliberations of the committee of the whole (which are not officially transcribed), and the breakdown on the vote was taken from *RMN*, Mar. 19, 1909, p. 1.

TABLE 6.5 *Landmark Legislation Introducing the Direct Primary, Colorado*

				Lower House				Senate			
Year	Bill	Law	Description	Vote "Yea"-"Nay"	Party Index of Like.	Eta² for Urban	Eta² for Comp.	Vote "Yea"-"Nay"	Party Index of Like.	Eta² for Urban	Eta² for Comp.
1909	H282		Direct primary								
			Motion to strike out enacting clause	25-27	X	.04	.01				
			Referring back to committee	39-11	X	.07	.07				
1909	S14		Direct primary	54-4							
			Making bill special order					22-10	82.5	.03	.00
1909	H2		Direct primary								
			Motion to move bill to front of calendar	45-8	68.0	.05	.07				
			Passage with amendments					22-13	81.7	.00	.01
			Concurring with senate amendments	29-34	34.6	.02	.19				
			Motion to table reconsideration of bill					19-16	66.7	.01	.04
1910	H2	4	Direct primary with assemblies to nominate candidates	47-8	43.9	.00	.12				
			Passage with amendments	44-8	44.3	.01	.06				
			House insists on its version – asks conf. comm.					18-9	5.3	.00	.01
			Passage of conf. comm. bill	55-4				20-6	23.1	.05	.03

Abbreviations: X = Minority party constitutes fewer than 5 voting members.

an underlying division within that body. The legislator responsible for introducing House Bill 2 had been a candidate for speaker, and all the Democratic members who voted for him subsequently followed his lead in opposing the senate revisions; Democrats who voted for his rival split down the middle (17 "yea" and 16 "nay"). This may only confirm one senator's assertion that "personal animosity . . . is at the root of the trouble."[64] A conference committee could not resolve the differences between the legislative chambers when the hundred-day time limit on the session expired.

Democratic governor John F. Shafroth called the legislature back into special session during the fall of 1910. He demanded that the Democratic platform pledges of 1908 be redeemed, including those pertaining to the direct primary.[65] Once again, the house and senate squared off over the propriety of holding party conventions in conjunction with a system of direct nominations. Eventually, house Democrats bowed to the will of the upper house, and the assemblies became a feature of the state's new direct primary system.[66] Party divisions widened in 1910 (evidenced by the Index of Likeness), perhaps only because the legislature was meeting just weeks before the general election.[67] The workings of House Bill 2, however, were eminently bipartisan. The state-administered direct primary was a prerogative of the major parties alone. A provision limited its application to parties that had secured 10 percent of the vote in the previous election – in a state that had long lent support to powerful third-party insurgencies. The narrowly bipartisan character of the bill was reflected in the comments of one legislator who "declared that there was no such thing as an independent voter. His heart was with some one party. He might get dissatisfied over the result of some convention but still deep in his heart he was a party man."[68]

---

[64] *RMN*, Jan. 6, 1909, p. 1; Mar. 14, 1909, p. 1.

[65] The legislature sat in session while the Democratic State Convention met; Shafroth secured renomination by the convention in the face of formidable opposition from his home delegation in Denver. *RMN*, Sept. 16, 1910, p. 2. The *News* insisted that Denver's Democratic organization, led by Mayor Robert W. Speer, was responsible for opposition to the bill. But there is no relationship at the county level between support for House Bill 2 in either house and the opposition Shafroth faced in the 1910 state convention, which the *News* also associated with the "Speer machine."

[66] *Colorado Statutes* (1910), Chap. 4, pp. 15–44.

[67] Republicans in the senate voted unanimously against the legislation, as did most of their colleagues in the house. But the key division in the 1910 legislature was that separating the house and senate Democrats over the status of assemblies.

[68] *RMN*, Feb. 18, 1909, p. 1.

Partisanship and bicameral bickering marked the progress of direct primary legislation in Denver. Unlike elsewhere, urban/rural divisions did not much manifest themselves in the lineup over House Bill 2. Two-party competition, however, did play a modest role in house roll calls – though not in the senate. Legislators from competitive districts were responsible for the house's refusal to bow to senate amendments in 1909.[69] Nonetheless, the impact of competition was limited to one house, while partisanship more nearly held sway in the other. In both chambers it was the G.O.P. that stood firmly committed to pre-primary assemblies. When house Democrats divided on whether to accept the senate amendments in 1909, they revealed a geographic and possibly an ethnic dimension to the controversy. All but one of the eighteen Democrats who voted to go along with the senate's pre-primary assemblies came from either Denver or the southern portion of the state. The latter were regions where Hispanic influence was greatest, and it may be that representatives of the state's minority voters feared losing some political clout in the absence of conventions.[70] Possibly these politicians understood that the demands of a balanced ticket offered one of the few avenues for public office for minorities, but, alas, the legislative record is silent on the matter. Any consideration of the statistical evidence for Colorado should bear in mind that the division was mainly over whether a primary should be preceded by assemblies; no significant bloc of legislators endorsed the status quo.[71]

[69] Analysis of only the Democratic legislators who divided 18 "yea" to 34 "nay" in 1909 on whether to go along with the senate bill produces an even higher Eta² of .34 – and it is the Democrats from the competitive counties who are voting in the negative. These results accord with those derived from the binary logistic regression results appearing in Table B.4 of Appendix B.

[70] In neighboring New Mexico, one of three states that resisted the allure of direct nominations for several decades, opposition was said to originate from "the Spanish American cultural group" who feared the measure "would lessen their political influence." Thomas C. Donnelly, "New Mexico: An Area of Conflicting Cultures," in *Rocky Mountain Politics*, ed. Thomas C. Donnelly (Albuquerque, N.Mex., 1940), p. 238. Southern Colorado here encompasses the county of Kiowa and below; the lone exception was a legislator from the far western county of Garfield. The three Hispanic-surnamed legislators (Amador and Garcia in the house, and Barela in the senate) all supported the pre-primary convention.

[71] Only two other states joined Colorado in writing a pre-primary convention into their election statutes at this time. In later years the system would be credited with allowing party organizations to hand a nomination to one of their favorites. One scholar reported in 1940 that victory in the state convention "virtually amounts to securing the state nomination" in the subsequent primary. See Roy E. Brown, "Colorful Colorado: A State of Varied Industries," in Donnelly, *Rocky Mountain Politics*, pp. 74–75. The same was also said to be true for more local offices. However, just because other state laws did not

In each of the states under review, legislation proposing to abolish the convention system met with more opposition than had past measures proposing merely to regulate it. The divisive roll calls in the four states aligned along two dimensions. The first was a partisan one that found Democrats more in sympathy with the new system for making nominations. One characteristic shared by Democrats in all four states was a higher frequency of contested delegations at their state conventions compared to the Republicans (see Figures 4.4 and 4.5). Nationally, Democrats acquired a reputation for being a more disorganized, contentious, and diverse coalition in the 1920s, and the characterization may have been applicable at the state level well before then.[72] Caucuses and conventions were more likely to sow discord among Democrats. Along its second axis, the direct primary divided urban and rural legislators in Michigan and New Jersey, and to a lesser degree in California. Candidates for statewide office in these states had already converted the indirect primaries in the major municipalities into direct ones by putting forward slates of delegates pledged to themselves. Additionally, in many urban areas voters already selected their candidates for local offices through party-run primaries. In rural areas, where the sparsely attended "office caucus" reigned and where state races mattered little, the system did not appear to be in need of repair. Rural residents in New Jersey and California did not much like the more formalized voting arrangements imposed on them by the new primary laws.[73] Most importantly, it was widely anticipated that candidates from urban areas would reap the benefits of a statewide direct primary. The apportionment of state conventions favored sparsely populated counties, and some feared that the turnout rate in rural areas would fall below that of the cities. Rural areas could not even hope to secure some lesser office as a consolation prize, as was the practice in the state convention. Democratic and urban legislators both embraced direct nominations as a system to better regulate and contain competition within their ranks. Opponents of direct nomination vocalized concern over party

mention pre-primary conventions did not mean that they were not held. It was reported in 1923 that the major parties organized pre-primary nominating conventions in about ten of the eighteen states that officially provided only for conventions after the primary. See Schuyler C. Wallace, "Pre-Primary Conventions," *Annals of the American Academy of Political and Social Science* 106 (Mar. 1923): 99. Official post-primary conventions mainly framed platforms and appointed party officials.

[72] David Burner, *The Politics of Provincialism: The Democratic Party in Transition, 1918–1932* (New York, 1967).

[73] "Charles A. Spier vs. Robert Baker et al." (1898), 120 Cal 370, p. 372; *Sussex Register*, Sept. 12, 1907, p. 4.

organization and responsibility, but many worried most about the threat it posed to their political careers.

Legislators moved cautiously in replacing a long-standing convention system with a novel electoral process, and the route they chose reveals again the practical considerations at work. In the two states that got an early start on revamping the nomination process (Michigan and New Jersey), legislators first applied the system to local offices before moving on to the state level. The debilitating effects of internal party warfare were more in evidence in local races than in state or congressional ones. It was far easier for a maverick candidate to mount a challenge for the state legislature than for governor. Statistical analysis of split ticket voting suggests that voters were more likely to scratch the ticket on local offices than for governor or president.[74] If a major purpose of the direct primary was to bring order to a disorderly process, the need was greatest at the local level. "Anyone familiar with local politics in this part of the state must testify that some of the rottenest of corrupt conventions have been those called to make county tickets,"[75] one Michigan newspaper opined in endorsing primaries for local offices. The objections of rural legislators that a primary for governor would reduce their influence did not apply when the office in question was county clerk or state assemblyman. Politicians preferred a step-by-step approach to refashioning the nomination process. This caution did not win them many plaudits from independent newspapers and organizations, but then their critics were not up for reelection.

Highlighting the instances when legislators lined up on opposite sides of a roll call should not distract attention from the many instances when they worked in unison. Much of the most important legislation bearing on the nomination process moved through the state legislatures with hardly any opposition. Occasionally, legislation was stalled by competing bills that all aimed to abolish the nominating convention but worked in different ways: this one envisioning a closed primary or that one including the U.S. Senate among the offices to be voted on. Once they had an opportunity to see the system in action, partisan-minded senators and assemblymen realized how it could shore up the major parties. Candidates defeated in the primary forfeited their right to run for the office in California.

---

[74] See the discussion accompanying Tables 4.1 and 4.2, and John F. Reynolds and Richard L. McCormick, "Outlawing 'Treachery': Split Tickets and Ballot Laws in New York and New Jersey, 1880–1914," *Journal of American History* 72 (Mar. 1986): 840–46.
[75] *DEN*, May 27, 1903, p. 1.

In New Jersey and Michigan, a party registration system coerced independent voters back into party ranks if they hoped to have a voice in the candidate selection process. California required candidates to endorse the party platform before certifying them as nominees. Colorado's law virtually excluded third parties from its provisions, making the primary a strictly Democratic or Republican institution.[76] Reformers had long maintained that the direct primary posed no threat to the major parties. State legislators eventually came to the same conclusion.

III

Like many electoral reforms past and those to come, the direct primary proved to be a disappointment to its most avid supporters. Doubts about the efficacy of the new laws arose as early as 1910. Low voter turnout mocked the reformers' image of a public-spirited John Q. Citizen impatient to make his voice heard. Few anticipated the post party period's mode of campaigning based on expensive electioneering practices that relied ever more on advertising to reach a distracted public. "We seem to assume that the voters . . . could and would, always and readily name by acclamation, the man of their choice," wrote Charles J. Bonaparte in 1909. The former president of the National Municipal League now dismissed that notion as fatuous. Bonaparte and others developed a new appreciation for the boss's "laborious and unpleasant duties." He and his henchmen engaged in work that "will be simply left undone if entrusted to the people at large."[77] More troubling still was the mounting evidence that political machines had used the device to further entrench themselves in power. "Talk about the people making nominations," grumbled one Iowa newspaper in 1910, "why the politicians already control the machinery more than they did under the old caucus system, and they are only kindergartners in the business as yet."[78] "Experience with the direct primary . . . has brought disillusionment," wrote a political scientist from

[76] A 1909 law also established a system of state funding of political parties at the rate of twenty-five cents for every vote cast for a party's gubernatorial candidate. *Colorado Statutes*, No. 141, pp. 303–5.

[77] Charles J. Bonaparte, "An Elective Boss," *Outlook*, Dec. 4, 1909, p. 773; Henry Jones Ford, "The Direct Primary," *North American Review* 190 (July 1909): 1–14; Issac M. Brickner, "Direct Primaries Versus Boss Rule," *Arena* 41 (Aug. 1909): 550–56; Arthur Wallace Dunn, "The Direct Primary: Promise and Performance," *Review of Reviews* 46 (Oct. 1912): 439–45.

[78] F. E. Horack, "Primary Elections in Iowa," *Proceedings of the American Political Science Association* 7 (1910): 185.

Michigan in 1916. "The system is not popular, it has serious shortcomings, and there is at present no serious demand for its further extension."[79] By World War I, enthusiasm for direct nominations had burned itself out across the country. During the 1920s, when political exposés denounced the enormous sums required to win a primary, a brief backlash induced three states to return to the convention system.[80] Despite the disappointment and negative publicity that it aroused, the direct primary remained a fixture of American politics. A cohort of politicians had come to power through its mechanisms and they had no incentive to return to the convention system. If direct nominations chastened those who placed so much confidence in the electorate, the system did address the needs of the hustling candidates who placed it on the statute books.

Opponents of the direct primary often condemned the system because of the type of candidates who flourished in its wake. "From the unanimous testimony, I have received, in Western States," President Jacob Gould Schurman of Cornell University complained, "I learned that the system of direct nominations, discourages self respecting and independent men from entering the public service and encourages the demagogue, the self advertiser and the reckless and unscrupulous soldier of fortune." The direct primary, he continued, "puts a premium on passing popularity. The man who trims his sails to catch the breeze of popular favor will secure the nomination." "The direct primary says that party is nothing," one Idaho politico sneered, "the man is everything."[81] Scholarly opinion in later years would echo these charges by associating the reform with the rise of a more candidate-centered electoral environment.[82] Contemporary

---

[79] Arthur C. Millspaugh, "The Operation of the Direct Primary in Michigan," *American Political Science Review* 10 (Nov. 1916): 725–26.

[80] *Literary Digest*, June 17, 1922, p. 10; July 10, 1926, pp. 10–11. Alan Ware, *The American Direct Primary: Party Institutionalization and Transformation in the North* (Cambridge, U.K., 2002), pp. 227–54; *Outlook*, Sept. 1, 1926, p. 8; Charles Edward Merriam, Harold F. Gosnell, and Louise Overacker, *Primary Elections* (Chicago, 1928), pp. 94–107. Merriam et al. note that this reassessment of the direct primary was confined to the northern states; in the South the white primary system more fully met the expectations of its proponents by acting as a disfranchising device. See also Dunn, "Promise and Performance."

[81] Brickner, "Direct Primaries," p. 553; Boyd A. Martin, *The Direct Primary in Idaho* (New York, 1947), p. 22.

[82] See David B. Truman, "Party Reform, Party Atrophy, and Constitutional Change: Some Reflections," *Political Science Quarterly* 99 (Winter 1984–85): 637–55; James J. Connolly, *The Triumph of Ethnic Progressivism: Urban Political Culture in Boston, 1900–1925* (Cambridge, Mass., 1998), pp. 81–82, 105–7; Martin Shefter, *Political Parties and the State: The American Historical Experience* (Princeton, N.J., 1993), pp. 76–81.

political commentators correctly understood that a new breed of politician was emerging at the turn of the century. They supposed that structural changes in the nomination process were responsible for the changes in candidate behavior. This survey of the last thirty years of the convention system suggests that the relationship between the independent and dependent variables was more nearly the reverse of what was and is commonly supposed.

The direct primary – and the laws seeking to control campaign expenditures, and the direct election of U.S. senators – were responses to the challenge posed by a new generation of aggressive elective office seekers. Around 1900, candidates in New Jersey, Michigan, Colorado, and California carved out a larger role for themselves in the nominating process. During the Gilded Age, a successful gubernatorial nominee could make his case with the assistance of a few friends and the postal service. Over time, candidates became more visible and vocal at conventions. These nominating bodies became less deliberative as roll calls on nominations became less competitive and the convention sessions shorter. The ticket's "headliners" – such as the party's gubernatorial nominee at a state convention – increasingly dominated the proceedings. Candidates gained control over the convention by electing loyal delegates in the primaries and county conventions. Landing a nomination after 1900 required travel to greet delegates and voters, oratorical skills, and even advertising. These new rituals of democracy were already in evidence when it came to local offices during the 1880s. Many of the more proactive gubernatorial aspirants had mastered the necessary skills by running for lesser offices such as mayor (Newark's James M. Seymour and Detroit's Hazen S. Pingree) or congressman (Denver's John F. Shafroth). From the standpoint of the hustling candidate, moreover, the convention system was an uncertain and rickety device. The complex and multilayered nomination process – running from primaries to county and then state conventions – offered too many opportunities for manipulation and consequent controversy and disaffection. Candidates could never be entirely sure that the delegates they enlisted and elected would not desert them at some stage of the convoluted nominating process.

Direct primary laws represented one of a series of measures taken by the major parties to bring more order to their proceedings. An increasingly contentious set of primaries and county conventions posed a major challenge for Democrats and Republicans alike. The convention system was designed to promote party harmony through negotiation and trade. It was ill suited to referee a political knockdown fight in a caucus, primary, or convention. In frustration, partisans turned to state regulation of the indirect primary, with laws to curb fraud and monitor the voting process. Early efforts at defining fraudulent practices in party functions and setting more uniform procedures for running the primaries set the parties on the path to the direct primary. Governor Emanuel L. Philipp lauded the steady progress Wisconsin had made in regulating nominations by law long before Robert M. La Follette popularized the direct primary. "No platform pledges had been made to reform the primaries; no campaigns had been conducted in the interests of such a reform; no public demand made through the newspapers had furnished the inspiration or pointed the way; no meetings were held; no bands were employed to please or torture the public ear." Philipp attributed the expansion in state regulation over the nomination process to "the impossibility of continuing to do party business in an orderly manner in mass caucuses in congested municipal wards.... No reasonable man can doubt for an instant that, had this movement been permitted to continue, there would have been a steady and gradual improvement in the primary laws."[83]

Greater regulation of political parties and of the electoral process in general during the Progressive Era was accomplished by those who stood the most to gain under the new rules of the game. Legislators in New Jersey, Michigan, Colorado, and California endorsed much of the most important legislation with hardly any dissent. Only senators and assemblymen representing sparsely settled districts mounted a spirited defense of the convention system. They could see that the advantages afforded rural areas through the apportionment of a state convention and its concern over a geographically balanced ticket would disappear under a system of direct nominations.[84] Urban politicians could embrace the direct primary as a mechanism that would increase their clout in the nomination process.[85] Third parties and independent candidates were largely frozen outside the process, and it was hoped that the new nominating

---

[83] Emanuel L. Philipp, *Political Reform in Wisconsin* (Madison, Wis., 1973), p. 10.

[84] John D. Buenker uncovered a similar axis of opposition in New England. See Buenker, "The Politics of Resistance: The Rural-Based Yankee Republican Machines of Connecticut and Rhode Island," *New England Quarterly* 47 (June 1974): 212–37. Ware finds a like division evident in Massachusetts but takes less note of it elsewhere. Ware, *American Direct Primary*, p. 136.

[85] Ware, *American Direct Primary*. See also John D. Buenker, "The Mahatma and Progressive Reform: Martin Lomasney as Lawmaker, 1911–17," *New England Quarterly* 44 (Sept. 1971): 397–419.

procedures would render them obsolete. Many charged that the most prominent supporters of the direct primary were those who saw it as the surer path to elective office. Direct nominations advantaged seasoned elective office seekers and incumbents in particular. The new laws gave candidates authority to draft a platform and appoint party officials.[86] Once in power, elected officials found their influence much enhanced under the new regime. Complaints of "executive usurpation" found expression in legislatures in New Jersey, Colorado and elsewhere, manifesting a more activist executive branch at the state as well as at the national levels.[87] Incumbency became a far more formidable weapon at the turn of the century. The term limits informally imposed on state officers in Colorado, California, or Michigan no longer applied once the decision was in the hands of voters. "Under this primary law it is practically impossible to defeat the governor in office for nomination if he uses his office to renominate himself," one Illinois politician averred in 1912.[88]

Direct nominations represented a shift in power within the party structure that benefited the parties' officeholders at the expense of their rank-and-file loyalists. It pitted the party in office against the party organization. Much of the impetus of electoral reform at the turn of the century amounted to "cutting out the middleman" in the person of delegates, ticket peddlers, and state legislators who appointed U.S. senators.[89] The direct primary went furthest in this respect by eliminating the delegates, the largest and most visible segment of "the organization." The convention system required that all parties operate with a sizable, if ephemeral, officialdom. Democrats, Republicans, Populists, and Prohibitionists recruited extensively among the electorate to staff nominating bodies for a multitude of political subdivisions. Conventions embodied the party itself; in word and action they affirmed that it was the needs of the party that came first – not those of any particular candidate. Voters singled out persons of standing in the community to represent them at party functions during the Gilded Age. Once candidates made themselves the center of attention the delegates lost status as well as their raison d'être. As candidates gained mastery over the convention they undermined its

[86] Thomas R. Pegram, *Partisans and Progressives: Private Interest and Public Policy in Illinois, 1870–1922* (Urbana, Ill., 1992), pp. 220–21; John W. Lederle and Rita Feiler Aid, "Michigan State Party Chairmen, 1882–1956," *Michigan History* 41 (Sept. 1957): 257–68.

[87] Shefter, *Political Parties and the State*, p. 79; Truman, "Party Reform," p. 645.

[88] Pegram, *Partisans and Progressives*, p. 170.

[89] Connolly, *Ethnic Progressivism*, p. 133.

ability to function as a deliberative body or as an honest broker between contesting factions. Weak party organizations of the American model were not well situated to block legislation putting an end to the convention system had they even cared to.[90] Many if not most organization men, especially those in urban areas, had concluded that the system was broken and could not be fixed. State, county, and local party conventions voted to put themselves out of business by endorsing the principle of direct nominations.

The effort to accommodate the hustling candidate entailed, as well, enhancing the role of a more engaged electorate. Voters had not been well served by the nomination process in place during the 1880s.[91] It was difficult locating the poorly advertised and hastily arranged caucuses and primaries. Those voters who did show up often found that local factions had negotiated away their differences and drawn up a single, consensus slate. Even when electors had options in their choice of delegates, it was usually not clear how their votes would influence party decisions down the road. Little wonder that few citizens troubled themselves with these preliminary party functions. Some were content to leave the duty of appointing delegates entirely in the hands of the county committee. Once candidates openly sought to use primaries and caucuses to elect their delegations, however, voters took more interest in the proceedings. During the 1890s, parties had to oblige the voters and the candidates by opening the indirect primary up to more electoral input. They formalized the process (especially in the shift from the caucus to the primary); they better publicized and coordinated the proceedings (by arranging for all voting to be done on the same day and time); and they expanded both the hours for voting and the number of places where it could be done. Allowing voters to mark their choice for a nominee rather than for a delegate took the process to its next logical step. In this respect, the interests of the voters, the candidates, and perhaps democracy itself were arguably better served by the direct primary.[92] Consequently, the movement to abolish the

---

[90] Truman, "Party Reform," p. 647.

[91] On this point, one study of the nominating process in selected towns during the Gilded Age agrees: Glenn C. Altschuler and Stuart M. Blumin, *Rude Republic: Americans and Their Politics in the Nineteenth Century* (Princeton, N.J., 2000), pp. 218–25. See also Connolly, *Ethnic Progressivism*, pp. 30–35; Philip J. Ethington, *The Public City: The Political Construction of Urban Life in San Francisco, 1850–1900* (Cambridge, U.K., 1994), pp. 71–72; Robert W. Cherney, *American Politics in the Gilded Age* (Wheeling, Ill., 1997), pp. 6–8.

[92] Yet, it is legitimate to wonder if voters were well served with ballots the size of a sheet of newspaper and two tiers of elections instead of one.

nominating convention enjoyed a measure of support among the public, but whatever enthusiasm or fervor the citizenry displayed was whipped up by the party in office.

Working in tandem with party regulars seeking to put their houses in order were the reformers. These members of the "better element" entertained no conspicuous interest in making a career of elective office. Few in their ranks desired to do the major parties any harm, but they were not primarily interested in "curing the mischiefs of faction." Reformers demanded "the freest, fullest and most convenient method in expressing [the people's] will,"[93] at least among those they viewed as respectable citizens. They desired to participate in the nomination process without "encountering a crowd, or being hustled or jostled by intoxicated men." They supposed that the direct primary would topple a political oligarchy represented by the boss and the machine. What most clearly distinguished the reform from the partisan mentality was the former's vision of a politically charged electorate (at least among the ranks of its "better citizens"). They saw a voting public that was, in Walter Lippmann's formulation, "at once omniscient and disinterested."[94] Many expected, at a minimum, to see an outpouring of good citizens at the polls to throw the rascals out. Few anticipated that so many otherwise good citizens would be so easily swayed by advertising or an ingratiating smile or perhaps would neglect to vote at all. Peter Finley Dunne's Mr. Dooley lampooned the earnest reformer-politician who imagined that he had won public office on the basis of his resume, when in fact:

He's ilicted because th' people don't know him an' do know th' other la-ad, because Mrs. Casey's oldest boy was clubbed by a polisman, because we cudden't get wather about th' third story wan day, because the Flannigans bought a piano, because we was near run over be a mail wagon, because th' saloons are open Sundah night, because they're not open all day.... Th' rayformer don't know this. He thinks you an' me, Hinnissy, has been watchin' his spotless career f'r twinty years, and that we've read all he had to say on the evils if pop'lar sufferage befure the S'ciety f'r th' Bewildermint iv th' Poor.[95]

An unbounded and unfounded faith in the electorate's interest and sophistication in matters political underlay a variety of electoral reforms of this era: the blanket ballot, voter registration, nonpartisan elections, and the

---

[93] Philipp, *Political Reform*, p. 7; *TTA*, Feb. 22, 1911, p. 1.
[94] Quoted in Leon D. Epstein, *Political Parties in the American Mold* (Madison, Wis., 1986), p. 16.
[95] *SFE*, Aug. 10, 1902, p. 2.

preferential primary.[96] The reform element would be among those most disappointed with the direct primary. But their influence was never such that they could compel the parties to undo what was done – if indeed reformers had anything to offer in its place.

Reformers, politicians, and the public endorsed regulation of political parties because of the special status these organizations occupied in the American political system. The nation's republican ideology disposed politicians and the public to view political parties in a different light from their modern-day or European conception. From the outset, Americans viewed the Democratic and Whig/Republican organizations not as classical political science would have it – representatives of particular constituencies or interests – but as embodiments of public sentiment. Americans of the party period were never comfortable with the notion of a party system of competing interests. Democrats and Republicans shared the notion that the proper role of the political party was to give expression to an overarching public opinion, protect the common good, and fend off special interests or "class legislation."[97] With each campaign, Democrats and Republicans quarreled over which of them represented "the people" and which "a greedy band of place seekers." The propriety of government oversight of institutions with so obvious a public purpose was never seriously in question in the Gilded Age. Hence, when bills appeared on the legislative calendar outlawing vote fraud in primaries or setting the hours of voting, few – inside or outside the legislative chambers – objected on the principle of laissez-faire. The major parties' quasi-public status, which preceded the direct primary, reflected a general perception of the political party as the embodiment of public opinion rather than as an aggregation of interests.

Achieving semiofficial status did not come without some cost for the major political parties. They were no longer in need of their organizational or electoral base to organize or to attend party functions or to engage in the mobilization campaigns of old. The public's ardor for the Democratic or Republican brands cooled noticeably, setting the stage for the much attenuated party systems of the twentieth century. Herbert Croly, the Progressive movement's prophet, recognized the trade-off inherent in regulating political parties. Unlike most Americans of his day, Croly persisted

---

[96] Reynolds, *Testing Democracy*, pp. 117–26; Robert H. Wiebe, *Self-Rule: A Cultural History of American Democracy* (Chicago, 1995), pp. 176–77.

[97] Ethington, *Public City*, p. 306; Elizabeth S. Clemens, *The People's Lobby: Organizational Innovation and the Rise of Interest Group Politics in the United States* (Chicago, 1997), p. 171.

in viewing the political party as "essentially a voluntary association" among persons with mutual interests. When controversy or dissension arose within the ranks, the appropriate response was for the organization to disband. "By regulating it and by forcing it to select its leaders in a certain way," he warned, "the state is sacrificing the valuable substance of party loyalty and allegiance to the mere mechanism of partisan association.... [Direct primaries] will make it more necessary for every voter to belong nominally to one of the two dominant parties; but the increasing importance of a formal allegiance will be accompanied by diminishing community of spirit and purpose. Such is the absurd and contradictory result of legalizing and regularizing a system of partisan government."[98] But Croly spoke up much too late. By the time he published his unorthodox view of the matter (1914), all but four states already had direct primary laws in place. If the Democratic and Republican labels lost some measure of popular appeal, the direct primary (along with the ballot laws) preserved their status as the oldest surviving political parties among Western democracies.

Placed in its historical context, the direct primary did not mark a pivotal point of departure in the nation's political development. America's "cadre-based" political parties were born with a weak organizational backbone relative to their European counterparts. The direct primary accentuated the dissimilarities by doing away with the one institution – the convention – that most nearly epitomized the party organization. Power within American political parties historically gravitated to those holding government office. "[T]he major political party is the creature of the politicians, the ambitious office seeker and office holder," writes the political scientist John H. Aldrich. "They have created and maintained, used or abused, reformed or ignored the political party when doing so has furthered their goals and ambitions."[99] Decades before the direct primary appeared on the books, the authors of the Constitution devised an electoral college whose function prefigured the role of the nominating convention. The nation's "wise men" would furnish the names of worthy men to serve as the nation's chief executive, leaving the final choice to Congress if a majority of presidential electors had not settled on a single individual. Within a short time, the very men who invented the electoral college reined in its independence to insure the election of their preferred party

---

[98] Herbert Croly, *Progressive Democracy* (New York, 1914), p. 343.
[99] John H. Aldrich, *Why Parties? The Origin and Transformation of Political Parties in America* (Chicago, 1995), p. 4.

slate.[100] The next generation of national leaders fashioned a new party system (incorporating the convention) to advance the political careers of prominent national figures. Two generations later, it was again the parties' officeholders who dumped the convention to make way for the direct primary. By the 1960s, the national or presidential convention was subverted by the same candidate-dominated dynamic that had done away with the state convention. None of these transitions should be seen as a radical break in the nation's electoral system. Instead, by constantly redesigning the nomination process to suit the interests of the hustling candidate, the direct primary and other electoral reforms fashioned a distinctly American political tradition.

[100] Richard P. McCormick, *The Presidential Game: The Origins of American Presidential Politics* (New York, 1982).

APPENDIX A

Collective Biographies of State Delegates

In the near total absence of official records of convention proceedings, local newspapers furnished the list of state delegates.[1] Information on occupations appeared in city directories published in the same year as the state convention.[2] Directories published the year after the state convention were consulted for delegates who were not found in the previous edition. Some names appeared without an occupation. In about half these cases, a directory published two or four years earlier revealed an occupation that was the one assigned for this study. Individuals traced back in earlier directories had to retain the same address. Persons with "No Occupation" in Figures 2.3 and 2.4 and Tables 3.1, 3.2 and 3.3 either had no occupation listed in the directory over a period of four years or, more commonly, could not be located in the earlier editions.

When the names appearing in each source exactly match, as they do in most instances, record linkage was simple and reasonably sure. There were a number of "close fits" that required a judgment call. In the interest of consistency and of mitigating subjectivity, the following guidelines determined when a match from the newspapers and directories was inferred:

1. First and last names had to conform – with rare allowances for variations on abridged first names or common nicknames; for example, "Augustus" in one source appears as "Gus" in the other.

---

[1] The one official list that was unearthed was the California Republican Party State Committee's "Roll Call of the Republican State Convention, 1882," Bancroft Library, University of California at Berkeley.

[2] Directories consulted included "Corbett's and Ballinger's" for Denver; "Crocker Langley's" for San Francisco; "R. L. Polk's" for Detroit; and "Holbrook's" for Newark.

2. When more than one individual with a given name appeared in the directory, an address singled out the individual living in or near (within 1 block) of the appropriate ward.

3. If the newspaper's delegate list did not include a middle initial, and the directory listed but one person with the same first and last name, a match was made even if the directory name included a middle initial. (Hence, if the newspaper lists a "Frank O'Neil," and the directory has only a "Frank P. O'Neil" and no other "Frank O'Neil," record linkage was established.)

4. If the delegate list did not include a middle initial, and the directory lists only persons with middle initials, a decision was made based on the delegate's address, as done in section (2) above. (The delegate list refers to a "Frank O'Neil" but the directory lists only a "Frank P. O'Neil" and a "Frank T. O'Neil." The guidelines call for selecting "Frank T." if he lives in the appropriate ward and "Frank P." does not.)

5. No match was made if the delegate list included a middle initial that did not match what appeared in the directory. (A delegate named "Frank H. O'Neil" was not presumed to be the "Frank W. O'Neil" who appears in the directory, even if this is the only "Frank O'Neil" listed therein.)

6. A caveat: In 3% of all cases the preceding guidelines were violated when a linkage seemed highly probable because of a very close approximation in name spellings. The exceptions applied either to uncommon or difficult-to-spell names ("George Kratzke" is "George Kratke") or when there might be some confusion about proper spelling ("Robert Feeley" in one source is taken to be "Robert Feely" in the other).

These procedures resulted in a number of "missing" cases because either (1) a delegate's name could not be found in the directory, or (2) more than one individual living in the appropriate ward shared an identical name, or (3) none lived within a block of the ward or district they would have represented. When delegates were selected "at large" (i.e., with no reference to the ward they represented) it proved impossible to choose between individuals sharing a name.[3]

---

[3] In four instances all the city's delegates to the state convention were elected at large: among Democrats this occurred in Detroit (1904) and Denver (1880, 1908); among Republicans only in Denver (1908).

TABLE A.I. *Unidentified or Missing State Delegates*

	Democrats		Republicans	
	Total	Percentage (%)	Total	Percentage (%)
1880–1886				
N of cases	572		515	
Unidentified	93	16.3	42	8.2
Not in directory	44	7.7	22	4.3
None in ward	22	3.8	11	2.1
Duplicates	27	4.7	7	1.4
Illegible	0	0.0	2	0.4
1898–1910				
N of cases	1,061		1,282	
Unidentified	213	20.1	259	20.2
Not in directory	122	11.5	151	11.8
None in ward	38	3.6	24	1.9
Duplicates	51	4.8	82	6.4
Illegible	2	0.2	2	0.2

Table A.1 offers a full breakdown of the number of unidentified (or "missing") cases for each party in each of the two time periods. The higher percentage of missing cases among the Democrats in the 1880s (relative to that of the Republicans) reinforces the impression that the social standing of the former was less imposing. The percentage ranged from 8.2% to 20.2% and increased over time in both parties, especially the Republican. About half the time when a delegate's occupation could not be ascertained it was because no person with the given name appeared in the directory. This figure increased over time and is consistent with indications that the social status of delegates in the Progressive Era was more modest than that of the delegates of the 1880s. "Duplicates," the circumstance of having two persons in the same district with the same name, also became more common, which is what one would expect as urban populations boomed. The percentage of cases when it was impossible to determine which duplicate was the delegate because none lived in the respective ward constituted between 2% and 4% of the samples. A minute number of names (6) could not be deciphered from the newspapers on microfilm.

It will be conceded that a small number of cases of mistaken identity almost certainly made their way into the database. The presence or absence of middle initials was likely the most common source of

TABLE A.2. *Percentage of Male Delegates to Republican and Democratic State Conventions by Occupational Groupings for Newark, Detroit, Denver, and San Francisco, 1880–1886, Together with U.S. Federal Census of Occupational Groupings for 1880*

	Census Pop. (%)	Republican		Democratic	
		Delegates (%)	Ratio	Delegates (%)	Ratio
Business leaders	2.4	27.7	11.54	12.1	5.04
Professionals	3.5	15.0	4.29	17.5	5.00
White collar	8.9	12.1	1.36	9.4	1.06
Government	1.5	9.3	6.20	5.2	3.47
Small retail	14.9	16.3	1.09	24.4	1.64
Skilled	39.8	14.6	0.37	21.7	0.55
Semi- and unskilled	29.0	3.2	0.11	6.1	0.21
No occupation		1.9		3.5	
Standard Dev.			4.17		2.06

TABLE A.3. *Percentage of Male Delegates to Republican and Democratic State Conventions by Occupational Groupings for Newark, Detroit, Denver, and San Francisco, 1898–1910, Together with U.S. Federal Census of Occupational Groupings for 1910*

	Census Pop. (%)	Republican		Democratic	
		Delegates (%)	Ratio	Delegates (%)	Ratio
Business leaders	5.8	15.8	2.72	12.3	2.12
Professionals	6.2	21.4	3.45	20.9	3.37
White collar	11.2	11.7	1.04	12.7	1.13
Government	2.7	12.8	4.74	12.7	5.37
Small retail	12.5	17.6	1.41	14.5	1.33
Skilled	25.4	12.6	0.50	16.6	1.33
Semi- and unskilled	36.4	5.3	0.15	12.4	0.49
No occupation		2.7		7.8	0.21
Standard Dev.			1.69	2.8	
					1.82

confusion. To cite a hypothetical example: the "Patrick Flynn" listed in the newspaper may have appeared as "Patrick J. Flynn" in the directory, but the rules of selection applied earlier would have picked out another "Patrick Flynn" if one appeared without a middle initial. This is possibly how most of the thirty-five common laborers appeared among the ranks of "the best representative men."

Tables A.2 and A.3 place the occupational percentages into context by contrasting them with like percentages for all adult males in the four cities as derived from contemporary federal censuses.[4] The "Ratio" column brings the delegate and population percentages together to reveal how different occupational groups fared when it was time to appoint or elect a state delegation from Newark, Detroit, Denver, and San Francisco. When the ratio value approaches 1.0, as it does for white-collar workers, representation in the convention about matched the group's proportion of the adult male labor force. Ratios higher than 1.0 occur when an occupational group constitutes an ever larger share of the delegations relative to their proportion of the working population, and numbers falling below manifest the opposite pattern. The probability of attending a state convention plainly improved as one moved up the social ladder. Unskilled and semiskilled manual workers constituted about one-third of the workforce in 1880 and 1910 but occupied only around one in twenty of the seats in the state convention. Skilled workers were also likely to be overlooked when it came time to appoint a delegation, though the disparity was less glaring. The bias worked most in the interest of the business elite in the 1880s but switched to favor government employees thirty years later. The disparities between representation in the workforce and in the state delegation became less marked over time, especially among Republicans. The trend was less evident among Democrats owing to the growing representation of government employees in their delegate ranks. Here is more evidence that concern about electing a reliable body of delegates produced a nominating body more broadly representative of the population. Fewer of the "best men" roamed the convention floor around 1910, where more of the "representative" variety sat in their place.

---

[4] Department of the Interior, Census Office, *Statistics of the Population of the United States at the Tenth Census* (Washington, D.C., 1883), pp. 875, 876, 889, 902; Department of Commerce, Bureau of the Census, *Thirteenth Census of the United States Taken in the Year 1910*, vol. 4, *Population, Occupation Statistics* (Washington, D.C., 1910), pp. 153–207.

APPENDIX B

Legislative Roll Call Analysis

Except in California, the *Minutes* or *Journals* of each legislative body provided an index that was first consulted to identify bills bearing on the regulation of the nominating process. Until indexing commenced in 1899 it was possible to track only those California bills that made it onto the statute books. Prior to that date, any bill that failed to become law in California has been overlooked. To be included in the analysis a bill had to have been voted upon by least one legislative body; a bill introduced and then buried in committee (the fate of most legislation) does not qualify.

This survey brought to light hundreds of proposals touching on the regulation of the nomination process between 1877 and 1910, the vast majority appearing in the last decade. The analysis singles out bills of "landmark" status that represent important departures from past practices. The first bill proposing to set the hours for polling at the primaries represented an important milestone; later measures that altered the hours for opening or closing the polls did not. Once the principle of state administration had been established, the recurrent efforts at tweaking the law rarely proved very controversial. Most of the roll calls pertain to a bill's "Third Reading," often the only time that each legislator's "yea" or "nay" is documented. When a bill was tabled or otherwise defeated before reaching a third reading, that vote is reflected in the tables. An especially controversial bill might have had to survive several roll calls. When this happened, the most closely divided vote appears in the tables; it represented the maximum level of opposition to the measure. The tables also record any motions to significantly modify a bill that resulted in a divided vote (defined as a roll call where the losing side garnered at least 15% of the vote).

In Michigan and Colorado the same *Journals* or *Minutes* that recorded
the votes included a table listing each legislator's party affiliation.[1] In
California and New Jersey this information was taken from the *California
Blue Book* for 1975 and the annual *Fitzgerald's Legislative Manuals*,
respectively. Information on urban population is based on the chronolog-
ically closest U.S. census. Indices for urbanization and party competition
were derived for the legislator's home county.[2] Urbanization refers to the
percentage of the county population living in cities of 7,500 or more.
The threshold is higher than the census bureau standard (2,500) but more
nearly represents a level where the sheer size of the population necessi-
tated a primary in lieu of the informal "office caucus." A 1901 California
law mandated primaries in all places with populations over 7,500.[3] The
level of party competition represents the absolute difference between the
Democratic and Republican percentage of the total vote for governor in a
legislator's home county in the preceding, off-year election. The election
results used are those issued by the respective secretaries of state.

BINARY LOGISTIC REGRESSION RESULTS

The Index of Likeness and analysis of variance appearing in the roll call
tables are somewhat crude tools. The relatively small size of the legislative
bodies (New Jersey's senators numbered 21) meant that the chi-square
results for the Index of Likeness are often not statistically significant. The
same problem applies to the analysis of variance that is responsible for the
Eta[2] values for competition and urbanization. In addition, both the Index
of Likeness and Eta[2] are bivariate measures – they examine the impact
of partisanship or competition in isolation from one another. The tables
do not reveal how the variables interact to improve overall explanatory
power, nor do they control for the effects of one independent variable on
the other.

Given the limitations of bivariate analysis, attention turned to more
robust statistical measures for studying legislative behavior. The first step
was to bring the threshold for statistical significance closer by expanding

[1] Colorado's legislative manuals begin listing party affiliation only in 1887. Prior to that
time, partisanship was inferred on the basis of the legislator's vote for speaker of the
house. In 1881 the vote on the speaker was not recorded in the minutes.
[2] In Michigan, Colorado, and California many rural legislative districts encompassed more
than one county. The indices of urbanization and competition are calculated for the
legislator's county of residence – not for the whole legislative district he represented.
[3] *California Statutes* (1901), Chap. 197, p. 606.

the "N of cases." When a bill was voted on by both legislative bodies in substantially the same form, the votes of the senators and the representatives are combined. The same aggregating procedure can be applied when different legislatures – over a span of years – have voted on a bill that is substantially the same from session to session.

The larger data sets achieved by combining roll calls across legislative chambers or over time have been subjected to binary logistic regression analysis. This multivariate procedure allows for a more thoroughgoing analysis of the factors inducing some legislators to support government regulation of political parties and others to oppose it. A standardized coefficient measuring the relative impact of each variable is produced, which is especially helpful in comparing the impact of a categorical variable (party) versus that of the two of interval type (competition and urbanization).[4] A positive value attached to a coefficient registers stronger support among Democrats or among legislators from counties that are the more urban or more competitive. The coefficients offer a more accurate assessment of each variable's influence since the multivariate approach controls for the other two independent variables. In addition, logistic regression produces a couple of measures for ascertaining how well the three independent variables account for the legislators' positions on the pending legislation. Nagelkerke's "Pseudo R Square" can be interpreted as a rough estimate of the proportion of variance explained. The presence of categorical variables in the mix (party affiliation and the roll call vote) renders this statistic somewhat unstable and less precise than the "R-Square" analysis associated with Pearson Correlation or ordinary least-squares multiple regression. An alternative approach to testing the "accuracy" of the model is to use it to see how it would assume a given legislator would vote, and contrast this predicted value with the actual one. As the "Percentage Correctly Classified" approaches 100% the statistical model represented by the standardized coefficients becomes the more convincing. Statistical significance is recorded for each of the variables as well as for the equation as a whole. Coefficients that meet a .05 level of statistical significance will be identified with an asterisk (*).

California

In California, two legislative sessions (1907 and 1909) dealt with three separate bills (AB 748, SB 829, and SB 3) that aimed at closing the

---

[4] The values for "urban" and "competition" have been standardized by converting them into their respective "z scores."

TABLE B.1. *Binary Logistic Regression Results for California*

	Providing for Closed Direct Primary	Regulating Conventions	Including U.S. Senate
Bill(s)	AB 748; SB 829; SB 3	AB 794	SB 3
Year(s)	1907–1909	1907	1909
Vote ("yea"-"nay")	75-92	47-53	58-54
Significance	.18	.00	.00
Nagelkerke's Pseudo R Square	.04	.30	.29
% correctly classified	57.5	67.7	71.4
Standardized coefficients			
Party	.453	2.234*	1.293*
Urban	.279	.371	.881*
Competition	.089	−.869*	−.136

* Statistically significant at .05.

primaries to all but party members. Table B.1 finds that the three bills collectively garnered 75 "yea" votes and 92 "nays." Even with the larger number of cases no statistically significant results emerged from the binary logistic regression. (Note here, as well, the low Pseudo-R-Square value [.04] and the percentage correctly identified [57.5%] that hardly improves on what could be expected by random guessing.) In short, the circumstance that induced some legislators to support an open primary and others to want it closed cannot be ascribed to their party affiliation, or to the level of urbanization or the amount of two-party competition in their home counties.

The roll calls on a defeated 1907 bill (AB 794) that aimed at regulating state conventions proved somewhat more comprehensible (67.7% correctly classified). Party affiliation and to a lesser degree competition both proved to have a statistically significant effect in the legislative voting alignment. A small body of Democrats (11 of 13) overwhelmingly backed a measure that would have somehow outlawed "trading" at state conventions and imposed further rules on their conduct. Most Republicans (50 of 86) voted the bill down. The measure enjoyed stronger support from legislators hailing from less competitive districts.

Finally, the vote in both houses in the 1909 session on the provision in Senate Bill 3, providing for a primary for the United States Senate seat, furnished meaningful results. The regression revealed a largely urban/rural split. The mean level of urbanization in districts represented by legislators who wanted to add the Senate seat to the array of offices to be voted on was 74.2%, while the same figure for those who endeavored to leave

TABLE B.2. *Binary Logistic Regression Results for New Jersey*

	Vote on Record's Direct Primary Bill	Vote on Direct Primary for Various Offices
Bill(s)	SB 79	SB 301; AB 535; AB 41; AB 6
Year(s)	1894	1906–1910
Vote ("yea"-"nay")	34-39	82-108
Significance	.00	.00
Nagelkerke's Pseudo R Square	.80	.64
% Correctly classified	91.8	84.2
Standardized coefficients		
Party	5.596*	5.125*
Urban	−.850	−1.042*
Competition	−1.450	−.041

* Statistically significant at .05.

the Senate off the ballot stood at 36.7%. Party affiliation barely met the standard for statistical significance as Democrats (7 to 19) opposed the inclusion of the Senate among the offices to be voted on and Republicans generally voted the other way (51 to 35).

New Jersey

In New Jersey, George L. Record's novel direct primary proposal of 1894 (Senate Bill 79) passed in the upper house (11 to 8) but was voted down in the lower chamber (23 to 31). When these votes are combined in Table B.2, a total of 34 legislators are found in favor of the experiment and 39 opposed. Party affiliation stands out as the only statistically significant coefficient. Republican opposition to the bill, therefore, accounts for its impressive R-Square value (.80) that logically correlates with the very high percentage of legislators' votes (91.8%) that would be accurately predicted using this regression model.

Between 1906 and 1910 the New Jersey Assembly voted on four bills (SB 301, AB 535, AB 41, and AB 6) that would have mandated direct nominations for governor or Congress. Here again, party stands out as the most important variable, but this time urbanization also meets the standard for statistical significance. Democrats joined with a minority of Republicans representing urban areas in support of the principle of direct nominations. The overall model accurately places 84.2% of the legislators in their respective "yea" and "nay" column. Multivariate analysis

TABLE B.3. *Binary Logistic Regression Results for Michigan*

	Direct Primary for Wayne County	Direct Primary for All State Offices	To Eliminate 40% Rule
Bill(s)	HB 114; HB 376	HB 173; SB 34	SB 292; HB 173
Year(s)	1899–1901	1907–1909	1905–1907
Vote ("yea"-"nay")	85-87	107-94	96-110
Significance	.56	.01	.06
Nagelkerke's Pseudo *R* Square	.02	.08	.06
% Correctly classified	55.2	58.2	57.3
Standardized coefficients			
Party	−.288	21.007	21.572
Urban	−.236	−.128	−.076
Competition	.130	.344	−.191
Upper Peninsula	.215	−.159	−1.442*

* Statistically significant at .05.

supports the proposition that the statewide direct primary was mainly a partisan issue; urbanization could play a secondary role in inducing some New Idea Republicans to break ranks. The level of competition in a legislator's county appears to have had no bearing on his opinion regarding the state-run direct primary.

Michigan

The combined explanatory power of the three independent variables in Michigan, even when joined by the regional effect of the "Upper Peninsula," proves to be very weak in Table B.3. The close votes in the 1899 and 1901 legislatures on two bills allowing for a direct primary in Wayne County do not appear to have been influenced by the independent variables. Neither the equation nor any of the independent variables meet a liberal standard for statistical significance. Future researchers must either operationalize urbanization or competition differently or, perhaps more profitably, look for yet other independent variables (occupation? age? incumbency? past political office holding?) to account for the close votes on this early direct primary measure.

Three roll calls in the 1907 and 1909 legislatures (HB 173 and SB 34) would have mandated direct nominations for all state offices. Although the overall model reaches the threshold for statistical significance, this is not the case for any of the independent variables. The explanatory power of the model – as evidenced by the Pseudo *R* Square (.08) and the percentage correctly classified (58.2) – hardly does much better than the vote over Wayne County's direct primary. Here is another prime candidate for further statistical analysis.

The recurrent efforts to lift the proviso in the state's 1905 law requiring nomination in convention if winners in the gubernatorial primary fell short of 40% of the total vote (SB 292 and HB 173) also largely eluded statistical explanation. Note, however, that while the full model barely misses statistical significance, the coefficient for the Upper Peninsula category is statistically significant. This is as one would expect given the breakdown in the vote provided in Table 6.4. Michigan legislators from the far north acted together to limit the application of the direct primary, even if the influence of the Upper Peninsula was somewhat diluted when other independent variables were brought into the analysis.

The failure of the logistic regression model to explain the behavior of Michigan's senators and representatives might appear counterintuitive given the results in Tables 6.3 and 6.4. Legislators from Detroit and Grand Rapids backed a direct primary – they were already using it for local races – but apparently senators and representatives from smaller cities viewed the reform with some misgivings. (Some of these smaller cities were in the Upper Peninsula.) Partisanship scores very high coefficients on the votes expanding the direct primary to cover other state offices and dropping the 40% rule. Democratic legislators backed these changes unanimously. However, the hundred seat house had room for but two Democrats between 1905 and 1909, and none sat in the senate during that time. There simply were not enough Democrats to allow partisanship to be an important factor. If Democrats controlled a larger share of seats – as they did in New Jersey – and still voted in unanimity the party coefficient would prove statistically significant and the model's overall explanatory power would improve. Michigan resists statistical interpretation, in short, partly because it was so very nearly a one-party state after 1900.

Colorado

Party affiliation was also an important factor in Colorado politics. Senators and representatives divided along partisan lines in 1907 over HB 100, which was designed to eliminate fusion candidacies. All the Democrats in the upper and lower chambers opposed the measure, while all but

TABLE B.4. *Binary Logistic Regression Results for Colorado*

	Prohibiting Fusion	Providing for Party Assemblies
Bill(s)	HB 100	HB 2
Year(s)	1907	1909–1910
Vote ("yea"-"nay")	56-34	66-59
Significance	.00	.00
Nagelkerke's Pseudo R Square	.86	.15
% Correctly classified	94.4	64.8
Standardized coefficients		
Party	−23.745*	−.569
Urban	−1.393	.214
Competition	.213	−.901*

* Statistically significant at .05.

5 of 61 Republicans voted "aye." The nearly straight party vote produced a highly reliable model (94.4% of the votes correctly matched) in Table B.4.

Legislation introducing direct primaries appeared in both the 1909 and 1910 sessions in the form of HB 2. The most controversial feature of the bill was its provision for party "assemblies" to vote on prospective candidates prior to the primary. The model manages to accurately forecast a legislator's position on the role of the assemblies only 64.8% of the time. Only the competition index produced a coefficient that was statistically significant. The assemblies became a fixture in Colorado's primary system due to the support of legislators from less competitive districts. The generally weak explanatory power of the independent variables in Colorado may reflect the complications presented by a classic compromise measure: some legislators claimed they opposed the assemblies provision because they wanted a pure direct primary and others may have opposed the assemblies because they desired no direct primary whatever.

The broad pattern in legislative voting alignments on party regulation afforded by binary logistic regression analysis accords with patterns appearing in the bivariate analysis of Chapters 5 and 6. Party proved to be the most decisive factor dividing the senators and representatives on various measures. Democrats proved firmer friends of direct nominations than did the G.O.P. in each state, though their numbers were too few in Michigan to be meaningful. Urbanization emerges as a notable factor when the goal was to expand the number of offices subject to the direct primary in New Jersey and California. Electoral competition, – or lack thereof – seemed to play an important role in encouraging some local parties in Iowa and perhaps elsewhere to experiment with the system of direct nominations (see Table 4.3). Its impact inside the state legislatures, however, was more muted. It surfaced in Colorado and California, where legislators from less competitive districts supported measures that gave the party cadre in Colorado's assemblies a bigger voice in the candidate selection process and supported efforts to regulate California's conventions. Only in Michigan did party or the other independent variables largely fail to emerge in the analysis. The only characteristic that could separate supporters from opponents of party regulation – at least as it regarded Michigan's 40% cut off rule – was the regional division between the Upper and Lower Peninsulas. It is clear enough why party affiliation could not matter much in an almost exclusively Republican legislature. The failure of competition and especially urbanization to influence the Michigan legislature must be left to additional research.

Bibliography

Books

Abbott, Carl. *Colorado: A History of the Centennial State*. Boulder, Colo., 1976.

Aldrich, John H. *Why Parties? The Origin and Transformation of Political Parties in America*. Chicago, 1995.

Altschuler, Glenn C., and Stuart M. Blumin. *Rude Republic: Americans and Their Politics in the Nineteenth Century*. Princeton, N.J., 2000.

Argersinger, Peter H. *Structure, Process and Party: Essays in American Political History*. Armonk, N.Y., 1992.

Bensel, Richard Franklin. *The Political Economy of Industrialization, 1877–1900*. Cambridge, U.K., 2000.

Boots, Ralph Simpson. *The Direct Primary in New Jersey*. New York, 1917.

Bryce, James. *The American Commonwealth*. Edited and abridged by Louis M. Hacker. G. P. Putnam's Sons edition. 2 vols. New York, 1959.

Bullough, William A. *The Blind Boss and His City: Christopher Augustine Buckley and Nineteenth Century San Francisco*. Berkeley, Calif., 1979.

Burner, David. *The Politics of Provincialism: The Democratic Party in Transition, 1918–1932*. New York, 1967.

Chambers, William Nisbet, and Walter Dean Burnham, eds. *The American Party Systems: Stages of Political Development*. New York, 1967.

Chase, James S. *Emergence of the Presidential Nominating Convention, 1789–1832*. Urbana, Ill., 1973.

Cherney, Robert W. *American Politics in the Gilded Age*. Wheeling, Ill., 1997.

Clemens, Elizabeth S. *The People's Lobby: Organizational Innovation and the Rise of Interest Group Politics in the United States*. Chicago, 1997.

Connolly, James J. *The Triumph of Ethnic Progressivism: Urban Political Culture in Boston, 1900–1925*. Cambridge, Mass., 1998.

Croly, Herbert. *Progressive Democracy*. New York, 1914.

Dallinger, Frederick W. *Nominations for Elective Office in the United States*. New York, 1903.

Darcy, R., and Richard C. Rohrs. *A Guide to Quantitative History*. Westport, Conn., 1995.

David, Paul T. *Party Strength in the United States*. Charlottesville, Va., 1972.

Davis, Winfield J. *History of Political Conventions in California, 1849–1892*. Sacramento, Calif., 1893.

Dill, R. G. *The Political Campaigns of Colorado with Complete Tabulated Statements of the Official Vote*. Denver, 1895.

Diner, Steven J. *A Very Different Age: Americans of the Progressive Era*. New York, 1998.

Dobie, Edith. *The Political Career of Stephen Mallory White: A Study of Party Activities Under the Convention System*. Stanford, Calif., 1927.

Donnelly, Thomas C. *Rocky Mountain Politics*. Albuquerque, N.Mex., 1940.

Epstein, Leon D. *Political Parties in the American Mold*. Madison, Wis., 1986.

Ethington, Philip J. *The Public City: The Political Construction of Urban Life in San Francisco, 1850–1900*. Cambridge, U.K., 1994.

Finegold, Kenneth. *Experts and Politicians: Reform Challenges to Machine Politics in New York, Cleveland and Chicago*. Princeton, N.J., 1995.

Flint, Winston Allen. *The Progressive Movement in Vermont*. Washington, D.C., 1941.

Fredman, L. E. *The Australian Ballot: The Story of an American Reform*. East Lansing, Mich., 1968.

Goebel, Thomas. *A Government by the People: Direct Democracy in America, 1890–1940*. Chapel Hill, N.C., 2002.

Hichborn, Franklin. *Story of the Session of the California Legislature of 1909*. San Francisco, 1909.

Hofstadter, Richard. *The American Political Tradition and the Men Who Made It*. New York, 1948.

Issel, William, and Robert W. Cherney. *San Francisco, 1865–1932: Politics, Power and Urban Development*. Berkeley, Calif., 1986.

Jensen, Richard. *The Winning of the Midwest: Social and Political Conflict, 1888–1896*. Chicago, 1971.

Josephson, Matthew. *The Politicos, 1865–1896*. New York, 1938.

Katznelson, Ira, and Helen V. Milner, eds. *Political Science: The State of the Discipline*. New York, 2002.

Keating, Edward. *The Gentleman from Colorado*. Denver, 1961.

Keller, Morton. *Affairs of State: Public Life in Late Nineteenth Century America*. Cambridge, Mass., 1977.

Key, V. O., Jr. *Politics, Parties and Pressure Groups*. 5th ed. New York, 1964.

Key, V. O., Jr. *Southern Politics in State and Nation*. New York, 1949.

Keyssar, Alexander. *The Right to Vote: The Contested History of Democracy in the United States*. New York, 2000.

Kousser, J. Morgan. *The Shaping of Southern Politics: Suffrage Restriction and the Establishment of the One Party South, 1880–1910*. New Haven, Conn., 1974.

Leonard, Thomas C. *The Power of the Press: The Birth of American Political Reporting*. New York, 1986.

Link, Arthur S., and Richard L. McCormick. *Progressivism*. Arlington Hts., Ill., 1983.

Lovejoy, Allen Fraser. *Robert M. La Follette and the Establishment of the Direct Primary in Wisconsin, 1890–1904.* New Haven, Conn., 1941.

Marcus, Robert D. *Grand Old Party: Political Structure in the Gilded Age, 1880–1896.* New York, 1971.

Martin, Boyd A. *The Direct Primary in Idaho.* New York, 1947.

McCormick, Richard L. *From Realignment to Reform: Political Change in New York State, 1893–1910.* Ithaca, N.Y., 1981.

McCormick, Richard L. *The Party Period in Public Policy: American Politics from the Age of Jackson to the Progressive Era.* New York, 1986.

McCormick, Richard P. *The History of Voting in New Jersey: A Study of the Development of Election Machinery, 1664–1911.* New Brunswick, N.J., 1953.

McCormick, Richard P. *The Presidential Game: The Origins of American Presidential Politics.* New York, 1982.

McCormick, Richard P. *The Second American Party System: Party Formation in the Jacksonian Era.* Chapel Hill, N.C., 1966.

McGerr, Michael E. *The Decline of Popular Politics: The American North, 1865–1928.* New York, 1986.

McSeveney, Samuel T. *The Politics of Depression: Political Behavior in the Northeast, 1893–1896.* New York, 1972.

Merriam, Charles Edward, Harold F. Gosnell, and Louise Overacker. *Primary Elections.* Chicago, 1928.

Millspaugh, Arthur Chester. *Party Organization and Machinery in Michigan Since 1890.* Baltimore, 1917.

Morgan, Edmund S. *Inventing the People: Popular Sovereignty in England and America.* New York, 1988.

Mowry, George L. *The California Progressives.* Berkeley, Calif., 1951.

National Conference on Practical Reform of Primary Elections. *Proceedings of the National Conference on Practical Reform of Primary Elections, January 20 and 21, 1898.* Chicago, 1898.

Noble, Ransom E. *New Jersey Progressivism Before Wilson.* Princeton, N.J., 1946.

Pegram, Thomas R. *Partisans and Progressives: Private Interest and Public Policy in Illinois, 1870–1922.* Urbana, Ill., 1992.

Philipp, Emanuel L. *Political Reform in Wisconsin.* Madison, Wis., 1973.

Pollock, James K. *The Direct Primary in Michigan, 1909–1935.* Ann Arbor, Mich., 1943.

Polsby, Nelson W. *Consequences of Party Reform.* Oxford, 1983.

Ranney, Austin. *Curing the Mischiefs of Faction: Party Reform in America.* Berkeley, Calif., 1975.

Rapport, George C. *The Statesman and the Boss.* New York, 1961.

Remsen, Daniel S. *Primary Elections: A Study for Improving the Basis of Party Organization.* New York, 1895.

Reynolds, John F. *Testing Democracy: Electoral Behavior and Progressive Reform in New Jersey, 1880–1920.* Chapel Hill, N.C., 1988.

Rogin, Michael Paul, and John L. Shover. *Political Change in California: Critical Elections and Social Movements.* Westport, Conn., 1970.

Schattschneider, E. E. *The Semi-Sovereign People.* New York, 1960.

Shafer, Byron E. *Partisan Approaches to Postwar American Politics.* New York, 1998.

Shafer, Byron E., and Anthony J. Badger. *Contesting Democracy: Substance and Structure in American Political History, 1775–2000.* Lawrence, Kans., 2001.

Shefter, Martin. *Political Parties and the State: The American Historical Experience.* Princeton, N.J., 1993.

Silbey, Joel H. *The American Political Nation, 1838–1893.* Stanford, Calif., 1991.

Smith, Hedrick. *The Power Game: How Washington Works.* New York, 1987.

Sorauf, Frank J. *Party Politics in America.* 2nd ed. Boston, 1972.

Summers, Mark Wahlgren. *Party Games: Getting, Keeping, and Using Power in Gilded Age Politics.* Chapel Hill, N.C., 2004.

VanderMeer, Philip R. *The Hoosier Politician: Officeholding and Political Culture in Indiana, 1896–1920.* Urbana, Ill., 1985.

Ware, Alan.*The American Direct Primary: Party Institutionalization and Transformation in the North.* Cambridge, U.K., 2002.

Ware, Alan. *The Breakdown of Democratic Party Organization, 1940–1980.* Oxford, 1985.

Wattenberg, Martin P. *The Rise of Candidate-Centered Politics: Presidential Elections of the 1980s.* London, 1991.

Wiebe, Robert H. *The Search for Order, 1877–1920.* New York, 1967.

Wiebe, Robert H. *Self-Rule: A Cultural History of American Democracy.* Chicago, 1995.

Williams, R. Hal. *The Democratic Party and California Politics, 1880–1896.* Stanford, Calif., 1973.

Woodruff, Clinton Rogers, ed. *Proceedings of the New York Conference for Good City Government and the Sixth Annual Meeting of the National Municipal League [1900].* Philadelphia, 1900.

Woodruff, Clinton, ed. *Proceedings of the Rochester Conference for Good City Government and the Seventh Annual Meeting of the National Municipal League [1901].* Philadelphia, 1901.

Woodruff, Clinton Rogers, ed. *Proceedings of the Chicago Conference for Good City Government and the Tenth Annual Meeting of the National Municipal League [1904].* Philadelphia, 1904.

Woodruff, Clinton Rogers, ed. *Proceedings of the New York Conference for Good City Government and the Eleventh Annual Meeting of the National Municipal League [1905].* Philadelphia, 1905.

Wright, James Edward. *The Politics of Populism: Dissent in Colorado.* New Haven, Conn., 1974.

Articles

Anonymous. "Doubts about the Direct Primary." *Literary Digest,* Oct. 10, 1914, pp. 672–73.

Aylsworth, Leon E. "Primary Elections – Legislation of 1909–1910." *American Political Science Review* 6 (Feb. 1912): 60–74.

Beard, Charles A. "The Direct Primary Movement in New York." *Proceedings of the American Political Science Association* 7 (1910): 187–98.

Becker, Carl. "The Unit Rule in National Nominating Conventions." *American Historical Review* 5 (Oct. 1899): 64–82.

Bernheim, A. C. "Party Organizations and Their Nominations to Public Office in New York City." *Political Science Quarterly* 3 (Mar. 1888): 99–122.

Blair, Emily Newell. "Every Man His Own Campaign Manager." *The Outlook,* Feb. 25, 1911, pp. 426–33.

Bogue, Allan G., Jerome M. Clubb, Carroll R. McKibbin, and Santa A. Traugott. "Members of the House of Representatives and the Process of Modernization, 1789–1960." *Journal of American History* 63 (Sept. 1976): 291–305.

Bonaparte, Charles J. "An Elective Boss." *The Outlook,* Dec. 4, 1909, pp. 773–76.

Boots, Ralph S. "Party Platforms in State Politics." *Annals of the American Academy of Political and Social Science* 106 (Mar. 1923): 72–82.

Brickner, Issac M. "Direct Primaries Versus Boss Rule." *The Arena* 41 (Aug. 1909): 550–56.

Buenker, John D. "The Mahatma and Progressive Reform: Martin Lomasney as Lawmaker, 1911–17." *New England Quarterly* 44 (Sept. 1971): 397–419.

Buenker, John D. "The Politics of Resistance: The Rural-Based Yankee Republican Machines of Connecticut and Rhode Island." *New England Quarterly* 47 (June 1974): 212–37.

Buenker, John D. "Sovereign Individuals and Organic Networks: Political Cultures in Conflict During the Progressive Era." *American Quarterly* 40 (June 1988): 187–204.

Burnham, Walter Dean. "The System of 1896: An Analysis." In *The Evolution of American Electoral Systems,* ed. Paul Kleppner, Walter Dean Burnham, Ronald P. Formisano, Samuel P. Hays, Richard Jensen, and William G. Shade. 147–202. Westport, Conn., 1981.

Chrislock, Carl H. "Sidney M. Owen: An Editor in Politics." *Minnesota History* 36 (Dec. 1958): 109–26.

Committee on Political Parties of the American Political Science Association. "Toward a More Responsible Two Party System." *American Political Science Review* 44 (Sept. 1950): 15–84.

Cox, Ora Ellen. "The Socialist Party in Indiana Since 1896." *Indiana Magazine of History* 12 (June 1916): 95–130.

Crossley, James Judson. "The Regulation of Primary Elections by Law." *Iowa Journal of History and Politics* 1 (Apr. 1903): 165–92.

Dunn, Arthur Wallace. "The Direct Primary: Promise and Performance." *Review of Reviews* 46 (Oct. 1912): 439–45.

Easley, Ralph M. "The Sine Qua Non of Caucus Reform." *Review of Reviews* 16 (Sept. 1897): 322–24.

Ethington, Philip J. "The Metropolis and Multicultural Ethics: Direct Democracy Versus Deliberative Democracy in the Progressive Era." In *Progressivism and the New Democracy,* ed. Sidney M. Milkis and Jerome M. Mileur. 192–225. Amherst, Mass., 1999.

Evans, Frank B. "Wharton Barker and the Republican National Convention of 1880." *Pennsylvania History* 27 (Jan. 1960): 28–43.

Filene, Peter G. "An Obituary for the Progressive Movement." *American Quarterly* 22 (Spring 1970): 20–34.

Ford, Henry Jones. "The Direct Primary." *North American Review* 190 (July 1909): 1–14.

Formisano, Ronald P. "The Concept of Political Culture." *Journal of Interdisciplinary History* 31 (Winter 2001): 393–426.

Geiser, Karl F. "Defects in the Direct Primary." *Annals of the American Academy of Political and Social Science* 106 (Mar. 1923): 31–39.

Godkin, E. L. "The Nominating System." *Atlantic Monthly* 79 (Apr. 1897): 450–67.

Green, George Walton. "Facts About the Caucus and the Primary." *North American Review* 137 (Sept. 1883): 257–69.

Haigh, Henry A. "The Alger Movement of 1888." *Michigan History Magazine* 9 (1925): 173–214.

Hand, Samuel B., Jeffrey D. Marshall, and D. Gregory Sanford. "'Little Republics': The Structure of State Politics in Vermont, 1854–1920." *Vermont History* 53 (Summer 1985): 141–66.

Hays, Samuel P. "The Politics of Reform in Municipal Government in the Progressive Era." *Pacific Northwest Quarterly* 55 (Oct. 1964): 157–69.

Hein, Clarence J. "The Adoption of Minnesota's Direct Primary Law." *Minnesota History* 35 (Dec. 1957): 341–51.

Hemstreet, William. "Theory and Practice of the New Primary Law." *The Arena* 28 (Dec. 1902): 585–95.

Holli, Melvin G. "Mayor Pingree Campaigns for the Governorship." *Michigan History* 57 (Summer 1973): 151–73.

Hopkins, John S. "Direct Nomination of Candidates by the People." *The Arena* 19 (June 1898): 729–39.

Horack, Frank Edward. "The Operation of the Primary Election Law in Iowa." *Iowa Journal of History and Politics* 19 (Jan. 1921): 94–124.

Horack, Frank Edward. "Primary Elections in Iowa." *Proceedings of the American Political Science Association* 7 (1910): 175–86.

Hotchkiss, William H. "The Movement for Better Primaries." *Review of Reviews* 17 (May 1898): 583–89.

Insley, Edward. "How to Reform the Primary Election System." *The Arena* 17 (June 1897): 1013–23.

Insley, Edward. "Needed Political Reforms." *The Arena* 29 (Jan. 1903): 71–75.

Kernell, Samuel. "Toward Understanding Nineteenth Century Congressional Careers: Ambition, Competition, and Rotation." *American Journal of Political Science* 21 (Nov. 1977): 669–93.

Key, V. O., Jr. "The Direct Primary and Party Structure: A Study of State Legislative Nominations." *American Political Science Review* 58 (Mar. 1954): 1–26.

Kleppner, Paul. "Voters and Parties in the Western States, 1876–1900." *Western Historical Quarterly* 14 (Jan. 1983): 49–68.

Lederle, John W., and Rita Feiler Aid. "Michigan State Party Chairmen, 1882–1956." *Michigan History* 41 (Sept. 1957): 257–68.

Ludington, Arthur. "Election Laws: The New Geran Law in New Jersey." *American Political Science Review* 5 (Nov. 1911): 579–85.

Lukes, Timothy J. "Progressivism Off-Broadway: Reform Politics in San Jose, California, 1880–1920." *Southern California Quarterly* 76 (Winter 1994): 377–400.

Mann, Ralph. "National Party Fortunes and Local Political Structure: The Case of Two California Mining Towns, 1850–1870." *Southern California Quarterly* 57 (Fall 1975): 271–96.

McClosky, Herbert. "Are Political Conventions Undemocratic?" *New York Times Magazine,* Aug. 4, 1968, p. 10.

McCormick, Richard L. "The Party Period and Public Policy: An Exploratory Hypothesis," *Journal of American History* 66 (Sept. 1970): 279–98.

Merriam, Charles Edward. "Some Disputed Points in Primary Election Legislation." *Proceedings of the American Political Science Association* 4 (1907): 179–88.

Milholland, John E. "The Danger Point in American Politics." *North American Review* 164 (Jan. 1897): 97–105.

Millspaugh, Arthur C. "The Operation of the Direct Primary in Michigan." *American Political Science Review* 10 (Nov. 1916): 710–26.

Noble, David W. "Progressivism." In *Encyclopedia of American Political History,* ed. Jack P. Greene. Vol. 4. 992–1004. New York, 1984.

Petersen, Eric Falk. "The Adoption of the Direct Primary in California." *Southern California Quarterly* 54 (Winter 1972): 363–78.

Petersen, Eric Falk. "The Struggle for the Australian Ballot in California." *California Historical Quarterly* 51 (Fall 1972): 227–43.

Reynolds, John F., and Richard L. McCormick. "Outlawing 'Treachery': Split Tickets and Ballot Laws in New York and New Jersey, 1880–1914." *Journal of American History* 72 (Mar. 1986): 835–58.

Rodgers, Daniel T. "In Search of Progressivism." *Reviews in American History* 10 (Dec. 1982): 113–32.

Roosevelt, Theodore. "Machine Politics in New York City." *The Century* 33 (Nov. 1886): 74–82.

Schlesinger, Arthur, Jr. "Faded Glory." *New York Times Magazine,* July 12, 1992, p. 14.

Shaw, William B. "The Direct Primary on Trial." *The Outlook,* Oct. 24, 1908, pp. 383–89.

Shefter, Martin. "Regional Receptivity to Reform: The Legacy of the Progressive Era." *Political Science Quarterly* 98 (Autumn 1983): 459–83.

Starring, Charles R. "Hazen S. Pingree: Another Forgotten Eagle." *Michigan History* 32 (June 1948): 129–49.

Taylor, William B., and Elliott West. "Patron Leadership at the Crossroads: Southern Colorado in the Late Nineteenth Century." *Pacific Historical Review* 17 (Aug. 1973): 335–57.

Throne, Mildred. "Electing an Iowa Governor, 1871: Cyrus Clay Carpenter." *Iowa Journal of History* 48 (Oct. 1950): 335–70.

Truman, David B. "Party Reform, Party Atrophy, and Constitutional Change: Some Reflections." *Political Science Quarterly* 99 (Winter 1984–85): 637–55.

Wallace, Schuyler C. "Pre-Primary Conventions." *Annals of the American Academy of Political and Social Science* 106 (Mar. 1923): 97–104.

Warden, G. B. "The Caucus and Democracy in Colonial Boston." *New England Quarterly* 43 (Mar. 1970): 19–45.

Weeks, O. Douglas. "The White Primary, 1944–1948." *American Political Science Review* 42 (June 1948): 500–510.
West, Victor J. "Round Table on Nominating Methods: The Development of a Technique for Testing the Usefulness of a Nominating Method." *American Political Science Review* 20 (Feb. 1926): 139–43.
Westbrook, Robert B. "Politics as Consumption: Managing the Modern American Election." In *The Culture of Consumption: Critical Essays in American History, 1880–1980*, eds. Richard Wrightman Fox and T. J. Jackson Lears. 145–73. New York, 1983.
Wicker, Tom. "Let Some Smoke In." *New York Times Magazine*, June 14, 1992, p. 34.

Unpublished Theses and Dissertations

Sarasohn, Stephen B. "The Regulation of Parties and Nominations in Michigan: The Politics of Election Reform." Ph.D. diss., Columbia University, 1953.
Warner, Robert Mark. "Chase S. Osborn and the Progressive Movement." Ph.D. diss., University of Michigan, 1957.
Wolfe, Arthur Coffman. "The Direct Primary in American Politics." Ph.D. diss., University of Michigan, 1966.

Newspapers

California

Los Angeles Times	*Redwood City Times and Gazette*
Mail (Stockton)	*San Francisco Chronicle*
Marin County Journal	*San Francisco Examiner*
Mountain Democrat (Placerville)	*Sutter County Farmer*
Mountain Messenger	*Tulare County Times*
Placer Herald	

Colorado

Aspen Democrat	*Denver Times*
Chaffee County Republican	*Greeley Tribune*
Courier (Georgetown)	*Gunnison News*
Denver Post	*Rocky Mountain News*
Denver Republican	*Trinidad Weekly News*

Michigan

Adrian Daily	*Genesee Democrat*
Big Rapids Current	*Mining Gazette* (Houghton)
Big Rapids Pioneer	*Niles Daily Star*
Buchanan Record	*Niles Democrat*
Detroit Evening News	*Ontonagon Herald*
Detroit Free Press	*Portage Lake Gazette*
Detroit Post and Tribune	*State Republican* (Lansing)
Evening Press (Grand Rapids)	

New Jersey

Burlington Gazette	Newark Advertiser
Cape May County Gazette	Newark Evening News
Daily State Gazette (Trenton)	Newark Sunday Call
Gloucester County Democrat	Penns Grove Record
Hunterdon County Democrat	Red Bank Register
Jersey Journal (Jersey City)	Trenton True American

New York

New York Times

Manuscript Collections

The Archives at the University of Colorado at Boulder Libraries

William Penn Collins Collection.
Colorado Federation of Women's Clubs Collection.
Edward P. Costigan Papers.
Edward Keating Papers.
George J. Kindel Papers.
National Republican League. "Souvenir of the Seventh Annual Convention of the National Republican League Meeting in Denver, June 26, 1894."
T. J. O'Donnell Papers.
Harper M. Orahood Papers.
Thomas M. Patterson Papers.
Jose Urbano Vigil Papers.

Bancroft Library – University of California at Berkeley

Daniel M. Burns Papers.
Committee of Fifty. "Address of the Committee of Fifty to the People [1882]."
League of Republican Clubs. "Plans for Effective County Organization."
George Cooper Pardee Papers.
Pillsbury, Arthur Judson. "Plans for Effective County Organization of the Republican Party in California." Tulare, Calif., 1898.
Republican Party of California. "Proceedings of the Republican State Convention, Sacramento, June 18th to June 19th, 1861."
Republican Party of California. "Proceedings of the Union State Convention Held at Sacramento on the 17th and 18th Days of June, 1862." San Francisco, 1862.
Republican Party of California. "Roll Call of the Republican State Convention, 1882."
Republican Party of San Francisco, California. "By-laws and Rules of the Republican County Committee for 1873–74."
Republican Party of San Francisco, California. "Proceedings of a Meeting Held at Platt's Hall, San Francisco, June 11th, 1872 . . . to Ratify the Nominations of U. S. Grant and Henry Wilson."

Republican Party of San Francisco, California. "Rules and Regulations of the Republican Party of San Francisco." 1881.

Bentley Historical Library – University of Michigan, Ann Arbor

Rice Aner Beal Papers.
Ferry Family Papers.
Harrison Greer Papers.
Chase S. Osborn Papers.

California State Library, Sacramento

California League of Republican Clubs. "Second Biennial Convention of the California League of Republican Clubs, Held at Los Angeles, Apr. 27–28, 1900."
California Republican Club. "Proceedings of the Republican League of 1900."
James N. Gillett Papers.
Warren T. Sexton Papers.

Colorado Historical Society – Denver

Colorado Federation of Jane Jefferson Clubs Collection
Job Adams Cooper Papers.
John Franklin Shaforth Papers.

Denver Public Library

William A. Hamill Papers.
Henry Moore Teller Collection.
Joel F. Vaille Papers.

Department of Special Collections at the Stanford University Library

Stephen Mallory White Papers.

Index

Abbett, Leon, 51, 77
Adams, Charles Frederick, 166
advertising, 64, 73, 80, 103, 104, 191, 192, 227, 229, 233
African-Americans, 12, 35–39, 127, 188
agriculture, 12, 14, 15, 16
Aichele, Julius, 118
Aldrich, John H., 235
Alger, Russell A., 68
Allied Political Clubs of New York, 159
Alpena County, MI, 216
ambition, 21, 61, 62, 79, 103
analysis of variance
    explained, 178
    with competition, 179
    with urbanization, 178
Arapahoe County. *See* Denver
Asian-Americans, 16, 37
Atlanta, GA, 159
attorneys general. *See* minor state offices
auditor. *See* local offices
Australian Ballot. *See* Ballots, official
automobiles, 102, 201

balanced tickets, 133, 134, 135, 138, 139, 224, 230
    and direct primary, 187
ballot boxes, 146, 169, 216
ballots, 77, 113, 126, 142, 146, 169, 211, 216
    "mixed" tickets, 127

official, 6, 8, 124, 130, 132, 161, 164, 165, 166, 167, 173, 185, 189, 198, 233
    pasters, 127, 131
Baltimore, MD, 113
Barela, Casimero, 38
Barker, Ren, 75
Barnes, William, Jr., 159
Barry County, MI, 190
bartenders. *See* semi-skilled workers
Beal, Rice Aner, 68, 69
Beard, Charles A., 5
Becker, Carl, 5
Berrien County, MI, 138
best citizens, 35, 160
Big Rapids, MI, 111
binary logistic regression, 243, 244, 246, 247, 248, 249, 250
Black, Winifred Sweet. *See* Laurie, Annie
Blair, James, 42
Bliss, Aaron T., 75, 152
Bonaparte, Charles J., 227
bossism, 70, 71, 92, 109, 125, 168, 180, 182, 183, 194, 207, 209, 227, 233
    and ballot reform, 165
Boston, MA, 159
Bradford, Mary C. C., 136
Bridgford, E. A., 135
Bryan, William Jennings, 15
Bryce, James, 71
Buckley, Christopher, 168
Buffalo, NY, 159, 161, 184